Scratch-Building
Model Railway Locomotives

Scratch-Building
Model Railway Locomotives

Simon Bolton

THE CROWOOD PRESS

First published in 2014 by
The Crowood Press Ltd
Ramsbury, Marlborough
Wiltshire SN8 2HR

www.crowood.com

British Library Cataloguing-in-Publication Data
A catalogue record for this book is available from the British Library.

ISBN 978 1 84797 768 7

Dedication
This book is dedicated to Paul for his amazing help with organization, editing and laughter.

Acknowledgements
My thanks to the following who have kindly allowed me to include their excellent photographs:
David Coasby, Paul Winskill, Steven Greeno, Gordon Gravett, Benjamin Boggis, Paul Macey, Keith
Ashford and Maurice Hopper.
    I would also like to thank all those society members and website forum contributors for their
assistance and kind comments.
    And finally, thanks to my father for having a lathe in the front room as I grew up.

Disclaimer
The author and the publisher do not accept any responsibility in any manner whatsoever for any
error or omission, or any loss, damage, injury, adverse outcome, or liability of any kind incurred
as a result of the use of any of the information contained in this book, or reliance upon it. If in
doubt about any aspect of scratch building model railway locomotives, readers are advised to
seek professional advice.

Typeset and designed by D & N Publishing, Baydon, Wiltshire

Printed and bound in India by Replika Press Pvt Ltd

CONTENTS

J15 Locomotive 7564 at Sheringham station on the North Norfolk Railway.

J15 scratch-built model.

PREFACE

For the beginner, scratch building can seem a daunting prospect: how do you start, what tools do you need, will it hurt? For me, scratch building has opened up a world of possibilities and creativity, allowing me to practise skills, collect ideas and methods, and come up with some of my own. I've been inspired by the enthusiasm and helpfulness of the people I have met through this project; they have been incredibly helpful and keen to share their time and expertise.

Being able to build the locomotives that I want and to be proud of the results is very exciting, and it is this excitement that I want to share. The aim of the book is to inspire the beginner to take up his or her place at the dining-room table (or work-bench) and begin to scratch build. I have chosen a pleasing locomotive (the J15) to scratch build, which, at the time of writing, is not available as a ready-to-run model. I have chosen OO as the main gauge to build in, as it is the most popular and accessible format. There is excellent trade support for scratch building in this gauge, and a great deal of online advice.

The book is structured with the aim that you will be able to scratch build a OO-gauge J15 locomotive following the stages set out. I have included my own drawings, with some slight simplifications to the dimensions to make life a little easier, lots of prototype photographs, sketches, and step-by-step photographs. To ease the process further, I would urge you to acquire a relevant set of scale drawings. However, it's not all hand holding: as the book progresses you are invited to make your own decisions regarding construction and detailing. Descriptions of different methods available and avenues for further research are given.

Like many skills in life, learning to scratch build is an on-going and highly enjoyable process, and I hope that you will be able to take what you can from the book and, most importantly, enjoy yourself as you do.

ABOUT ME

I have been scratch building model railway locomotives on the kitchen table since my early teens, and as my skills have improved, so have the kitchen tables. I have taught both adults and children for many years, and firmly believe in the positive effects of making things, crafting objects, and the pleasure to be gained from creating something for yourself.

I would be very pleased to be contacted with any questions about your scratch building or to hear about your progress. Please go to my website for contact details and further resources: www.artfulengineering.co.uk

Simon Bolton

CHAPTER ONE

WHY SCRATCH BUILD?

DEFINITIONS FIRST

My understanding is that scratch building, within the terms of model railways, is the production of models by choosing and using raw materials, tools and skills that you find appropriate and that suit you. Scratch building is a wide-ranging term – in fact, as far as I'm concerned, it can mean anything from modifying kits and ready-to-run items to making the component parts of a model, right up to producing your own wheels, motor and fittings.

WHY DO IT?

I really enjoy scratch building. I enjoy making something that wasn't there before, I enjoy having things that are a little bit different, and I get an immense feeling of satisfaction from having made something myself. It means becoming completely immersed in a project that involves problem solving, and the acquisition and utilization of skills to produce

a tangible solid object. Moreover this is believed to have beneficial effects on our mental health, in that clearing your head of extraneous worries and concentrating solely on the task in hand is very good for you. So if nothing else, the model railway hobby is an economical and pleasant form of therapy.

Scratch building, then, is the perfect fit for escaping the everyday trials of life and refreshing your mind for new challenges. And as a by-product, you end up with some beautiful models.

You may, of course, find the challenge difficult to handle and be tempted to hide your miniature offering in the back of the cupboard. This is normal, too; the most effective learning can come from making mistakes, picking yourself up and carrying on. This is literally the case in learning to walk: did you give up, vow never to do it again, and go off down to the pub in a huff? No, you got back on your horse and drank your milk. Soldering is like that (the pub just helps).

One of my earlier projects, a Great Western 2-4-2 Birdcage tank loco in 7mm scale: almost completely scratch built bar the wheels, motor and fittings – and am I proud of her!

CHOOSING A SUBJECT

I'm going to describe how I scratch build model locomotives starting with simple methods, and then introduce complementary techniques, which are arguably more complex. The more practised you become at something and the more you challenge yourself, the easier it becomes. Scratch building may seem daunting at the beginning; however, it soon becomes compelling and you'll wonder why you were wary of starting.

The wide range of approaches suits me: I'm not an engineer; I buy ready-made wheels and motors; and I also buy or commission detailing parts such as chimneys and domes. I'm not a fast worker (almost glacial in fact); I'm very meticulous (a Virgo apparently), and I tend to plan most projects in my head as I go along, with the occasional foray into sketchbooks or on to the backs of envelopes.

Locomotives are the subject of this book as they have particular challenges and are generally more complex than other forms of rolling stock, such as coaches and wagons. When you can successfully build a locomotive you won't have any trouble with a fish van.

There is now an enormous and still growing choice of superb ready-to-run models in the most common OO gauge and increasingly on either side of the size spectrum in N gauge and O gauge. Paradoxically, this abundance may be decreasing the availability of kits as manufacturers are forced to consider more rarefied prototypes, which may not sell in sufficient bulk to be practicable. There are probably always going to be some locomotives that are not going to be commercially available – at least, not in the near future.

Building something allows to you to produce exactly what you want. It is generally cheaper than buying an off-the-shelf model, especially if you don't include the construction time (and that's the fun bit). You can have any loco you want from any time period or railway company. You could make a unique model of a loco on a specific date exactly as in a treasured photograph. It may be a loco that you spotted, or one that you rode behind and one that means something to you emotionally: an evocative and tangible memory in three dimensions.

You might want a static 'museum' specimen with everything included: all those bits and pieces underneath and inside that make the real thing work. Or it might be an imaginatively fictional 'freelance' model, not to mention the occasional 'Thomas' to enthral the younger generation.

If you're after something quite different you could try one of the 'rarer' gauges, such as 3mm scale and S gauge. These have their own particular advan-

The Lady Armstrong, *an Armstrong–Whitworth diesel electric shunter that provided a large proportion of the motive power on the impecunious North Sunderland Railway (when it wasn't broken down and replaced by a local taxi service).*

tages: 3mm has greater heft than N gauge and still takes up less space than OO gauge, while S gauge goes the other way, fitting nicely between the size and weight of O gauge and the more compact OO gauge (and in imperial measurements at a size ratio of 1 to 64).

There are all the narrow-gauge variants, too – or you could even have a gauge or scale all of your own. A particularly beautiful example is the layout *Pempoul* modelled by Gordon and Maggie Gravett to a unique scale of 1 to 50 – and a French prototype to boot.

SCALES AND GAUGES

Just to clarify, 'gauge' normally refers to the distance between the rails, a reduction of the full size 4ft 8½in (1.44m). For example, OO-gauge track has a gauge of 16.5mm, which is slightly narrower than it ought to be. 'Scale' is the ratio by which the real thing is reduced to model size; again in OO this is 4mm to 1ft (30cm), where each foot of the real thing is represented as 4mm on the model – which makes OO track just a little over 4ft (1.2m) wide.

In S scale everything is divided by sixty-four, and you can have a great deal of fun immersing yourself in scratch building.

As I mentioned, OO gauge is a historic compromise of 4mm scale for everything but the track, and consequently the width apart of the wheels. One of the reasons often cited for this is that it was difficult to fit the bulkier electric motors of the earlier twentieth century into locomotives at a scale of 3.5mm/foot, or HO (half the size of O gauge at 7mm/foot).

Maurice Hopper's lovely little S-scale layout **St Juliot**. *The audience are watching the author (standing) struggle ineffectually with the three-link couplings.*
MAURICE HOPPER

So they kept the track at HO and made all the rolling stock a little bigger.

This curiosity has promoted the growth of various complementary gauges that aim for a progressively more realistic appearance. EM stands for 18.2mm (it was widened a bit from 18mm) between the rails. The even more precise gauge of 18.83mm can be found, championed by such societies as Scalefour. And when I say championed, people can be *very* enthusiastic about, and protective of, their particular choices in all aspects of railway modelling.

APPROACHING SCRATCH BUILDING

This book describes the more traditional ways of construction by cutting and shaping materials, generally by hand. There are new and thought-provoking ways to produce models, and resin moulding, laser cutting, computer-aided design and 3D printing are becoming increasingly commonplace. It seems that the model railway community is often amongst the early innovators, and embrace new ways of doing things – and there is a great deal of information available out there if you find yourself drawn to these exciting developments.

The main emphasis of this book is to provide a step-by-step guide to building a locomotive in arguably the most popular gauge – OO gauge (4mm scale) – and to briefly describe techniques from other gauges/scales. Virtually all the approaches lend themselves to any of the scales, though there are quirks that are more applicable to some than others.

I have built up my skills through practice over the years, choosing methods from books, society journals, magazine articles and, more recently, internet forums. Joining a club has allowed me to pick people's brains, and I have learned a lot from visiting exhibitions. There are usually excellent demonstrations by skilled modellers who will happily show you the things that work best for them; you can explore the differences and work out what is best for you.

The processes I describe in the book are the ones that work for me. I use simple tools, and haven't got a lathe or milling machine. This is not because I don't want them: at the moment I just don't have the room. I am very much looking forward to acquiring some hefty hardware when there's enough space for it not to interfere with domestic life – but until then it's the kitchen table.

Historically, model railways were built (out of necessity) from whatever materials were cheaply and

An inspirational scratch-built locomotive by Gordon Gravett running on Pempoul – a superb example of what can be achieved with practice.
GORDON GRAVETT

easily available. People were happy to bash something beautiful out of a biscuit tin with a hammer and a pair of pliers – including the drive mechanisms. The necessary skills were routinely taught at school (if you were a boy…), and it was an everyday occurrence to watch your granddad whittle something useful for the household with a selection of tools from his well stocked shed. People fixed anything that broke. These pleasures and skills, and the confidence to use them, are now not as commonplace.

Happily now there is a roaring trade in detailing parts available from small manufacturers, and the practice of buying motors and wheels is almost ubiquitous and equally well catered for. There is also a resurgence in old-fashioned manual skills and creativity, which is reflected in the continuing interest in model railways. You only have to look at the wonderful examples of real-life scratch building, the steam locomotive 'new builds', to see how railways can still capture the imagination.

MAKING A START

Before you take the plunge you might want to get in some practice: perhaps soldering together an etched kit or modifying a shop-bought locomotive. Whilst I would recommend that you do this (I did and still do), it is not essential. If you are scratch building you are not going to make a mess of an expensive kit or ruin your favourite r-t-r (ready-to-run) loco. If you do make a mistake, and you will, you can dismantle the relevant bits and start again, or throw away a wonky component and make a new one. I have boxes full of rejected bits and pieces, which is frustrating *and* educational.

The chief motivation in deciding to build your own model may well be, as it is for me, the sheer pleasure of construction. I can sit and admire a half-completed model or set of pieces with great satisfaction as I work out how next I am going to put them all together. However, if you find yourself in difficulty I would advise you to step away from the work-bench and have a walk. If you're good at imagining shapes in 3D, then a tricky piece of construction may magically resolve itself inside your head while you're happily loading the dishwasher.

I find acquiring new skills, or making steady progress in existing ones, very rewarding, not just in modelling but in all walks of life. And many of those are transferable to modelling: measurement, imagination, patience, perseverance, a positive attitude and a pair of reasonably steady hands. There are no barriers to age or sex. The number of children at exhibitions seems, happily, to be holding up steadily, and more and more women are glad to demonstrate and discuss their modelling techniques in public. In fact I find that women are generally far more *able* to discuss things.

As a teenager I always loved the 'how-to' features in *The Railway Modeller*, and I hope that this book will do for the reader what those articles did for me. Latterly I have found magazines such as the *Model Railway Journal* inspirational. Seeing superb workmanship shouldn't put you off – equally, listening to that little voice over your shoulder telling you that you'll never get there won't help either. You can aspire and build and be very happy with something you've made, and as you learn from your mistakes you'll be even happier.

It may also be one of those tailor-made opportunities for you to sit down with your son or daughter, niece or nephew, spouse or concubine, and learn together. Children enjoy the creative process just as much as they did in the days of Meccano; look at the ongoing popularity of Lego or the proliferation of snowmen and sand-castles whenever the weather conditions allow.

There are specific skills that you will need for scratch building locomotives, and there's no time like the present to get hold of a soldering iron and a piercing saw and wave them around in a meaningful fashion. These are the hardest things you'll have to tackle, and like anything else, they take practice. You will have to roll with the blows of the occasional disappointment and disaster – though each new challenge becomes easier with familiarity. Actually, *the* most catastrophic scratch-building catastrophe is that of dropping your much loved model on to the floor. And you can do that just as easily with something straight out of a box.

CHAPTER TWO

WHAT TO BUILD?

Scratch building enables us to have a completely free choice of what we want to model. It also requires us to know why we want it. You might set your heart on an example of an unusual locomotive, or maybe decide to take up the challenge of producing a specific member of a class. There are lots of different locos out there, and the more you look, the more you will find: oddities, experiments and one-offs, and stuff for which there is little information and for which you'll need to dig around in obscure books and follow murky internet trails.

The smaller scales allow smaller layouts in restricted spaces, or they provide the opportunity for wide, sweeping lines with long trains in open countryside or urban settings. Larger scales take up much more room. The bigger you get, the more detail you might want to include and the fewer models you'll need to fill the available space. Do you want a static model in a display case or something that can nip round your garden in the rain?

The locomotives in this book, unlike many of the real things, are propelled by small electric motors,

so if you want any other form of power (clockwork, battery, radio control, live steam) you'll be able to find further information in all the other books, magazine articles and the internet that are out there.

Finally, how much detail do you want? Can you get parts or is there a kit?

MY CHOICE

I have chosen as my main example an LNER J15 (formerly GER Y14) in 4mm/OO gauge, as there isn't a readily available kit (as I write) and no current ready-to-run (r-t-r) model – though no doubt there will be by the time you read this sentence. The J15 is a beautiful British 0-6-0 inside cylinder tender locomotive with a low slung, rather cat-like demeanour. Long-lived and numerous, they tackled both goods and passenger trains over a large geographical area, from tiny country branches to main-line services, ranging from the wide open spaces of East Anglia to the wilds of Scotland.

It has no outside valve gear, and all the mechanical excitement carries on unseen between the frames,

The LNER J15, a striking example of Victorian locomotive design.

which makes things very much easier. The loco and tender are not encrusted with rivets, just enough to add texture, and there is a reasonably small number of quite charming variants and modifications. The tender also allows for some slightly less mechanically involved practice in scratch building.

Alan Gibson, as well as occasionally producing a kit of the J15 in 4mm and 7mm scales, complements these with many excellent castings of the bits I don't generally like to make (and some of the ones I do). These bits are an absolute boon to the scratch builder both new and experienced; they are also quite easy to get hold of from traders at shows or internet websites, and you might be able to pick up some useful odds and ends from swap-meets and eBay.

Wheels and associated mechanical parts are straightforwardly available, and the biggest problem to tackle, I discovered, was fitting a motor into the rather petite boiler. However, this was helped by modern small motors being highly efficient and powerful.

I have a number of wonderfully atmospheric prints of J15s in service, particularly No. 65447 on the East Suffolk line in early BR days, one I knew well growing up there in the 1970s. There is also a glorious example, No. 65462, preserved on the North Norfolk Railway. A model of a J15 ticks all the boxes for me: comparatively simple to build, lots of easily available information, a real one to take detailed photos of, an emotional connection, and just the thing for my (long) planned model of Saxmundham station. And I already had a lot of relevant literature cluttering up the house. A perfect place then, from which to start to scratch build a locomotive.

However, if you are not completely enamoured by the J15, there are plenty of very similar designs of 0-6-0 tender locos from many of the other railway companies that you could attempt instead, using exactly the same techniques. Or even something completely different? If so, do you have suitable photographs? Is there a preserved example? I'm continually surprised by how many steam and diesel locos there are in preservation in the UK – and was also alarmed to discover that my favourite diesel, the North British Class 22, is not amongst them. If you are a diesel fan, Chapter 15 looks at a scratch-built example and should be of interest. (A word of warning regarding a preserved loco: there may well have been necessary or unexpected changes throughout its life in preservation, so take care to look at original information as well.)

I must add that my life-long infatuation with all things Great Western has been almost overturned by the many splendid locomotive types that I have uncovered whenever researching away from home. Do take the time to look beyond your primary interest, as there is plenty out there to take your fancy.

SOURCES OF INSPIRATION

I take great pleasure in the process of collecting photographs and articles. I've spent ten years accumulating them for a projected 7mm layout of Culmstock station on the Culm Valley line. I've got folders of the stuff and am still finding new things. eBay is a very good (though sometimes expensive) source of photographs. The internet of course can be very helpful, particularly – and rather ironically – when unearthing obscure book titles and magazine articles.

There are many companies advertising in magazines and online who have archived a wealth of railway images and will supply downloads, hard copies and slides. Most of them provide printed catalogues, or you can search and order online. *Locomotives Illustrated* and similar periodicals are great for historical information and a good range of photos, while old modelling magazines are excellent for more esoteric drawings and information. The number of fine quality books with superb illustrations is expanding, and despite the growing distance in time, interest in the more obscure nooks and crannies of British railway history seems to be building.

The libraries of many model railway clubs are packed with archival gems, and you can spend many happy hours rooting around in them; and it is still possible to persuade your local library to order books for you. If you are very fortunate you might come across something like *Yeadon's Register* for your choice of loco; I have the volume that shows virtually every J15 at various times during the long life of the class.

A selection of the printed material I collected for the J15 build – even more stuff is on the computer.

PLANNING AND RESEARCH

There are many different ways in which you can prepare for your build, although the amount of research necessary for the completion of a successful locomotive model is quite subjective. Some people are content with a good drawing and a couple of photos of their chosen class of loco – or even just the one photo.

PHOTOGRAPHS

You can take numerous digital photos if the real thing is on hand, either with a clear idea of those parts and details in which you are interested, or just so many that what you want is bound to show up. It is almost obligatory that something important ends up just off frame or masked by smoke, or by the crew of the loco or another photographer with their copious family standing in front of you.

It is quite difficult to find photos of your particular loco in pieces, either when being built or repaired, or

crashed or broken up, and these are invaluable when you do. In the case of the J15, I still couldn't quite see how the smokebox saddle was shaped until I found the photo (opposite) in the magazine *Joint Line*, the house journal of the Midland and Great Northern Joint Railway Society who own the only preserved example. In fact I managed to contact the photographer, Mr Keith Ashford, who is overseeing the J15's current rebuild, and he kindly supplied me with some invaluable photos for this book.

By the time this book is in print, she should be back on the rails and you can go and see her in Norfolk. If not, you could contribute to the fund to rebuild her. I'm very hopeful that I may soon be the proud sponsor of one of her washout plugs – though they won't let you take it home apparently.

People may have exactly the information that you need, and are usually very pleased to be asked. Some of the photos I've used have been very happily offered for our entertainment and education – or there's al-

The J15 boiler undergoing repair, showing the smokebox saddle underneath. KEITH ASHFORD

ways your imagination or a similar locomotive type to take a good guess from. I use photographs particularly when detailing models, often estimating the dimensions by eye. A lot of the photos I took of the J15 are provided in the book for this purpose.

DRAWINGS

There may be numerous sources of drawings to help you in your build, or you might want to draw your own. Many modellers start with General Arrangement (GA) drawings: these are drawings of the full size loco, and show every detail that enabled engineers to build the real thing. They are works of art in themselves. If you want to know the shape of something you can't see, a GA will almost certainly show it, from above, below and either side, and as such their main disadvantage is that they tend to be very complex and can be difficult to read. Services such as the National Railway Museum Search Engine are making GAs much more easily available.

It can be very helpful to prepare your own sketches from a GA as you will get to know the loco better and gain a feel for how it is put together. I've included my drawings where I used them as an aid to construction: I apologise now for any inaccuracies, and have simplified some of the measurements to ease construction.

I would recommend that you try to get hold of at least one drawing from the following sources. Detailed outline drawings may be obtained from Skinley Drawings, and in the case of LNER locos such as the J15, Isinglass produce an excellent range featuring a great deal of useful prototype information from a variety of viewpoints. There are also some beautiful drawings available from the website of the Great Eastern Society, or you can download some nice ones from the Connoisseur Models website, who incidentally produce a lovely J15 kit in 7mm scale. In fact you're spoiled for choice with the J15.

If you are lucky in your googling you can obtain some very good drawings from the internet, which can be printed out and resized by photocopier. And of course there are a great many illustrations available in magazines and books and from specialist historical societies.

Do try and stick to one drawing as there may be slight differences between them, and always check against the prototype measurements in case there are any inaccuracies due to scaling up or down, or the paper stretching. I also compare drawings against my photos for any oddities, and if the photo is different I amend the drawing.

In short, find or prepare a drawing that works for you, make sure it's accurate enough to be useful to you, and stick to it.

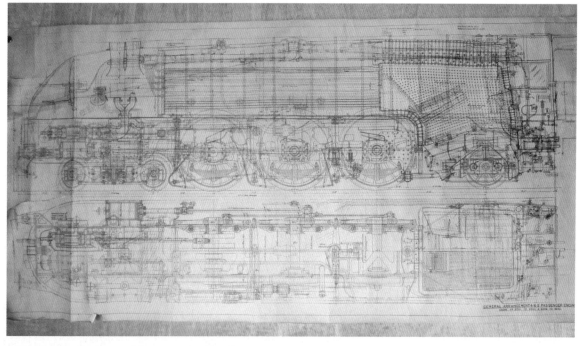

An example of a General Arrangement drawing.

PREPARING TO BUILD

WORKING ON THE RAILWAY

Knowing how the real thing works can be indispensable when building a model. It allows you to understand why some of the bits and pieces are where they are, and hopefully to notice if you've left something off.

If you are really keen to find out about the gadgets that get things going, sign up for a day's loco driving (or get someone to give it to you as a present). Besides being one of the most exhilarating things I've done for ages, it taught me more about how to run a model railway properly in one day than attending a whole raft of exhibitions. The effort needed just to get the thing to stop and start is quite startling, and the amount of heat and noise is astonishing. It's enormous fun, too – and now, of course, I want a model of the loco that I drove and fired.

If you visit the National Railway Museum at York you can witness how the real thing actually works. There is a sectioned Southern Railway Merchant Navy class locomotive on display, peeled open like a sar-

dine can. Colour-coded pathways show you where the steam was produced and where it went to do its marvellous work. The exhibit is accompanied by a team of highly knowledgeable staff, who know the whole business backwards and are very pleased to share their knowledge. And there's a café, which is wonderful.

There are also some excellent books documenting the development and use of steam traction, which are thoroughly interesting in themselves. Learning about the mechanics of steam locomotives, particularly when having not been around to see them on the real railway, has been very satisfying and quite alarming. (Did you know that a very high temperature mix of steam and oil under pressure is extremely corrosive?)

I remember being very surprised the first time I discovered that there isn't really an enormous electric motor inside the boiler, with the piston rods being driven back and forth by the driving wheels. I was also quite taken aback to learn that the boiler isn't just a large space full up to the top with water, sloshing wildly about inside. It's got a lot more going

The best birthday present you may ever receive.

So that's what goes on inside.
PAUL MACEY

on in there than that. This sort of insight may also help you find your way more easily around instructions and drawings.

You could join a preserved railway as a volunteer, and learn at close quarters with plenty of sound advice and experience immediately available. If nothing else, I'd recommend joining a railway club for plenty of knowledge, facilities and companionship – and you have the chance to show off your models to people who really appreciate them.

TECHNICAL TERMS

As you may have just discovered, there are a great number of technical terms involved in loco construc-

tion. Many bits and pieces have more than one name, and some of those seem confusingly interchangeable depending on personal preference; some can even be named differently depending on the railway company from which they originate. The ones in this book are those I know and use, and I offer my apologies for any offence caused by unintentional terminological sloppiness. These terms are shown in the photograph overleaf of another of my all-time favourite locomotives.

INFORMATION AND ACCURACY

If you come across an unfamiliar term, don't be anxious about looking it up or asking someone what

Some fine gentlemen enjoying the delights of the test track at the Model Railway Club in London, including an O-gauge J15.
DAVID COASBY

1. Guard irons
2. Buffer stock
3. Buffer beam
4. Vacuum pipe
5. Bogie
6. Bogie wheels
7. Smokebox saddle
8. Smokebox door
9. Smokebox dart
10. Smokebox
11. Chimney
12. Boiler band
13. Boiler
14. Inside motion
15. Dome
16. Footplate
17. Splashers
18. Firebox
19. Driving wheels
20. Coupling rods
21. Brake block
22. Brake hanger
23. Handrail knob
24. Washout plug
25. Safety valve
26. Whistle
27. Cab
28. Rainstrip
29. Tender
30. Tender axle-guard

Naming of parts on LNER B12 4-6-0 locomotive No. 8572 on the North Norfolk Railway. DAVID COASBY

it means. For example, I used to find the wheel arrangement conventions confusing. Take the J15: 0-6-0 indicates that there are no little (carrying) wheels at the front, there are six big (driving) wheels in the middle, and no carrying ones at the back of the locomotive.

If you are having problems with acquiring information for some of the more obscure prototypes, then all is not lost. The only information that I could initially find for a Furness tank loco that I wanted to build was that the driving wheels were 5ft 8in in diameter – that and an (almost) side-on photo. But from just this, it is possible to determine some idea of the other main dimensions: all it takes is a ruler, a calculator and some hard thinking. You could get the photo resized to suit your scale just by working out the ratio from the known size of the wheels and the actual measurement from the photograph; this is what I did.

Of course there will be inevitable inaccuracies due to distortion, but you'll get a reasonable idea, particularly if you go for the largest measurements such as the boiler length. The height of the buffers from the rail tends to be fairly standard, as does the height from the top of the chimney to the rails – that is if it is going to be able to couple up to other bits of railway equipment or go under any bridges. Then you can spend a pleasant few hours knocking up your own drawing.

Alternatively you could ask for help from such sources as the excellent and very friendly RMweb, which I did after finishing my drawing, and was provided with a link to a very good outline drawing absolutely full of measurements. And I was generally only 3in in 35ft out on my estimates, which was very satisfying. Soon after that, I was pointed in the direction

of a very reasonable second-hand book also full of Furness Railway locomotive information.

The point is, the more information you've got, the more accurate your model can be. However, it is possible to have a go using just one photo if that works for you. It is another Universal Law that someone will provide you with all the information you need as soon as you've finished – and that's good, too; you can always build another one.

Please note that some photocopiers can introduce distortion. So if you are sneakily using the machine at work, take a ruler to check the dimensions are still as they should be. I usually spend a few extra pence getting one of the surviving high street printers to do me a few good copies on nice stiff paper.

There are any number of societies that produce periodicals packed with opinion on your particular penchant, and they are only too happy to help out. Importantly for the scratch builder they may also produce and make available many of the bits and pieces that can be harder to come by. And if you want your modelling to be a sociable activity, they are a good place to start.

A selection of society magazines stuffed with information and modelling articles.

CHAPTER THREE

WORKING WITH TOOLS AND MATERIALS

THE WORK PLACE

Firstly you need to consider your environment – and this means not just the seating arrangements. If you are used to lots of people and things going on around you, find yourself a place where you don't feel left out. Alternatively, if you're easily distracted, make sure you're hidden away in peace and quiet where you have control of your surroundings and you won't be tempted to go off chatting with the neighbours every ten minutes. This applies in particular to those terrors of modern time-wasting: emails, social networking and the internet.

You'll probably have to compromise, so it is worth considering what would be your ideal and getting as close to it as possible. You don't want small fingers to be able to find their way to your half-finished model or hot soldering iron, and you may have to clear up after each modelling session. Whatever your space, if you're anything like me you'll find it becomes quickly cluttered. But it's surprising how effective you can be in a very small area as long as you keep control of your materials and tools.

Light is an important consideration, and if natural sunlight is not available you will need to supply it in

Dining room table work-bench and OttLite – remarkably tidy; it always looks better with a nice bunch of flowers.

Tool tidies save a great deal of time – and the right tool is always handy, so that you're not tempted to make do with the wrong one.

sufficient quantities artificially. Watch that it's neither too bright nor an uncomfortable source of heat; I use an OttLite desk lamp, which does all that. A binocular headband magnifier is also great for small work; make sure that it's properly adjusted and not causing you to strain your eyes.

I use the dining room table when it's not being used for its primary purpose, or we eat in the kitchen. There's plenty of natural light and quite a lot of human traffic, including regular piano practice, so I don't feel that I'm missing something. And it's easy to get to the radio so I can leap up and switch it off if I don't like the programme. Some scratch builders manage to build fantastic models on a tray balanced on their knees, sitting in front of the television or in a hotel bedroom.

I try to keep the tools I use most often in pen and pencil tidies, while those I use more seldom are in a small toolbox on the floor. As you gain experience you find particular tools more suitable, and discard others. My most aged ones tend to have a patina of rust caused by the spray from the more caustic fluxes I used to use.

HEALTH AND SAFETY ESSENTIALS

- If you are using a mini-drill, wear a pair of protective glasses
- Get a proper stand for your soldering iron, and don't leave it where inquisitive little fingers and paws can get to it
- Treat your soldering iron with extreme care: it's incredibly hot and could be lethal. Don't accidently dunk it in your coffee cup or try to catch it with your knees if you drop it
- Work in a well ventilated space so as to avoid fumes building up, and only smoke in the back garden
- Be careful when under the influence: be sure that alcohol is the only poison you're drinking
- Have a big box of plasters close to hand, as blood can tarnish metal terribly

So you can see that safety precautions are fairly painless, in fact just good old-fashioned common sense.

HEALTH AND SAFETY

Health and safety issues are inevitable, since scratch building necessarily involves lots of very sharp things, incandescently hot objects and occasionally a noxious chemical, not to mention tiny items flying at high speed in unexpected directions. I have a friend who is a health and safety trainer for charity volunteers and it's a tough job, but when his trainees realize that what they are learning might actually save life, limb and law-suits, they really warm to the idea.

TOOLS

To use an angling metaphor, when you fish, a great deal of your success in catching and landing your quarry successfully is due to touch: feeling the gentle twitch of the line at the first tentative nibble of the fish, choosing the right time to strike with the right amount of energy, and then carefully reeling in your thrashing adversary.

Getting the feel of your tools will allow you to use them as well as possible: knowing when a file or saw begins to bite, knowing when to stop as you feel a sudden resistance. Using a tiny drill or tap in a pin vice, scoring a line in a sheet of metal, forming a bend in a piece of wire or loco body component: all these and more require you to concentrate on how they feel, and a lightness of touch is key. Anyone who has watched a child attack a piece of wood with a saw will know what I mean: they go at it with ferocity and speed, producing a result that might have been done with a sledge hammer.

It takes time and patience to achieve mastery with tools.

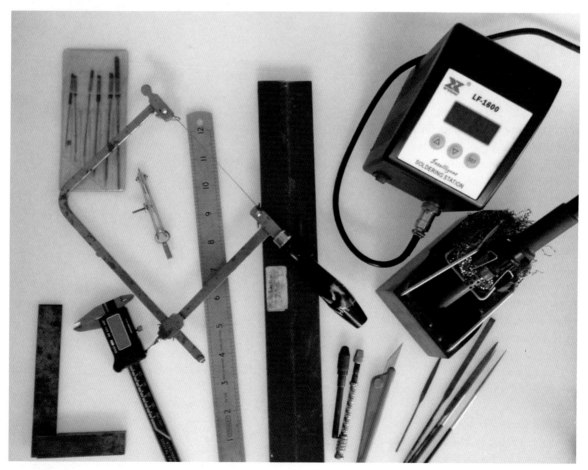

The essential tool selection.

THE ESSENTIAL SELECTION

I find that the following tools are absolutely essential for scratch-building in metal:

- Hefty soldering iron
- Piercing saw
- Electronic digital calipers
- Pair of dividers
- Steel rule
- Set-square
- A few good files
- Craft knife
- Bending bars
- Pin-chuck hand drill

You will find your own favourites.

Whatever your preferences, you do need to be able to make and transfer measurements easily and accurately, mark out shapes on metal, cut, bend and break it to size, shape it carefully to fit, and join all the bits together securely.

Once you've got the hang of the tools and their feel it's amazing how skilled and versatile you can be. The following section discusses the use of each one, plus a few extras.

MEASURING

DIVIDERS

These take the measuring out of measuring because you can copy dimensions quickly and accurately from drawings or components and transfer them to the metal without any ruler. To avoid scratches you can replace one point of the dividers with a thin brass rod. Take care that you scribe lines in a firm flowing motion, not with the circular scribing that you did at school with a pair of compasses.

VERNIER CALIPERS

These can change your life. They take all the horror out of measurement (except perhaps the cost of the batteries), are simple to use, and can be as accurate as

you want. Just make sure that they are zeroed properly with the handy switch, and make sure they are showing you millimetres or inches as required (they do both). No fiddling disconsolately with dials: there is a digital display to show you exactly what you want to know.

Use them to measure inside things, the diameter of holes, and the distance between edges and markings. Find out how thick your metals are and the size of your drills, nuts and bolts. They even have sharp edges to mark things with (although you really shouldn't).

RULERS OR STRAIGHT EDGES

You will still need a ruler, even if you're not keen to measure with it. I have a small 6in and larger 12in metal one, with divisions in half millimetres and whatever fractions of inches you might find useful. You can run a knife blade down the incised lines of the divisions straight on to your work to mark lengths accurately. The straight edge itself is, of course, great for scoring straight lines (though watch you don't remove the tips of your fingers). I also use them to support brass and nickel sheet when I'm bending it in the bars.

GRIPPING

BENDING BARS

These are a fantastically versatile tool. You can use them as a vice to hold stuff or flatten bendy bits of metal. Their most useful function is to break pieces of sheet metal to size. You just need a reasonably deep scored line, then clamp the part into the bars along the score line and bend back and forth, supporting with a ruler or wood block. You can even use this method to make really narrow (and otherwise expensive) strips. Nickel silver is easier as it snaps more easily; brass tends to be softer and doesn't break as cleanly.

PLIERS

These come in a bewildering array of sizes and shapes and you need to consider what you want them to do. I have three main ones, all small: flat-nosed, round-nosed and some little pointy ones. They're great for

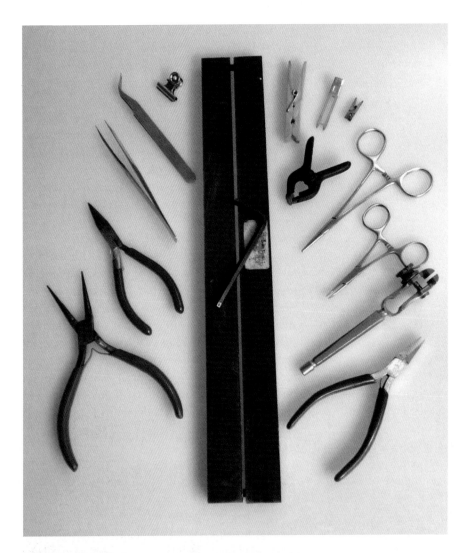

Gripping tools.

shaping metal rods, tubes and flat pieces. Basically, whatever you wrap round them will take the shape of the nose. The flats are particularly good for straight, sharp bends and breaking off small pieces of metal that would be fiddly in the bending bars. The round and pointed ones are great for such things as handrails and detailing components.

You can just hold things with them, and I have a secret weapon for that which is even better.

MEDICAL FORCEPS

These forceps are relatively new to me, and I would suggest that reasonably cheap locking ones would suffice. They are phenomenally good for holding small bits and pieces (they are supposed to clamp blood vessels closed during operations). The clamp on the handle locks them closed to a varying degree of firmness, and the serrated jaws are flexible enough to give a little and not squash stuff that you're trying to hold. You can use them whilst soldering as they're made of stainless steel, and they don't quickly transfer the heat to your fingers. I don't know how I did without them.

TWEEZERS

These are also good for holding and positioning things. I have curved and straight pairs both with exceedingly pointy ends. Due to the physics of trying to hold something still with very tiny pressure points you can exert great force and things will ping off into oblivion. It can be infuriatingly difficult to keep items in the correct position with them, though they do have more finesse than the slightly clumsier forceps and are invaluable for manipulating small items such as nuts, washers and crankpin components.

CUTTING

PIERCING OR JEWELLERS' SAW

These are great: you can go round corners and cut delicate complicated shapes with great dexterity. It is a difficult thing to use at first and, like soldering, one of the most useful skills to acquire. A variety of blades is available: those for jewellers' saws are usually listed in a range from 8/0 (fine) through zero and up to 4 (the coarsest). Finer blades have more teeth per inch and are generally thinner. I tend to use the finer ones,

6/0 to 4/0, for most jobs, mainly because I'm too lazy to change the blade – it just takes longer and the finer blades are more likely to break. Buy a pack of assorted ones and try them out for yourself. You do need to set everything up correctly.

The teeth should 'bite' as the saw is drawn downwards so that the blade is stretched, not compressed, as it cuts. I work out the direction of the teeth by drawing the blade carefully across my thumb nail. The blade is then clamped into the frame, which is tensioned by pressing one end down onto a firm surface and tightening the frame screw. (There's no shame in getting someone to help you here.)

You will need a little cutting stand (or piercing saw table) to support the work; mine clamps to the table and has a circular hole in it to accommodate the blade. Often you have to pass the saw blade through a small starter hole in a piece of work to begin cutting, which is very fiddly, making everything even more of a challenge.

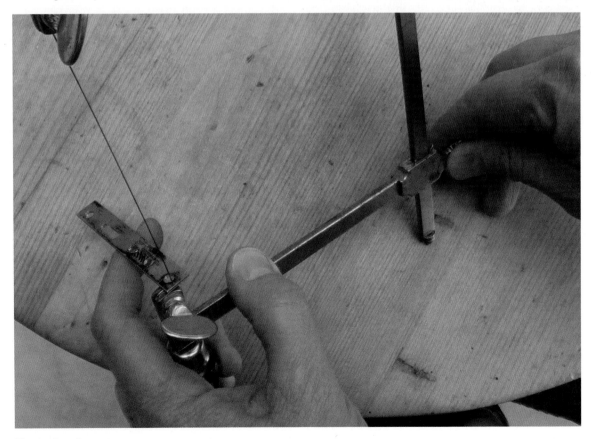

Tensioning the saw.

Once all that's done, position everything carefully on your table and draw the blade lightly where you want to start. It can help if you steady it right up against the woodwork of the table so that you cut a little slot in it. Don't get the blade caught in the slot because it will break.

Continue to cut gently. Get a feel for the bite of the blade for when it starts to stick, and you'll gradually reduce the rate of breakage. This will decrease as you become more accustomed to the process (I promise) and is infuriating every time it happens because you have to set up all over again. I rarely break a blade now, generally only if I'm tired or in a hurry.

A shape cut from the centre of a piece will need a starter hole to get the blade in. You will also need to drill holes to help you negotiate tight corners. I have included these in some of the drawings in the book. I find that you can actually make abrupt changes of direction by keeping the blade in the same place and as you saw up and down, gently rotate the saw frame (not recommended until you have some experience).

If you have to cut a piece larger than the reach of the frame, you'll have to start again from another direction.

Try to follow your marked lines; as you practise you'll be able to cut almost exactly along them. Keep to the waste side, and file back when you've finished sawing. Sometimes a blade can go a bit wobbly through wear, in which case change it for a new one that cuts straight.

Large pieces can take quite a bit of time; have patience, it's a very rewarding procedure. You could branch out into jewellery and watch-making too.

TIN SNIPS

I don't use these often, preferring the piercing saw. They can remove large chunks of metal or tiny slices if you're careful – the thicker the metal the more difficult the job. The main disadvantage is that they cause distortion. Smaller pieces will distort the most. You can always flatten pieces out carefully afterwards.

DRILLS

I use pin-chucks (small hand drills) a great deal; they are slow and easily controlled. Holes can be started off in the right places, and really tiny drills can be used without an outrageous breakage rate.

It's best to get a reasonably expensive pin-chuck that holds drills between 0mm to 1mm and others for larger sizes. You can get handles with four different swappable collets (the bits that hold the drills). I find it best to have a number of separate chucks holding different sizes of drill. If the holding end of your particular chuck is uncomfortable you can use a drawing pin as a swivel.

Slide the drill as far as it will go into the collet: about 5mm projecting is good as it's less easy to break, and take your time. You can widen the hole in stages using progressively larger drills. The smaller you start off, the more accurate you should be.

If you put a good sharp needle in your pin-chuck you can use it as a very accurate scriber against a straight edge. Hold it firmly and score a cross on to your metal in the correct place, and a small drill will find the centre by itself; you'll feel the click as it does. Then simply twist gently to start the hole.

Always use a nice bit of hardwood to support your workpiece, as the drill can be damaged as it breaks through the metal.

Relatively recently I have discovered the wonderful little Archimedes drill, which has a screw mechanism that can speed up the whole process. I describe its use later in the book. I also have a small, powerful mains mini-drill with variable speed control that I occasionally use to drill holes, although I find it most useful for cutting, grinding and polishing. It has a good hand grip near the collet and can be precisely controlled. I find it much easier to start holes using a pin-chuck, and then widen them using the mini-drill. Incidentally, before I bought my present one I used to use quite a hefty Black and Decker battery power drill – chunky yet able to drill down to 0.5mm.

I occasionally use a stand for the mini-drill; if this set-up suits you it can be highly accurate and save time, particularly using the drill table to keep things in line. It doesn't really do it for me, however, as I like to be able to feel what's going on.

Buy yourself a generous selection of drills from 0.3mm up to 2mm in 0.1mm stages, with plenty of duplicates for the more often used sizes such as 0.5mm and 0.7mm. I also have drills from 2mm to 4mm in 0.5mm stages.

Another interesting thing that metal can do when drilled is to form a raised collar round the outside of the hole you've carefully made. This can be handy if you want a hole with a raised lip, such as a mud-hole cover. If you don't want a lip, twiddle a larger drill in the hole with your fingers to get rid of it. It's useful to produce a small indent into the hole to allow such things as axle-bushes to 'sit' properly.

BROACHES AND REAMERS

These are used to make holes larger. Be sure not to use big drills in thin metal: it won't work and can be excitingly dangerous, if not downright ruinous, to both your model and health in general. A large drill will tear thin metal and jam inside the tear, causing the piece to whip round like a propeller blade, deftly removing any wayward digits.

Less exciting and much more effective is to use a broach or a reamer. Reamers are the tapered ones, and are used to make holes progressively larger. I use the calipers to find the general required diameter and mark the place on the blade of the reamer in felt-tip so I know when I'm getting there. Mine has the surprising tendency to cause a slight hexagonal shape to occur, though I've no idea why.

The parallel ones are broaches, and are used when you want a specific and accurate hole diameter such as for axle sizes. Finally there's the set of little tiny ones, which are good for accurately opening out tiny holes in small stages.

REMOVING UNWANTED METAL

FILES

I have a large collection of files. My earliest set of small or needle files is rusty from exposure to sol-

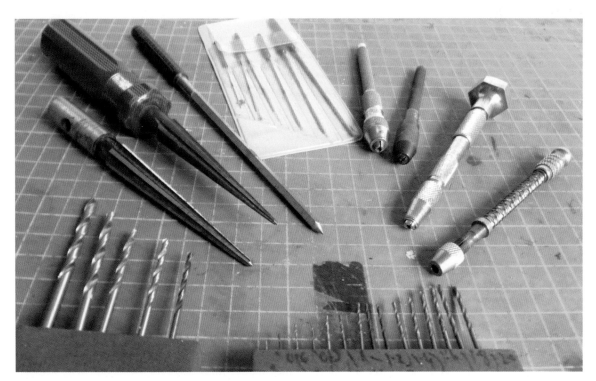

A selection of broaches, reamers, drills and pin-chucks.

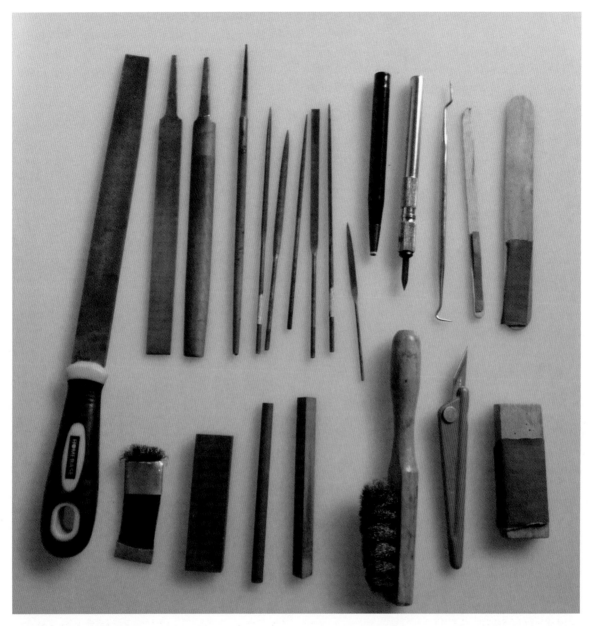

Tools for removing metal.

dering flux and are collectively clogged with solder and white metal. It is possible to clean them by heating them in a gas flame and quickly brushing off the molten clag (watching out for flying specks of incandescent material). However, it is safer if you just settle for the brisk application of a wire brush and forget the heat.

A much better policy is to have a set of good files that are used exclusively for filing metal. They should be sharp and of good quality – that is, a bit expensive. Try not to let them rattle around against each other; it is best to keep them in a stand. There are some excellent articles regarding their use, including a particularly fine one on the 2mm Scale Association website, which I urge you to read for a connoisseur's approach to filing.

When using them, clamp the work down as firmly as possible, and with a hand on either end of the file, move it gently at about 45 degrees to the length of the piece you are filing. Don't go at it like a terrier with a rat. You can smooth the piece off afterwards by 'draw filing', which is moving the file at 90 degrees along the piece; this takes off all the tiny bumps. Keep an eye on what you are doing, as it is very easy to take off too much. As with sawing, file to the line that you have scribed.

I use a small range of needle files: flat, triangular, square, half round and round; all of them are Swiss Cut No. 4, which is quite fine. You can feel them working and their use can be very therapeutic. A set of Swiss Cut No. 2 are a coarser cut and will take more metal off more quickly. I also have a lovely tiny little file from Squires which I use for very fine work, and miraculously haven't either broken or lost, yet.

Then there are great big files, with enigmatic names. It's good to use the largest that you can, because if you take off the most metal reasonably quickly you'll get a straighter edge instead of lots of ridges – though just watch that you don't take off too much. I have a massive rough flat file that I put flat on the table, and then I rub the work along it, to keep edges flat and parallel. Then I have a few indeterminate 'mummy bear' size files, flat and round, which I use for taking the cusps off edges or for larger work.

Favourites will grow on you, and you'll know which ones are going to end up as solder scrapers. And if you are a file connoisseur, all I can do is apologise.

SHARPENING STONES

After a recent article in the *MRJ*, I've started using sharpening or oil stones as an accompaniment to files. A small diameter round one is particularly useful; it's smooth and graceful and can take off a surprisingly large amount of metal. You can also use flat ones on the bench. However, they do make rather a mess, and can scratch deeply. Using them to keep your craft blades sharp is also handy, and I am really growing to like them.

WET AND DRY PAPER

This is great stuff for polishing and the final removal of metal. It won't take great lumps off, so don't try to use it as a file. It comes in a variety of grades: I tend to use the finer stuff, stuck with double-sided sticky tape to bits of balsa, coffee stirrers and brass tubes. It will polish your work, getting rid of minor scratches and removing the lighter file marks. Buy a packet of assorted grades.

FIBRE-GLASS SCRATCHING BRUSHES

I hate these brushes; I'm scared of (and scarred by) them. They consist of a bundle of fibre-glass fibres in a holder, providing a surface with which to abrade material away. People swear by them; I swear at them. The fibres break off and get everywhere, including in your fingers, and if you try to blow the bits away, possibly in your eyes. They polish things up prettily, won't gouge or scratch metal surfaces, and can round off lumps of solder nicely (without removing them), but they will hide in crevices and leap joyfully into the middle of your drying paint-work. Some people use medical gloves to tame them, or even use them under running water. I say don't use them at all.

If you have to, use a small pad of fine wire wool held in tweezers instead, or a Garryflex rubber sanding block. Regular washing after soldering will keep your model clean and ready for painting without having to resort to these methods of surface preparation.

OTHER USEFUL TOOLS

Vices: I have a small one that clamps to the table top; it can be useful to hold the bending bars in, and is particularly good for holding work for filing. It acts as a massive heat sink if I try to use it when soldering (wooden blocks and small clamps are much better). Vices can be good for squashing stuff, though generally I use my bending bars instead; this is definitely a matter of choice.

Razor saws: These come in a variety of widths and breadths. They are useful when you want a narrow

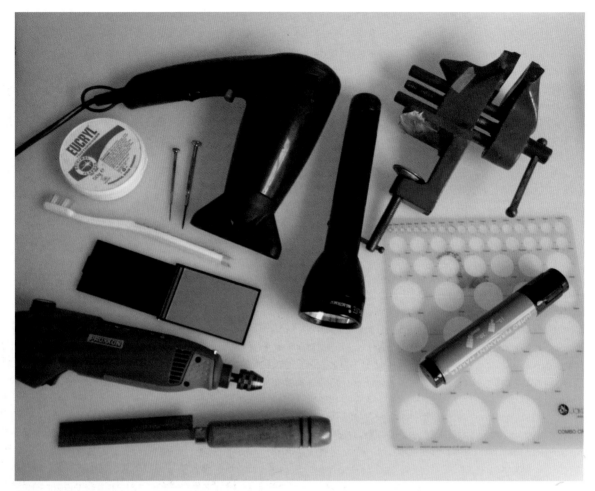

Other useful tools.

straight cut to a reasonable depth. I don't use them much to cut large pieces because I find the bending and breaking method more effective. They are good for 90-degree cuts in tubes and metal sections.

Watchmakers' screwdrivers: These are cheap and invaluable for dealing with the variety of tiny nuts and bolts involved in scratch-building. A little lump of Blu-tack on the blade will help you keep hold of bolts as you position them. You can also use them to scrape solder out of tiny recesses – or to fix your glasses – or your watch.

Great big permanent marker pen: These pens are excellent for showing markings on metal, and

easy to wipe off with meths; a selection of different coloured thin marker pens will allow you to write on metal surfaces, too.

Circle templates and French curves: These plastic templates are invaluable for producing your own drawings, and great for marking out curves and circles. They are readily available in stationery shops.

Scrapers: I have a triangular scraper, which is very useful for removing unwanted solder, having nice sharp edges and a point. Watch you don't scratch the metal too deeply, and keep the scraper sharp using a stone. As with all tools, give it a wipe if it gets flux on it, and gently de-rust it with a piece of wet and dry.

Other useful scrapers include sharpened watchmakers' screwdrivers (which have a nice flat chisel blade), old needle files and dental probes.

Torch: Besides being useful in a power cut, a small hand torch is invaluable if you drop something on a smooth floor (not a carpet, nothing will help you find anything from a carpet except a hoover…): just lie the torch on the floor and slowly revolve it. Any tiny item will throw a long shadow and is much easier to see (as is fluff and food and so on).

Hair dryer and little mirror: We've rifled through the contents of the doctor's bag and the dentist's surgery, now it's the turn of the hairdressing salon. A hair dryer is indispensable for drying models after you've washed off the detritus of soldering or are preparing them for painting; the little mirror offers you a different viewpoint when soldering, and an important new perspective when positioning different components.

Most importantly, buy these items cheaply for yourself and *don't* use those belonging to the house-hold authority – you'll be very unpopular.

Toothbrush and tooth powder: There are many choices of cleaning materials that are effective in removing flux and other impurities. I use a toothbrush, hot water, and *Eucryl* tooth powder – cheap, effective, and easy to rinse. If brushing dislodges a component, then it hasn't been fixed on properly. Always put the plug in the sink.

METALS – SHAPES AND SIZES

Every time I go to a show I like to stock up on a few bits and pieces of metal. Naturally you'll run out of the very stuff you haven't got when you ab-solutely need it, so it's always best to have some spare.

USEFUL METAL SHAPES

- Straight brass rod: in diameters 0.3mm, 0.5mm, 0.7mm, 0.9mm and 1.0mm
- Brass wire in coils: usually 0.5mm and 0.7mm diameter – a good complement to the straight stuff
- Square-section brass wire in coils: 0.3mm, 0.5mm and others – fantastic stuff for detailing
- Half-round brass wire: straight or coiled and in a variety of sizes; great again for detailing jobs – you can straighten any of the coiled wires by holding one end securely in a vice and pulling the other end with a pair of pliers until you feel it 'give' or it breaks (take care)
- Phosphor bronze wire, soft iron wire and nickel silver wire: can be used for pick-ups, couplings, springy bits or for any other exciting, innovative ideas
- A variety of brass tubes: you can get really tiny tubes that will take 0.3mm wire or even smaller, and go up to many centimetres in diameter. The ones that telescope into each other are great for building up detail pieces; the larger ones are fantastic for boilers, fire- and smokeboxes and anything between
- A variety of square-section tubes in brass: you can get L- and H-section pieces too

All these materials are initially quite expensive, the really tiny pieces in particular. However, just build up a bank of them: you often find tubing and other pieces going cheap in model shops and at shows, so buy it up even if you don't need it at that moment – you may one day.

METAL SHEET

Go for sheets no bigger than A4 size, depending on your needs, and of two or three appropriate thicknesses. For 2mm to 7mm scale models I use 0.015in and 0.020in almost exclusively. 0.010in can be useful although it is rather thin and the brass is particularly prone to bend-ing and denting unhelpfully, while anything much thicker than 0.020in can be difficult to work.

Nickel silver is lovely: it is silvery and easier to solder, it seems harder and holds its shape well. It is slightly more expensive than brass.

Brass is an attractive golden colour; it is softer, soaks up heat quickly, and is easier to bend into complex shapes. However, it will dent easily.

I use a mixture of both metals, partly because I like the way they look together. Find what suits you.

NUTS AND BOLTS

Stock up on nuts, bolts and washers every time you go to a show. I have a range of imperial sizes from 16BA (almost magically tiny) to 6BA (great big bruisers). Buy a selection: the bolts come in different lengths, and you can always saw them shorter. Bolt heads also differ; I like cheese-head, which are blocky and easier to locate with a screwdriver as they project out of the model. Countersunk heads are conical and can disappear flush into the side of your model if you countersink the hole with an appropriate size drill. With tiny bolts you do have to be careful not to force them, as they can break.

Special spanners or 'nut turners' are available, which makes the fiddly process of doing up the nuts much easier. Washers of all sizes are also really useful for detailing.

TAPS AND DIES

Taps cut screw threads into pre-drilled holes, and dies run threads around rods. These are both very useful if you don't want to solder nuts and bolts to components in order to provide fixing points. I have a few and use them rarely, preferring soldering. They are rather easy to break.

Now that we are fully equipped we can move on to one of the key skills in scratch-building: soldering.

CHAPTER FOUR

SOLDERING AND JOINING METALS

At the beginning of the main build I've tried to incorporate as little soldering as possible. As you go on you'll want to do more and more: it's a skill, and it's good to learn new skills because apparently it keeps old age at bay just like Sudoku and playing the violin.

There is a huge amount of information on the internet about soldering and soldering irons. I used to use cheap ones until two broke down on me rather quickly, and then I invested in a fantastic digital temperature-controlled iron from Hobby Holidays — and now I wouldn't use anything else. It goes up to molten (about 400°C), and there's a fancy LED temperature display. It warms up really quickly so you can switch it off when you don't need it and thereby lengthen the life of all its bits and pieces.

With practice you'll be able to solder the smallest of components with a delicacy of touch that would surprise even your granny.

WHAT IS SOLDERING?

I believe the basis of successful locomotive scratch building is that of being able to solder. Here is my definition, as far as I understand it, of the process that enables you to solder effectively:

> Molten solder flows into a clean joint between adjoining metal surfaces and bonds them together.

The surfaces to be joined should be as clean as possible so that the solder can do its job. Bright shiny metal is clean, so give everything a rub with a piece of wet and dry until it sparkles.

The solder must be molten in order to flow and stay molten long enough to flow to where you want it to go. As metal quickly redistributes heat you have to keep the whole joint hot enough, so no weedy little irons: I generally have mine at 350°C, which usually does the job. The 'bits' — the wedge-shaped metal pieces at the end of the iron — are quite large, and they need to be in order to transfer enough heat for any excitement to happen. As you solder more and more you'll find that bigger bits can be better; just use tiny amounts of solder and a small area of the bit.

For efficient heat transfer, the bit needs to be 'tinned' — that is, covered in a thin layer of solder before any attempt is made to make a joint. Just wipe the bit on the brass-wool cleaning surface on the soldering iron stand, and touch the end to add some solder.

In the project I also describe a number of solder-light examples for those who are really not keen — though most know they want to learn.

SOLDER

I use four different types of solder, which are characterized by their melting point. The temperatures can vary slightly.

145°C: This general-use solder makes strong joints and melts at a low enough temperature that small details can be joined to larger pieces of metal without too much heat dissipation. It can also be used near to joints that have been made with higher temperature solder without disturbing them.

180°C: This is great stuff; it has a bit of silver in it and will flow very easily as long as the joint is hot enough. I do all my initial soldering with it.

224°C: This may be called 'gap-filling' solder. You put on a big glob of it and then file it to shape, such as when you want to produce a rounded corner. It can be a little tricky to get it to go where you want it, and may melt back to a glob if you solder nearby. You do need to think carefully when you want to use it.

100°C (low melt): I like this one as it solders white metal to brass without having to tin the brass first with 145°C, and if you're quick it doesn't melt the white metal.

Always read the instructions before deciding which solder will be best for the job

FLUX

There are as many opinions on flux as there are solders. Flux is an enabler, in that it chemically cleans the metal surface and drags the molten solder into the joint by capillary action as it evaporates. Fluxes are acid based and corrosive (you can even use Pepsi Cola, which says a lot), and the stronger ones will add a generous layer of rust to any metal object within spitting distance of your soldering iron. They also come as a paste, which melts with the heat of the operation and is more controllable than the liquid forms. Noxious fumes may float above your workbench, which the household authorities and your doctor may object to.

I use a wonderful water-based safety flux available from the website of Building O Gauge Online. It is very user friendly and is actually called Safety Flux; it is nowhere near as corrosive as the others, and doesn't seem to poison the air. It can spill rather easily if you leave the top off. You will still need to clean your work after each session.

OTHER AIDS TO SOLDERING

It is important to hold things steady when soldering. Sometimes pieces just won't stay still, or the solder won't go where you want it, and when it does work the piece will move slightly and you'll have soldered it solidly in the wrong place. When this happens, step away from the soldering iron and do something less stressful, like putting the children to bed, and then try again.

I find my home-made bench-hook to be an invaluable piece of kit. This is a square foot of nice flat kitchen-cabinet Formica with a piece of one-inch square pine screwed at each end to the top and bottom edges. One piece is fixed underneath to steady it against the bench, hence 'bench-hook', and the other is on the top surface so you can push things up against it. On it I use small blocks of wood to hold things in place. Balsa is good, though it can leave an odd residue when it burns, so I use a piece of business card between it and the work. Metal drawing pins go easily and firmly into balsa and will hold small or large pieces securely.

Holding things steady: the bench-hook and assorted wood blocks.

Rather surprisingly for a chemical coward like my-self (I'm sure this comes from watching my chemistry teacher slowly poison himself) I have discovered that Blu-tack is great for holding things in place. Avoid touching it directly with the iron, and it seems im-pervious to heat and flux. Do experiment carefully, however, as there are many different types, some of which may give off fumes or leave some atrocious residue.

There are also miniature clothes pegs, small metal clips, tweezers and the fabulous forceps. Always try to have one of the pieces that you're trying to solder secured solidly on the workbench, mostly to avoid accidents. And there's fingers, though I wouldn't rec-ommend them: they burn.

HOW TO SOLDER

Once you're ready to go, find some scrap brass or nickel, and clean the faces and edges where you want to make a joint with a piece of wet and dry.

With one piece flat on your work surface, hold the other at right angles (you almost always have to hold things at right angles). Do check with a square if you need to; indeed, you can use the square as a handy stand if you want, though take care it doesn't act as a massive heat sink by interposing a piece of card. You can even use magnets to hold pieces if you are very careful to keep the soldering iron away from them, as the bit will be strongly attracted. Then proceed as illustrated in the photographs overleaf:

- When you're satisfied with the relative positions of the metal, use a paintbrush or cocktail stick to apply plenty of flux along the joint.
- Tin and wipe the bit and put a small blob of solder on the tip. Tinning is the art of having a thin layer of solder on the bit, which conducts the heat to the joint (it doesn't mean an *enormous* blob).
- Apply the bit carefully to the centre of the joint, and smartly move the iron away as soon as the hissing begins and the solder starts to flow.

   This is called 'tack soldering', and what you should have is a blob of solidified solder just hold-ing the pieces together: it allows you to check that all is still square and in place before attempt-ing something more permanent.
- When satisfied, solder two small tacks a few millimetres away on each side, and check again. Then seam the joint by running a loaded iron from the centre outwards to one end.

   Complete the seam from the centre to the op-posite end of the joint.
- The last illustration shows the finished piece with a fully seamed joint, ready to become part of the starship *Enterprise*.

All this is so that you have a chance to check that everything is as you want it before making the final strong joint, and it also goes towards avoiding the pitfalls of the metal expanding with excess heat. If you were to start by tacking at each end and work-ing inwards, you might find a great deal of unwanted buckling. Something else you should take care to avoid is unsoldering the joints you've already made by lingering for too long, which can be particularly infuriating.

Of course, not all joints are that simple or that shape: the secret is to watch the solder. When it's liquid it's all shiny and will run into the joint – you can see it moving, and you'll know it has gone where you want it to. Use enough to strengthen the joint without flooding it, and be careful to give it time to solidify before you move anything. You'll see it go 'matt', and this sometimes takes longer than you might expect.

Don't linger with the iron. If the solder doesn't move properly it's almost certainly because the joint isn't properly clean or the iron isn't hot enough. Let everything cool down, including yourself, and start again. Practise, practise, practise, and you'll find it be-comes second nature (most of the time).

And don't forget the hair dryer: this is absolutely the must-have tool when soldering. Always wash your work afterwards and dry it properly: the cheap hair dryer will do this cheerfully and quickly. Get one or borrow that of your loved one – but don't lend them your soldering iron in return: tell them to get their own.

Apply plenty of flux along the joint.

Tin and wipe the bit and put a blob of solder on the tip.

Apply the bit to the centre of the joint.

Solder two small tacks on each side. Then seam the joint from the centre out to each end.

The finished piece.

OTHER SOLDERING OPTIONS

You can use a small blowtorch such as those used in cookery to coagulate your crème caramel. They are fun and lethal. They will give you pin-point localized heat and a lot of it, and can cause buckling if you're not very careful. I very rarely use mine: I'm scared of it.

I have a resistance soldering unit, which is as near as you're going to get to the Doctor's – as in the television programme *Dr Who* – sonic screw driver in model railway circles. It's great for holding things down, as you only heat the probe (it has a probe) when you've got everything in place. You do need a metal base plate to conduct the large amount of (non-lethal) electricity, which I can never keep clean enough, and it can spectacularly disintegrate small metal components.

I've struggled with mine and have almost stopped using it, so it doesn't show up otherwise in this book. But many people love them, and a particularly keen proponent of their use is Mr Raymond Walley, whose fascinating website has an excellent description of how he uses them. He should be the next Doctor.

In fact there are any number of articles on all sorts of soldering techniques, both in print and on the

Metals and materials.

internet, to whet your appetite. There is no alternative to practice however, so get going on that.

GLUES

Keep a selection of your favourite glues available. I loathe superglue: I hate the fumes and hardly ever stick anything, other than my fingers, together with it. However, I have discovered odourless superglues, which seem to be much more user friendly, at least to this user.

I use Araldite Epoxy Resin glues, mostly for attaching details such as chimneys and domes. They dry slowly and give an excellent, strong bond, and I get on with them. They also have such esoteric uses as cosmetic rivet simulation, of which more later.

Really, the best glue is the one that suits you, though I should remind you of the old adage, 'Don't glue it if you can solder it' – or something along those lines.

So, fore-warned and fore-armed, let's get started.

CHAPTER FIVE

THE CHASSIS AND COUPLING RODS

Possibly the main barrier to beginning to scratch build is that of knowing where to start. If you're having a bit of a wobble just think baby steps: every journey starts with the first step, and so on. When I joined my local model railway club as a teenager I vividly remember being asked to build the decorative awnings for a Great Eastern railway platform shelter in 4mm scale and given a photo of Ipswich station. I hadn't a clue what to do and had to be provided with drawings, plasticard, a previously constructed example as a model and a bit of a talking-to. Now I could do it with just the photo.

So with that memory in mind, I've provided drawings, descriptions and photos that I hope will be of help, and have broken down each part of the build into separate stages. I shall describe these stages in build order.

THE CHASSIS

The chassis is a rather generic term for the frames and associated parts underneath the loco that the pretty bit sits on top of. In the case of both the prototype and the model it is where the power of the loco is transferred into forward or backward motion.

RIGID VERSUS FLEXIBLE

There are countless different and passionately held schools of thought regarding chassis design. Everyone

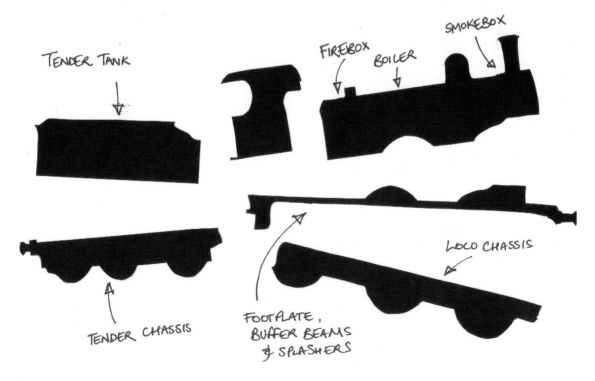

The main components of most locomotive builds are the chassis, footplate and splashers, cab, firebox, boiler and smokebox.

The simple chassis: there's something about modelling in metal that is very satisfying.

MAIN COMPONENTS

- Three pairs of Romford 19mm driving wheels and axles for OO gauge – three insulated wheels, three uninsulated*
- Pack of Romford brass axle bearings
- Pack of Romford crankpins
- Romford axle/crankpin screwdriver
- Comet 50/1 gearbox
- Mashima MHK-105 small flat-sided can motor
- Three 9.5mm frame spacers
- Markits loco brake gear etch
- 0.020in nickel-silver sheet

* Unless you are using a 'wiper' system of current collection.

You are of course at liberty to make your own choices of items and materials.

wants their locos to run as sweetly as possible without falling off the tracks, and there are a number of different ways of dealing with this, some of which echo the real thing in allowing the wheels and axles to move up and down in response to changing levels of the track.

Many OO locomotives are successfully built with a 'rigid' chassis – they have no form of suspension. Proponents of rigid chassis say that all you need to do is make sure that your track is well laid, and that any form of springing or compensation is an unnecessary complication. A rigid chassis has a set of axles held securely in circular bearings (usually brass bushes) with rigid coupling rods, even where those of the prototype are articulated to allow the wheels to move up, down and sideways. In the spirit of simplicity the main build of this book incorporates a rigid chassis.

If you are interested in a more flexible chassis or examples of other forms of suspension there are details in later chapters.

Whatever your interests, this simple chassis build provides good practice for some of the metal forming and soldering techniques you will come to enjoy when scratch building.

ELECTRICAL CURRENT COLLECTION

Unlike real steam engines where power provision is on board, the majority of model railway systems use electricity collected from the track through the wheels. Some way of connecting the wheels to the motor is then necessary. To keep things simple I decided to use what is generally known as the American system, in which the loco collects current through the wheels on one side and the tender collects it on the other. It has the great advantage of not needing any physical current collectors, which means you

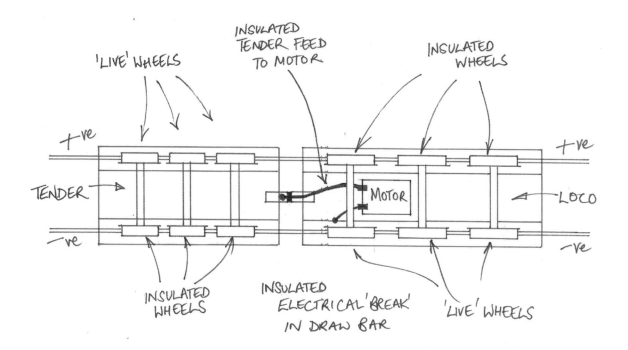

The 'American system' of current collection.

don't have to worry about short circuits between the two vehicles.

If you prefer the more common system of current collection using wire 'wipers' that bear on the wheel tyres, you'll find a few ideas later on in the book. If you decide to use wipers, the whole wheel will need to be insulated.

You will need three sets of Romford wheels. These have one live wheel on each axle with the other insulated. Make sure you check when you buy them: you can tell which is which from the visible ring of insulating material between the metal tyre and the plastic wheel centre on the insulated wheels. You might want to label them to prevent time-consuming mistakes – a spot of red marker on the back is good.

THE COUPLING RODS

This is where it all begins. The coupling rods on a locomotive transfer the rotation of the axle driven by the cylinders to all the other coupled axles. Getting the rods right is key to a free-running model loco. If there is a suitable pair available and you don't feel like making them you can buy them; I often do. There are a number of manufacturers who could supply you with a very nice pair of J15 rods in 4mm scale.

However you get hold of them, they are vitally important as they provide a fixed template for where you are going to put the wheels on the chassis. And they make a very good start for practising your marking out, drilling and piercing-saw skills.

GETTING STARTED

Nickel-silver is a good metal to use for the rods; it has a steel-like finish, and 0.020in is a good working thickness. You should now proceed as illustrated in the photographs:

- Use a set square to establish an exact 90-degree corner.
- Mark the square edge at 98mm with a craft knife. Try not to measure from the end of the ruler:

The rods are important, both on the real thing and on a model. They are quite massive chunks of beautifully worked and accurately shaped metal. This shows the business end of a 'solid' or 'plain' rod.

J15s had two different types of coupling rods: fluted and solid. Fluted ones have thicker metal top and bottom edges to strengthen them, as shown here on No. 7564.

it's easier and more accurate to move it on, say, 10mm – and don't forget to add that much to your final measurement.

- Use the square to scribe a straight line with a craft knife. This was the longest square I had, so after marking I used the steel rule to continue to the other end of the sheet. You could use a Stanley knife for a deeper cut.
- Put the sheet in the bars, lining up the score-line carefully with the edge of the bar. Make sure the piece you want is the section clamped inside the bars to prevent distortion while bending.
- Clamp the bars securely in a vice or to the table. Then, supporting carefully with something firm

such as a piece of wood or steel rule, bend firmly upwards – though not too far. It's important that you get the support right up against the bars so that you don't get a wiggle happening instead of a break.

- Move the support to the top surface and bend down firmly on each side.
- Replace the support underneath and bend up again. Repeat until you feel the metal begin to fracture along the score line.
- Continue to bend until there is a clean break.

It's tricky the first few times, and more so with a relatively large or thick piece of metal. As usual, take it

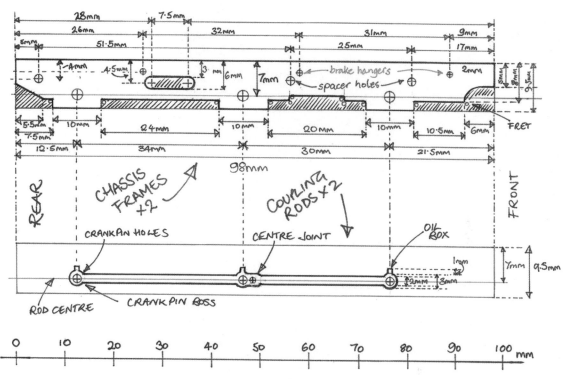

Dimensional drawing of chassis side frames and coupling rods.

gently, back and forth, bending a little bit further each time until you feel it begin to give. Have patience – perhaps practise on a smaller piece first. If you do get a slight wiggle near the break you can always squash it flat in the bars afterwards.

You will now have a rectangle, 98mm wide. Take care to 'dress' the broken edges nicely with a file to remove any roughness; it's easiest to rub the metal gently back and forth on a large file placed flat on the work surface.

Establish a 90-degree corner.

Mark the square edge with a craft knife.

Use the square to scribe a straight line with a craft knife.

Put the sheet in the bars, lining up the score-line carefully.

Clamp the bars in a vice or to the table and bend firmly upwards.

Move the support to the top surface and bend down firmly on each side.

Replace the support underneath, and bend up again.

Bend until there is a clean break.

MAKING THE STRIPS

Next we need to make the strips that will become the chassis side-frames and the rods. Proceed as described in the following four photos; do it four times and you'll end up with four little strips all exactly the same.

You could make these strips by buying a strip of 10mm-wide nickel silver and breaking off the correct length pieces. This is easier, though more expensive – but you don't get to practise your bending and breaking skills.

Use the steel rule to set your dividers to 9.5mm. Take the measurement from the end of the ruler as we are going to transfer it by running the point of the dividers along the edge of the metal.

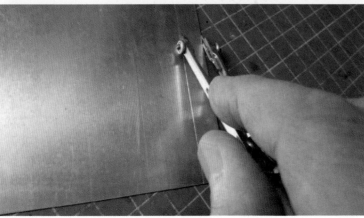

Run the dividers firmly along the square edge of your sheet, taking care not to distort the measurement by pressing too hard. You can deepen the scribe line afterwards with the set square and a craft knife.

It's time to bend and break again. This time I've clamped the bending bars to my workbench with a massive G-clamp (in case you haven't got a vice) using a piece of wood as a support here instead. You might find this easier.

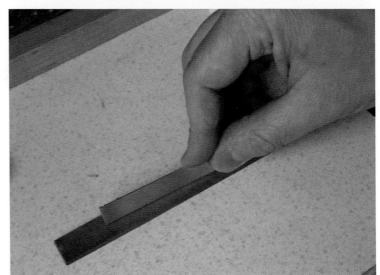

Remember to dress the edges gently with a file: just smooth away any roughness.

THE RODS THEMSELVES

To make the rods, proceed as follows:

- Clamp two strips carefully together – here I'm using a peg – ensuring that the bottom edges and at least one pair of sides are exactly together (the others should be as well, though it doesn't matter if they're slightly off).
- I like to use clothes pegs and hair grips – much more useful than their intended purposes. Tack solder at three points on the top edge – the

middle and the two ends. Simply deposit a good splash of flux in the middle and a nice blob of 145°C solder on top. That's all you need – don't linger, you don't want to make a really solid joint, just enough to hold the bits together while you work on them. Then do the same for each end near the pegs.

Check all is as it should be using the square. Remove any lumps of solder that might be getting in the way. Ensure the bottom long edge is smooth and straight by rubbing carefully on a

Clamp two strips carefully together.

Tack solder at three points on the top edge.

file, and then on some wet and dry lying on your work surface.

- It's important to scribe the outline of the rod directly on to the metal rather than use a paper template; it's a long, thin, straight shape, which is difficult to cut out accurately from a drawing and easy to distort when sticking down. A quick wipe with your marker will give you just the surface for scribing and a bit of unexpected excitement from the fumes.

- Scribe a parallel line at 7mm from the bottom edge (the top edge will be lumpy with solder)

down the metal using dividers. Take great care to produce a true, straight line. If you're very careful you can deepen the line using the steel rule and craft knife.

We're going to drill the crankpin holes exactly along this line. If they're not exactly on the line the chassis will rock about the centre wheels. This can be sorted out later, but as ever, it's best to get it right first time.

- Taking your measurements from the diagram, mark across the line using the steel rule and craft knife to locate your crankpin holes.

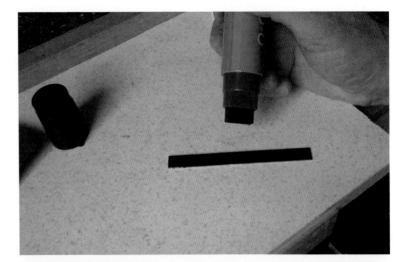

Wipe with a marker pen.

Scribe a parallel line using dividers.

- Run a scriber gently along the long, horizontal line until you feel it click into the crossing line; then a careful tap with a small hammer will give you the perfect lead-in for your drill: this is called 'centre-popping'. Repeat for the other two holes.

Remember to check your measurements all the time. It's a good idea to get into the habit of marking the frames with rear (R), front (F) and top (with an arrow) so you don't get confused as to which way up you are. Use a 0.5mm drill in a pin-chuck to start the holes, as the smaller you go the more accurate you will be. The holes are easy to open out later.

As we're not using a machine drill it's important for the holes to be at 90 degrees to the metal to keep the wheel centres accurately aligned. An Archimedian drill is very controllable – hold it at 90 degrees (use a square to check) and run the little collar up and down, drilling happily away.

Take a deep breath of satisfaction and go and have a cup of tea because we're going to leave the rods alone for a while. Put them somewhere safe.

Mark across the line to locate your crankpin holes.

'Centre-popping'.

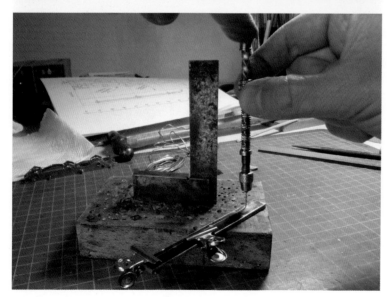

The holes should be at 90 degrees to the metal.

MAKING THE FRAMES

Looking at the drawings and photos you can see that the chassis frames that the axles pass through have all sorts of holes and ins and outs; they are not just flat rectangles, and are very distinctive on the J15s. The more you capture this shape the more pleasing and true to life your model will be.

Now we're going to assemble all four of the pieces we have made – the two coupling rod blanks (which are still soldered together) and the two frame blanks.

First, clamp your coupling rod blanks to the frame blanks, matching up the bottom edges and sides. I've used some different clamps for a change, rather dinky little paper fasteners.

When you're absolutely sure everything is securely in line, tack solder them all together, like last time. Then using the coupling rod holes as a template, drill right through the frame blanks. These are then your

The murky recesses of the real thing.

Clamp your coupling rod blanks to the frame blanks.

axle holes and they are an exact duplicate of your coupling rod centres. Providing everything has been kept in line, your chassis will run.

Gently slide a craft knife between the rod blanks and frame blanks. Rock them back and forth and it should be quite easy to separate the two sets, making sure each pair is still firmly held together.

All is not lost, by the way, if things do become un-soldered, as you now have matching sets of holes through which you can fasten a pair of nuts and bolts and carry on.

Put the coupling rod blanks back in their safe place.

SHAPING THE CHASSIS

There are three sets of different sized holes to be made in the chassis blanks: axle holes, spacer holes and those for the brake rigging. I would recommend that you mark and drill them one set at a time as it's quite easy to muddle them up and drill them to inappropriate sizes.

Axle holes: Open out your axle holes in stages with gradually increasing sized drills until you reach 3mm – go up in 0.2mm steps to 1mm, and then 0.5mm steps to 3mm. These will hold the axle bushes, or bearings, for the axles. They can be opened out finally to fit (with a reamer) after the two sides are separated.

Spacer holes: Then mark in the three spacer holes, and centre-pop and drill those to 0.5mm. Open out to 2mm. The centre one is positioned to clear the Comet gear-wheel. (If you're using a different gearbox just lay the gear-wheel over the central axle hole to check clearances and move the spacer hole if you need to.)

Position brake blocks carefully.

The drilled chassis-frame blanks.

Brake hanger holes: Finally mark and drill the three brake hanger holes to 0.5mm. (The diagram measurements are to suit Romford wheels and Markits brakes. If you are using other makes, work out the position of these holes by laying a wheel on the blank and lining up the brake.) Brake blocks need to be positioned so they won't cause electrical shorts or actually act as real life brakes.

Once that's done you can clean the marker off with a wipe of meths and some wet and dry and marvel at your metalwork. (I do this because all the drilling and so on tends to wear the marker away and makes it difficult to see any new marking out.)

Now with a fresh layer of marker, scribe in the details of the frame shapes. We'll start by cutting out the lozenge shape that you can see on the diagram on page 45. These holes make the frame lighter and allow easier access for maintenance; they are a distinctive feature of the J15's frames. Proceed as follows:

- Mark and drill the lozenge cut-out holes to 0.5mm, and open them up to 2.5mm. It's wise to mark with cross-hatching a 'waste' area as a visual reminder of which holes to join together. You don't want to be doing that between the axle holes.
- Using a fine blade, set up the piercing saw, threading the blade through one of the lozenge holes and tensioning it by pressing down on the end of the frame before tightening the frame screw. (If you are a beginner with the piercing

Mark and drill the lozenge cut-out holes.

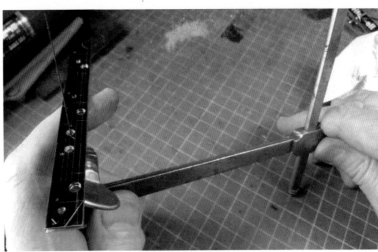

Using a fine blade, set up the piercing saw.

Position the work carefully on your saw table and saw out your lozenge shape.

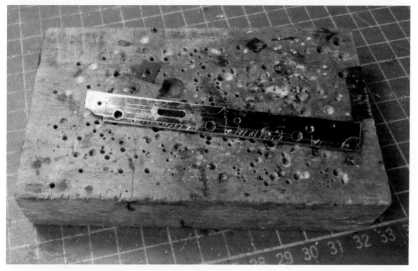

File carefully to the scribed lines.

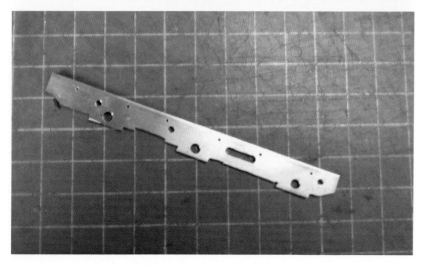

Saw the bottom edge of the frames to shape.

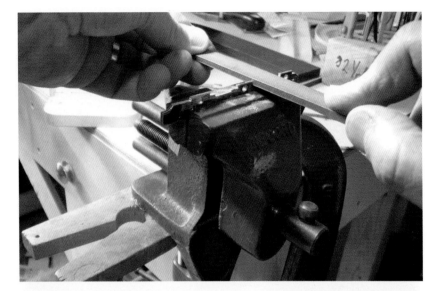

Use the largest possible fine files to get a good straight edge.

Use a fine flat needle file and 'draw' file for a smooth finish.

A square needle file is very good for beginning inside curves.

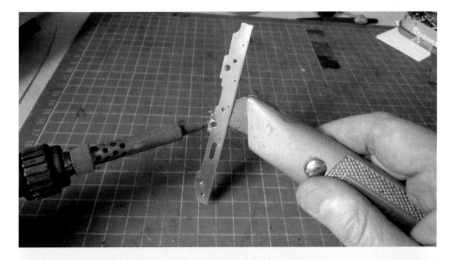

Carefully separate the frames with a Stanley knife.

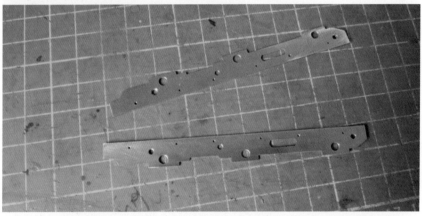

Finally clean them up with a wire brush and a bit of wet and dry.

saw, just remember your first beer: a momentous step towards maturity, possibly ending in disaster, but it didn't stop you becoming an expert. You may want to practise on scrap pieces of metal.)

- Position the work carefully on your saw table so that the part you are sawing is properly supported, to prevent excess vibration and your blade immediately going 'ping'.

  Start the cut with a gentle upward motion, and when you feel you've got a bite, saw down gently, releasing slightly as you saw up. You'll get the hang of it. Try to stay within the lines. When you get to the hole at the other end take care as you saw through into it; then have a breather, turn the work around and set off back to where you came from. Easy as colouring in with wax crayons.

- All you have to do now is tidy up by filing carefully to the scribed lines. Try not to let the file dig into the curved part of your carefully drilled holes.

  Before you shape the bottom edge of the frames you'll need to drill some new holes to allow the saw blade to follow the sharp changes of direction. The holes are labelled on the diagram on page 45. Drill them to 0.7mm and make sure they are in the waste area.

- It's a simple job now to saw the bottom edge of the frames to shape, including the cut-outs at the front and rear.

- Use the largest possible fine files to get a good straight edge; when working up against an inside corner make sure you use the 'blank' face of the file to stop you removing more than you want from where you shouldn't.

- To finish off, use a fine flat needle file and 'draw' file for a smooth finish with no marks. Take care to keep your lines straight; there is a tendency to form curves – don't.
- I find a square needle file is very good for beginning inside curves. Gently pass the pointy end of the file round the curve as you move it forwards. By all means use a half-round file to finish off. Counter-intuitively, I don't recommend a round file to make curves as they can dig in and make file-shaped bites.
- Carefully separate the frames with a Stanley knife by rocking gently. If they are a bit reluctant, use the soldering iron – very carefully – to help.
- And there you are; don't they look lovely? Clean them up with a brisk wire brushing and

a bit of wet and dry. Perfect. Admire them and congratulate yourself.

FITTING THE BEARINGS

This is very exciting: you are about to produce a rolling chassis. You'll need your brass axle bearings and frame spacers. For the engineers amongst you, the bearings we are using are actually known as 'flanged bushes'. You should proceed as follows:

- To start, open out the axle holes a tiny bit at a time with a reamer until you can press the bearings into a tight fit.
- I measure the outside diameter of the bearings with the calipers, and transfer that measurement

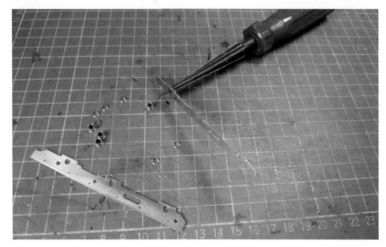

Open out the axle holes a tiny bit at a time.

Measure the outside diameter of the bearings with the calipers.

Keep the reamer at 90 degrees and twist gently.

Twiddle a bigger drill around the rim on each side of the hole.

Put your bearing back in.

to the reamer with a black marker: that gives you warning when you're getting close. These holes have to be a tight fit for the bearings. Take it slowly.

- Keep the reamer at 90 degrees and twist gently (you can feel it biting) – make it smooth and take it slowly. Check frequently for a fit. Keep an eye on the felt tip marker on the reamer blade too. Support the work better than I'm doing in the photo by holding it nearer to the reamer, otherwise it may bend.
- When you get a good snug fit, press the bearing in gently. If you've got a really snug fit, it won't want to come out again and you might have to help it out by pressing gently against a wood block.

  To ensure the bearing fits snugly against the frame, twiddle a bigger drill around the rim on each side of the hole to clear any swarf and 'break' the edge to allow the bearing to 'sit'.

- Put your bearing back in: make sure it's on the outer side of the frame and solder it in from the inside, laying the frame flat on a wood block and card. There should also be a piece of wood between the metal and those fingers. (Don't do as I do…) Repeat for all six of the bearings.

ERECTING THE CHASSIS

The next stage for the chassis is to connect the frames together using the brass spacers (these are brass rods cut accurately to length with countersunk bolts threaded into each end). Proceed as follows:

- Using a 4mm drill in a pin-chuck, gently recess the spacer holes to accommodate the countersunk bolt heads of the frame spacers. Take care not to open out the holes completely, just enough to stop the screw heads touching the backs of the wheels – about halfway in.
- Attach the spacers, tightening the screws gently and firmly. As the holes are in identical positions and the spacers are well engineered, the frames will be at exactly 90 degrees to each other and in line.

  Check this by laying your new frames upside down on something very flat, such as a piece of plate glass. Alternatively the hob of a ceramic oven is excellent, providing it's cool and clean. (Be stealthy in its use, and cleaning it will make you more popular.)

The frames should lie beautifully flat without rocking. If not perfect first time, loosen the screws a little, very lightly press the frames down on your flat surface, and re-tighten the screws. Whoop, holler and leave the kitchen before you are discovered.

WHEELS

The Romford wheels we are using are the nearest available size at 19mm diameter. This is measured

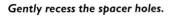

Gently recess the spacer holes.

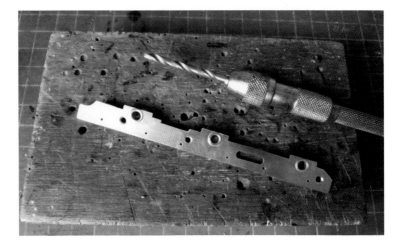

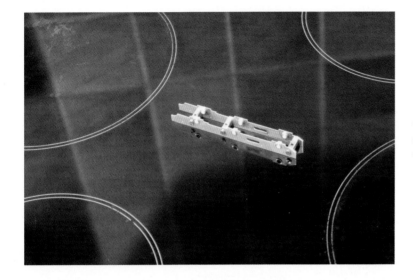

Check the chassis is square by laying your new frames upside down on something very flat.

across the wheel rim, not the outer flange, and scales slightly smaller than the 4ft 11in of the real thing. It is very little difference, and generally better to have a smaller wheel to allow for easier clearances in the model. A very useful feature of these wheels is that the axles automatically set the wheels at the correct back-to-back measurement for your chosen gauge. You can buy a little gauge to check them if you want, or if you're using a different make of wheel that you need to set yourself.

If you're using Romford/Markits wheels let's have a trial run fitting them. The special screwdriver tool they produce makes life much easier – I would rec-

ommend that you get one when you buy the wheels. Proceed as follows:

• Fit the crank-pins first before you lose them. They consist of a thin screw thread separated by a collar from a thicker thread. The thicker end locates into the off-centre hole in the front of the wheel face.
• Screw them in carefully at 90 degrees, making sure you don't get them cross-threaded (and wonky). The prongs on the screwdriver locate into the little slots in the collar. Screw them in gently, and don't over-tighten them.

Have a trial run fitting Romford/Markits wheels.

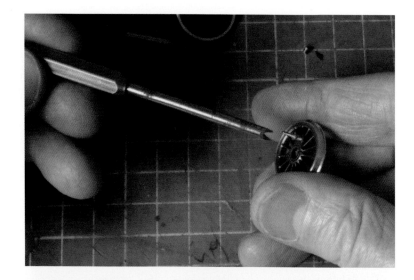

Screw the pins in carefully at 90 degrees.

The wheels locate on to the square shoulder of the axle end.

Locate the little slotted collar over the protruding thread at the wheel front.

Insulated and uninsulated driving wheels.

Place a wheel on each axle.

- The wheels locate on to the square shoulder of the axle end. Push the axle in gently and you'll feel it locate into the square hole. Check that the wheel sits at 90 degrees to the axle, and that it is fully in position.
- Locate the little slotted collar over the protruding thread at the wheel front. Use a pair of tweezers, and try to do all this over a plastic tray as it saves a lot of time hunting around on the floor if you drop anything. Locate the prongs of that versatile screwdriver into the collar slots, and tighten gently.

A word on those wheels: if you are following this build to the letter then you'll be using three pairs of wheels with insulated and uninsulated sides. You can tell them apart by looking at the area between the plastic wheel centre and the metal rim: on the insulated wheel there is a thin insulating layer between the two. It's a good idea to use a spot of marker to identify the uninsulated (that is, live) wheels, thereby saving many tears of frustration later.

- Place a wheel on each axle; get into practice by doing all the insulated (or the uninsulated) ones first. Thread an axle through the bearings and fit the opposite wheel. Don't worry too much at the moment about which direction your crankpins are pointing. You're going to get used to taking the wheels off and on.

Repeat twice more, and there you have it: a rolling chassis. Hurrah, now you can get some track and

Take measurements for the splasher spacings.

play, make chuffing noises and happily roll your little beauty up and down the kitchen table (not off it).

While the wheels are on you can take measurements for the splasher spacings. Hold a piece of card up against the wheels and chassis frame and draw round the wheels.

SHAPING THE COUPLING RODS

Locate your coupling rod blanks and check they're still soldered together. If they do come apart at any time, don't panic, just open out the crankpin holes carefully enough to take a 12BA nut and bolt and bolt them together. The centres of your crankpin holes can be used as guides for your dividers to scribe out circles for the crankpin bosses. Then using the straight edge, scribe lines 1mm either side of the horizontal centre line for the main body of the rods.

Mark in the large centre joint facing towards the front, and then add the oil boxes. Draw in all the details now, before you get busy with the piercing saw.

Mark in the large centre joint, then add the oil boxes.

Saw approximately around the scribed outlines.

This job is slightly trickier than shaping the frames because the rods are thinner and more fiddly; you've had lots of practice, however, so off you go:

- First open out the holes to suit your crankpins – 1.2mm for Romfords; go carefully as they have to be a precise fit.
- Hold the blanks in a hand or table vice, and steady your hands against the work surface. Saw approximately around the scribed outlines. Use needle files to achieve the final shaping: go carefully. Form the outside curves with flat files; the sharp edge of a triangular file will help get into any angles. Take it slowly and gently.

When you're satisfied with the shape of your rods, then it's time to separate them – really carefully if they're still soldered together: you don't want to bend them. Gently rock a craft knife blade between them, and they'll happily part company – and if they're reluctant give them a quick dab with the soldering iron. Then clean them up with a wire brush and a piece of wet and dry.

Despite the rods being rigid we can add some decoration to give the impression of their more complex functions:

- Having shaped the representation of the joint in the rod centre with a hole drilled already for the job, we can add a rivet simply by soldering in a 14BA bolt and filing it near flat (completely flush on the back).
- You can lightly file the metal of the rod centres to make them slightly thinner, which produces a little step up to the thicker crank-pin bosses.
- You can represent the corks on the top of the oil boxes. First file the end of a piece of 0.7mm rod

flat. Then tin it with the minimum of 145°C solder, apply it to the top of the oil box, add flux and lightly touch the joint with the soldering iron. Snip and file to length.

- Clean up the rods and trial-fit the crankpin collars. They should be a precise fit without being tight, because they have to turn in the hole as the coupling rods revolve. They fit through the holes in the coupling rods and screw quite tightly on to the threads of the crankpins.

Show them to your suitably astonished relatives and put them away somewhere safe where the cat can't eat them.

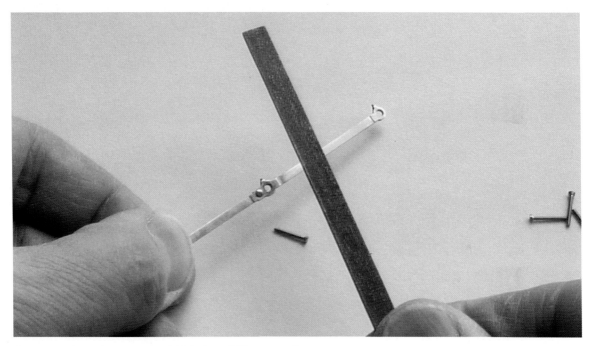

Add a rivet by soldering in a 14BA bolt and filing near flat.

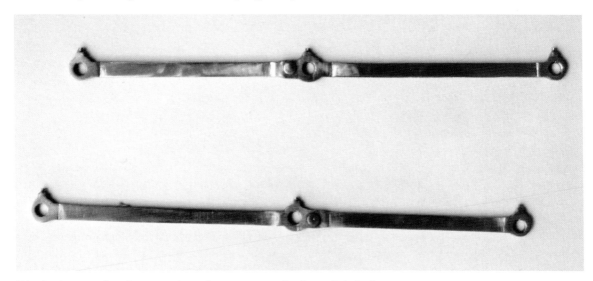

File the front surface between the rod centres to make them slightly thinner.

You can represent the corks on the top of the oil boxes.

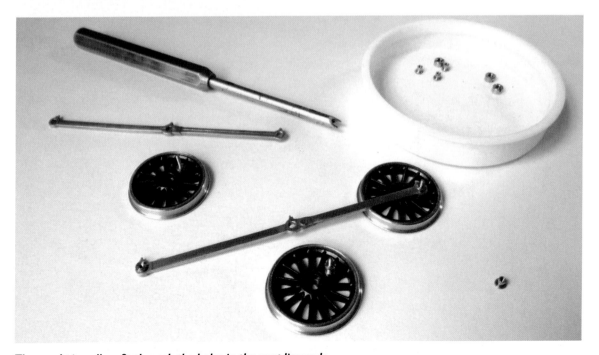

The crankpin collars fit through the holes in the coupling rods.

CHAPTER SIX

GETTING YOUR CHASSIS RUNNING

This stage can be most infuriating and could mark the point where you throw everything up in the air and have a good old-fashioned temper tantrum, and then just get on with it. Alternatively you could leave it for a while and build the loco body and then come back to it. Or it could all work beautifully first time.

Putting it simply, first you have to set up the motor and gearbox so they run sweetly, then you must position them in the chassis – still running beautifully – with all the wheels, rods and associated engineering ticking away like a well-oiled sewing machine, with a reliable system of electrical supply. And you'll need to be able to fit on the loco body afterwards.

So, let's do it one step at a time.

MOTORS AND GEARBOXES

Many providers of motors and gearboxes make available, on paper or online, a set of life-sized outlines of their products so that you can check against your drawings that they have a good chance of fitting before you buy them. Print them out on clear film, or trace them on good old-fashioned tracing paper and try them out for size.

If you don't want to fit a fly-wheel on the rear axle of the motor you can buy motors without the second axle sticking out of the back, otherwise you'll have to grind it off if it's getting in the way, which is quite a job. Get someone to do it for you, or ask for advice from your supplier.

If you have a motor available try out the real thing for size. The drawing helpfully shows this motor to be a little too big and I went for a smaller one instead. DRAWING WITH PERMISSION OF ISINGLASS MODELS

As I want the model to travel smoothly and slowly I went for a gear ratio of 50:1. The ratio between the two gears determines the sort of speed at which your loco will travel. This depends also on the size of your driving wheels. The J15 was designed primarily to move sizable goods trains around and didn't need to move quickly. The ratio actually describes the number of times the wheel axle will revolve compared to that of the motor: so for every fifty turns of the motor axle your driving wheel will revolve once. The High Level Kits website has an excellent resource for working out gear ratios.

I've used a simple Comet etched gearbox. Cut the fold-up box from the etch, file off any tags and fold at the half-etched lines. Use the square to check everything is at right angles, and run a fillet of solder along the fold for strength. The bearings (which have a thin shoulder to accommodate the gear wheel) are then soldered in place with the shoulder on the inside in a similar manner to soldering the bearings to the chassis frames. Make sure the gearbox sides are square to the end and parallel to each other.

There are small screws fixing the gearbox to the motor. They are a particular length so they don't intrude inside the motor casing and ruin all the delicate innards. Try really hard not to lose them. Use tweezers to hold them, a proper tiny screwdriver, and a

tray beneath. I always steady the motor with a blob of Blu-tack to help things along.

The gear wheel needs to be prevented from moving about using some washers. These may be included on the fret of your gearbox, or you can buy handy packets or etches of them. The worm-wheel needs to be as central as possible to the worm and is held in place by the washers.

To work out the right thickness of washers you'll need, slip some between the worm-wheel and the gearbox sides for a snug fit. It may be easier if you use a 3mm rod instead of the axle as the square ends can be awkward. After years of fiddling around with all these washers, I've recently discovered that if I solder them carefully together it makes them much easier to fit each time. You live and learn.

Now since time immemorial Rizla cigarette papers or Izal toilet paper have been used to set up gearboxes. The worm and worm-wheel need to have a close, but not too close, relationship and a thin sliver of paper should give you that relationship; it's a balance between too much friction and unnecessary wear due to a sloppy fit. Proceed as follows:

- Loosen the motor fixing screws very slightly. Fit the worm so it's not right up against the motor; it needs to be central to the worm-wheel. Tighten

The long thin gear is a worm that sits on the motor axle. It engages at right angles with the worm-wheel on the wheel axle that turns the wheels.

the tiny grub screw on the worm (you can buy packets of spares).

- With the worm-wheel in place between the sides of the motor mount, slip an axle through the whole lot. Poke or wind a thin rectangle of paper between the worm and the worm-wheel. Tighten the grub screw on the worm-wheel, and gently twist the motor mount so that the paper is trapped quite firmly between the teeth of the two.

They should then be properly meshed. Tighten the motor-mount screws, and you're done.

If the worm-wheel gets in the way of one of the motor-mount screws, ensure the one you can get at is tight, then take the worm-wheel out and tighten the other fixing screw. You're going to have to take the worm-wheel off again anyway, which may test your patience.

So now you have a correctly meshed, properly set-up gearbox, and it is time for a bit of fun. Connect up the terminals of the motor to your controller, and, holding everything carefully, let her rip! There shouldn't be too much noise, although it's not going to be silent, and there shouldn't be a shower of tiny

Fitting the paper between the worm and the worm-wheel.

Let her rip!

Put the wheels on too.

brass confetti coming from the gearwheel, which I have had.

Let it run for a few minutes, both backwards and forwards, gradually building up the speed. Check it's not running too hot. If something seems wrong, you may have to repeat the set-up procedure – and again – and again. When you're satisfied you can have even more fun and put the wheels on too. Check you've done the axle nuts up tight, and watch out for flying objects.

There is a serious point here, because if we test that everything is running well at each stage, then when it stops working – if it stops working – we'll know to look at the last thing we did to see what caused it. That's the theory anyway.

At this point you might want to very carefully solder a pair of wires to the terminals on the motor. However, if you want to wait until most of the fiddling is over, then use some crocodile clips for the time being (it can cause your soldered joints to fail).

I like to use a fly-wheel in my locos. These are rather nicely shaped solid brass wheels that will add an extra bit of 'oomph' to the loco's slow running. Basically they keep the motor turning if there's any interruption to the electricity supply, and can add a real sense of momentum to the way everything moves; they make shunting exciting, too. They can be difficult to fit inside small locos; there's just room enough

in the J15. I bought a really small one from Roxey Mouldings. You can leave it off if you want.

MOTORIZING THE CHASSIS

This is a good part of the build because it brings us to the end of one process and the start of another. The power-house of your scratch-built locomotive will be well on its way to completion – although fiddling is still the order of the day.

We're aiming here for a simple working motorized chassis complete with coupling rods. One good thing about Romford (other wheel makes are available) is that they have those previously mentioned square-ended axles that help to locate the wheels. Importantly this causes the opposite wheels to have a specific relative position of a half or quarter turn: in railway parlance this is called 'quartering'.

When the wheels are joined by the coupling rods they act together as a single unit. The driven axle (the one with the motor or pistons) pulls the others round with it, and this gives the loco more traction because they all work as one. Various counter-productive forces occur if the wheels on the other side of the loco are not slightly ahead or behind. They are generally a quarter of a turn ahead, and they all have to be exactly in line with each other. Romford wheels do all this for you without the hard thinking. (If you're using other makes of wheel then you might need to do it yourself, which is described later.)

Proceed as follows:

- Offer up the motor and gearbox to the centre wheel bearings. You may find that the gearbox

bearings for the worm-wheel are too wide to fit between the axle bearings in the frame.

- To provide a perfect fit for the gearbox, thin the axle bearings a little with a large, medium-grade file. You do need to keep the edges square, and it's a good idea to lay the chassis frames on the work-bench; keep the file parallel. Turn the

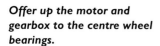

Offer up the motor and gearbox to the centre wheel bearings.

Thin the axle bearings a little with a large, medium-grade file.

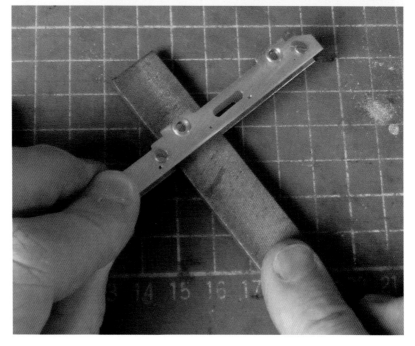

chassis over occasionally so that you file an equal amount from each bearing to ensure the gearbox is central.

Check frequently for a good fit. Here is a good time to practise using the calipers to check the outside measurement of the gearbox bearings and the inside measurement between filed ends of the axle bearings.

• When you have a good fit, polish the ends of the axle bearings until smooth with a piece of fine wet and dry wrapped around a flat wooden stirrer.
• Slide the gearbox between your carefully polished middle bearings, and insert the wheel axle through the whole assembly. You'll need to trap the worm-wheel and its washers as you push the axle through.
• Now attach the driving wheels to the motor axle, ensuring one side is live and the other insulated, it doesn't matter which side. It is important, however, that on one side the

crankpin is 90 degrees further round than the other.

Check that the motor is still running nicely.

• Next, put all the insulated driving wheels on one side and the live ones on the other, and check that the crank-pins are all in the same relative position on each side.
• With great excitement, attach a coupling rod to one side; make sure it's pointing forward. You'll need to slip a Romford crankpin collar into the hole in the rod; it should be able to revolve smoothly.

When you tighten the collar with the Romford screwdriver it shouldn't revolve while the rod moves around it: too much slop will cause binding, so take care. Minute adjustments can be made with a broach until you're satisfied. Again it's a matter of feeling when it's right, and it's important to get a nice, smooth movement.

Polish the ends of the axle bearings until smooth.

The wheels at quarter position.

Using finger pressure, push the chassis gently along.

Now then, before you rush for your controller dial, loosen the grub screw on the worm-wheel so that the axle can revolve freely through it. Using finger pressure, push the chassis gently along a piece of track or your workbench: it should gently roll along. Many people judge success by letting the chassis roll down a slight incline unaided.

If there is binding, check that:

• you've actually got the wheels at 90 degrees on each side;
• the worm-wheel grub screw is loose;
• the coupling rods aren't too tight on the crankpins;
• you didn't widen those coupling rod holes too much;
• the chassis spacers are nice and tight.

Running in the chassis.

The chassis may demonstrate a slight reluctance to roll as it runs in, but because its construction is so simple it is almost certain that things *will* work properly. However, if you want to run it in, prop up one end on some wood blocks, or hold it in a hand-vice, and gently ramp up the power in forward and reverse for half an hour or so. Don't overdo it and *don't* leave it unattended. Anything that is going to come loose will do.

But let us assume that your chassis rolls beautifully, in which case tighten the worm-wheel grub screw and apply some power leads to the motor – and off it goes! Marvellous! Enjoy it – show it to people – sit and watch it go backwards and forwards while you have tea and biscuits! You've earned the pleasure.

CONSIDER YOUR TRACK LAYOUT

You will need to give some thought to the curves that you would like your locomotive to negotiate. As the OO chassis is quite narrow you've already got some leeway, although you might find that the rigid chassis and coupling rods restrict its travel.

Try the chassis out on the sharpest curves of your layout, or a piece of track with the smallest radius you hope to have. If things are really tight you may have to have a re-think about either your track-work, or making a more flexible chassis. In which case, take a look at the chapter on the sprung EM chassis, which will provide some modifications you could make.

If the track curves are generous you may wish to restrict some of the sideways travel of the inner and outer axles (the centre axle is fixed by the gearbox). A few washers slipped between the wheels and the chassis as you put everything together will suffice. You can spend some time experimenting.

If you're happy with the spacers as they are, a drop of Loctite on the screw threads will keep everything done up nice and snugly. Some people like to replace the screwed spacers with soldered ones, and if you want to do this, then refer to the chapter on the EM chassis to give you some ideas.

That's it for now. We're going to build the loco body next (or the tender if you want), and we'll come back to detail the chassis after that.

CHAPTER SEVEN

THE LOCOMOTIVE FOOTPLATE

The footplate is the first part of the body that you will have to make, and as such is a little awkward. You can't see much of it in photos or on the real thing because it is obscured by all the parts on top and underneath, and you can only really see its full dimensions from above. To work out its shape you will need some imagination, photographs, a good drawing and perhaps a little general knowledge of the real thing. We already have the chassis to help us, and in model form we have to make sure that the footplate will accommodate the motor/gearbox mechanism, the wheels, and any other modifications that become necessary due to scaling down to model form from the real thing.

The dimensions of the diagram (below) have been taken from the length and wheel position of my own chassis. Yours may vary slightly, so once you've marked everything out on your metal, take a while to check it against the card template you made earlier, and adjust it accordingly.

To form the footplate, proceed as follows:

- Break off a rectangle of 0.015in nickel-silver to the dimensions shown in the diagram. Cover the

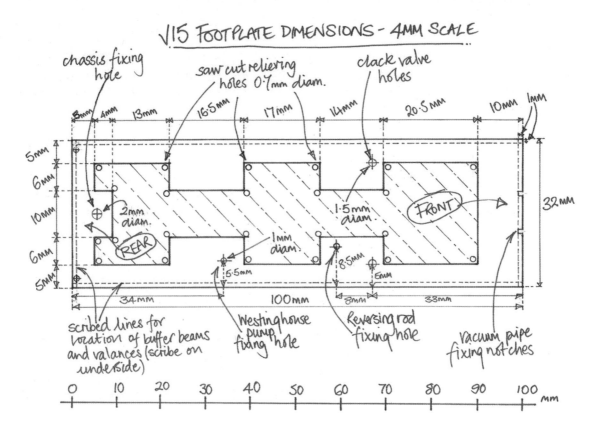

Footplate dimensions.

An enigmatic photo of the real thing. You can see the cut-outs in the chassis that accommodate the wheel-bearing assemblies, also the centre splashers, and the cab sides with the operating wheel of the reverser and the reversing rod itself. Brilliant. KEITH ASHFORD

surface with marker pen and scribe the outlines of the wheel cut-outs. Cross-hatch the waste area.
- Mark and drill (0.7mm drill) all the saw-relieving holes inside the waste area as shown to allow you to saw round the shape.

- Use the piercing saw to cut between the holes, keeping to the waste area.
- File and clean up for a neat finish. Then drill the rear chassis fixing hole, then the other smaller holes for the footplate-mounted details.

Marking the footplate.

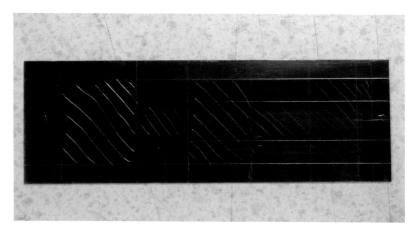

Mark and drill the saw-relieving holes.

Cut between the holes.

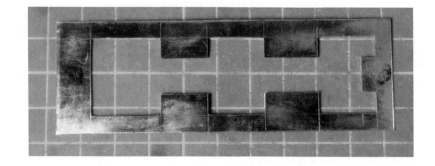

File and clean up for a neat finish.

THE BUFFER BEAMS

The front and rear beams are of the same breadth with differences in the details related to their function. The rear beam on tender locomotives is sometimes called the drag beam (or other things) for fairly obvious reasons. It comes between the locomotive and tender, which has its own diminutive pair of buffers that rub against a set of corresponding plates.

The front beam has a far more conventional set of holes for the buffers and a slot for the front coupling hook.

- Break the beams from a piece of 0.015in nickel-silver. Mark and drill the holes for the buffers

and the various slots. Join the slot holes with a piercing saw and file smooth with a tiny file. The rear slot has a pair of buffing plates made up of small squares of 0.015in nickel-silver and soldered in place.

VALANCES

These are strengthening pieces that run the length of the underside of the footplate.

- Take two strips of 0.015in nickel-silver and tack solder them together. The top edge must be smooth and straight with the ends at right angles. Mark their shape using your circle template

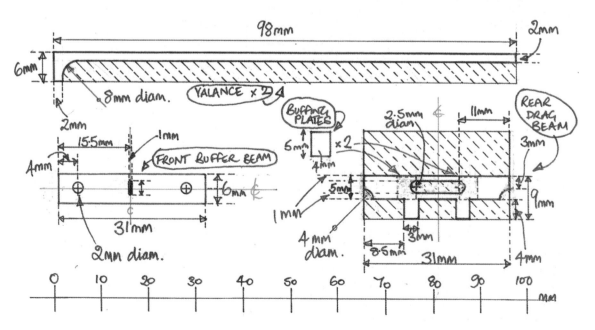

Valance and beam dimensions.

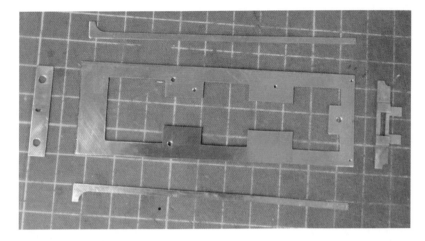

The component parts of the footplate.

for the curves. Saw and file to shape and very carefully separate the two pieces.

FOOTPLATE ASSEMBLY

Now you'll need to solder these bits together. Have a little practice on some scrap if you're feeling nervous. Unlike many kits there are no slots or tabs to show you exactly where everything goes. I use the dividers to scribe a centre line, and lines to locate the beams and valances. Of course you'll have to wipe off the marker to solder effectively. The lines are visible enough, and as they're on the underneath it doesn't matter if they're a bit deep.

Start with the front buffer beam – it's shorter and simpler and helps locate the valances. Proceed as follows:

- Mark a centre line on the back of the beam and locate it accurately with the centre line on the footplate. Ensure it lines up properly against the locating line. You can steady it with a wooden coffee stirrer or tweezers, clamp it with a clothes peg, or keep it still with some Blu-tack or drawing pins on balsa – whatever works for you. Do be aware that if you hold it with your fingers you might as well be touching the end of the soldering iron.
- Apply plenty of flux with a brush. Wipe your iron, tin it with a small blob of 180°C solder, and tack near the centre. Check everything is still in place,

and put another tack a little way from the first on either side – and be quick to avoid melting the first solder joint.
- Check everything again with a set square – it should be in line with the beam at 90 degrees to the footplate. Add some more flux, tin your iron, and spread one of the tacks to the end of the beam. Do the other side, then quickly join them up in the middle, and you've made a seam.

You don't need huge amounts of solder, though it doesn't matter if you end up with rather a lot as it's on the inside. However, you will need to clean out most of it as the chassis and valances fit closely against the joint. If it all goes horribly wrong, have a break, then unsolder, clean up and start again.

Once the front buffer beam is in position you can tack and seam each valance in turn. These are a little more tricky as they are long and thin, more difficult to keep in place, and liable to buckle if you use too much heat.

- 'Break' the corners of the valance where they meet the joints of the beam and footplate; just file a little off the sharp corner to allow them to 'sit' more easily.
- Position the first valance with the curved front edge to the front of the footplate. It should sit nicely against the back of the buffer beam. If not, clean out some more solder and check that everything is square.

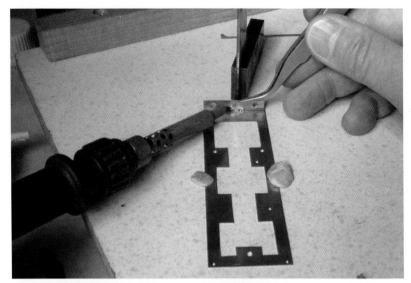

Apply plenty of flux and tack near the centre.

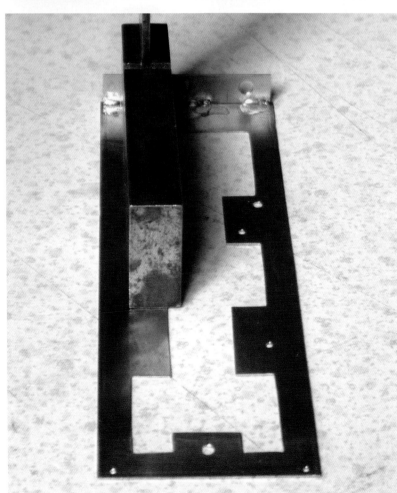

Spread the tacks, join them up in the middle, and you've made a seam.

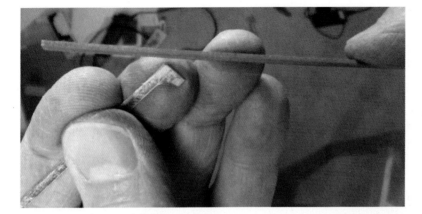

'Break' the corners of the valance.

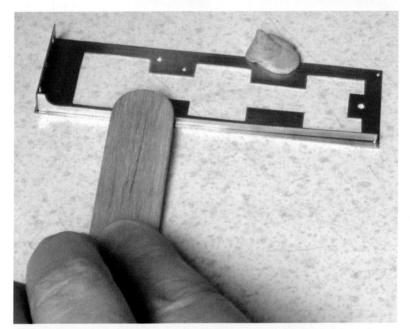

Position the first valance.

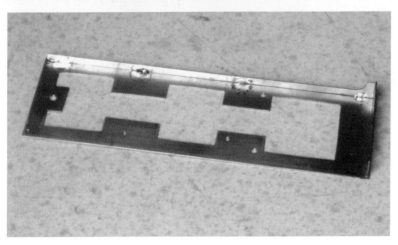

Tack the valance to the footplate.

- Tack the valance to the footplate with some little tacks near the centre. Check and then seam.

Watch out for buckling between the tacks, and don't linger with the iron so the buffer beam becomes unsoldered. If nothing happens with the first touch of the iron, then check everything is clean and that the iron is properly tinned.

- Repeat for the opposite valance. As they are the same length and you've got the front beam on perfectly square, they should be in exactly

Repeat for the opposite valance.

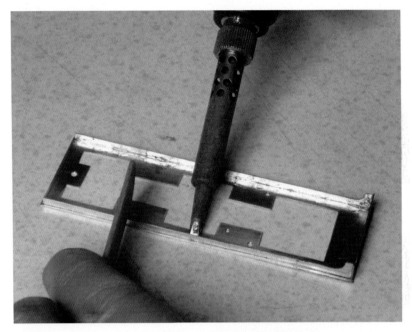

Tack on the drag beam at the back.

the right position for you to add on the rear beam.

- Tack on the drag beam at the back. If you've used a small amount of solder and done everything from the inside, you'll have a series of clean joints. (Just like mine…)

If you need to clean up, use scrapers and craft knives and finish off with wet and dry or a wire brush. Incidentally, it's very satisfying to watch the solder flowing into joints, particularly if you can see it making a lovely neat joint on the outside. If too much solder appears on the outside of the joint you may be able to draw it back inside by fluxing the inside of the joint and applying the iron. Get into the habit of watching the solder move: it's instructive and quite surreal.

Now the foundation to the locomotive body is done: fantastic!

FITTING TO THE CHASSIS

The ends of the chassis should fit neatly behind the buffer beams, and the wheels should pass through the splasher cut-outs with a fraction of space to spare on either side of the rim. If the chassis sides are slightly too long, file a little off the front ends to fit.

When you've done that, pass an 8BA nut through the rear spacer and footplate hole and gently tighten with a bolt to hold everything in place. We will fit a keeper plate to the front when the chassis has been detailed; for now, all we need to know is that the chassis fits. (If the frames are a little too long, file them back slightly at the front. Don't worry if they are a little short.)

- You do need to check that the splasher cut-outs give enough clearance for the wheels – approximately 0.5mm on each side. Sit the footplate on the chassis and take a good look at it. Lovely. Now is the time to mark and file them for a good fit: you don't want too much clearance as it may affect the size of your splashers.

Once that's sorted, are you tempted to try it on your piece of track? If you want to fit the motor into the chassis for a test run you'll probably find that the footplate inside edges between the rear and centre splashers will need to be filed away a little to accommodate it. Mark with the dividers by eye, and file away just enough to let the motor slip through with 0.5mm on either side. Put those crocodile clips on, and off she goes. If she doesn't, check for short circuits or

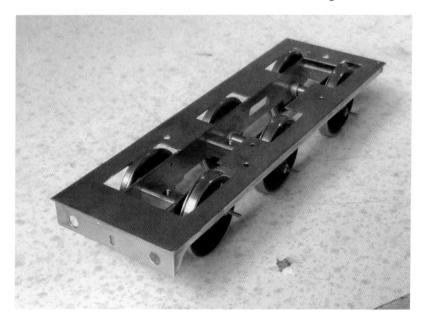

Test-fitting the footplate to the chassis.

Check again that the wheels will have room inside the splashers.

anything touching anything else that it shouldn't – take the footplate off and see what's going on.

When you're satisfied, remove the chassis, whittle yourself a little block of wood to fit (Jenga blocks are just right), and carefully place your footplate on it. It'll help keep things square and less vulnerable to damage, and it looks good.

• Check again with your card template that the wheels will have room inside the splashers. The added height of the footplate should help.

That's the main footplate complete: now for some splashers and a cab.

CHAPTER EIGHT

ABOVE THE FOOTPLATE

THE CAB

Now that the footplate is all nice and solid we can start to build up the rest of the loco body. The cab is next as it provides a good anchor point for the boiler, and it's a big chunk of construction that gives a good feeling of progress.

This is the first part of the build where we can really see the shapes and sizes needed directly from the photo. As steam loco design evolved throughout the Victorian era the cab was added as rather an afterthought to provide some cover from the weather for the valiant crew. Reminiscences record that it was still both freezing cold and boiling hot inside, so you can't please everybody. Many examples of the J15 had makeshift additions to try and improve things, and these variations make interesting modelling.

My choice of loco, No. 65447, had a raised cab roof (to accommodate increasingly tall drivers?) and a set of hooks under the edge of the cab roof with a matching rail on the tender to drape a piece of sheeting across.

THE CAB SIDES AND FRONT

The procedure for making the cab sides and front is as follows (refer to the diagram on page 90):

- First, tack two rectangles together so as to shape both sides at once. Drill holes for the handrails and shape the cut-outs before separating the two pieces.

  I tried to avoid the little splasher ends at the bottom, and added them to my model later. In retrospect it's much easier to fret them out of one piece, as in the diagram. Just make sure the sides are truly parallel, as the cab front and ultimately the boiler attach to these and need to be at 90 degrees.

- I use a French curve to transfer the curves from the diagram to the blanks for the cab sides. Rather surreal I think you'll agree. It's a good idea to mark the areas of the curve that you're using directly on to the template so that you don't forget which bit you're using.

- Shape the cut-outs (the side windows) carefully with small flat files and then half-round files, as they give character to the loco. Take your time and do it with small strokes travelling around the curve. Refer to your photos until you are happy with the result. (You might want to practise on a piece of scrap first.)

- Now is a good time to solder a captive 8BA bolt to the rear of the footplate. It will later be hidden by the raised cab floor. You can either do this by metal blackening the nut and bolt (as described in the chapter on building the tender), or as in the photograph, where a short bamboo skewer (from a roll-mop herring) can be screwed into the nut to keep the thread clear of solder, and located through the hole in the floor. Press everything down into a balsa block, and solder with a good blob of 145°C and plenty of flux.

- Cut the cab front from a rectangle of 0.015in nickel-silver using the French curve to mark the top curve. Open out the window holes (spectacles) to fit the etched spectacle plates (window frames) using increasingly large drills to about 2mm, and then continue with the reamer.

- Saw and file to shape the large cut-out in the cab front. This accommodates the end of the motor and will be hidden by the back head.

Before soldering the spectacle plates, which are very fragile, it's a good trick to lightly tin them first before you cut them out. Use only the slightest wipe of 180°C solder to tin them. This strengthens them

The cab side of No. 7564: a good solid piece of metalwork with some interesting details.

CAB SIDES (x2) CAB FRONT AND ROOF

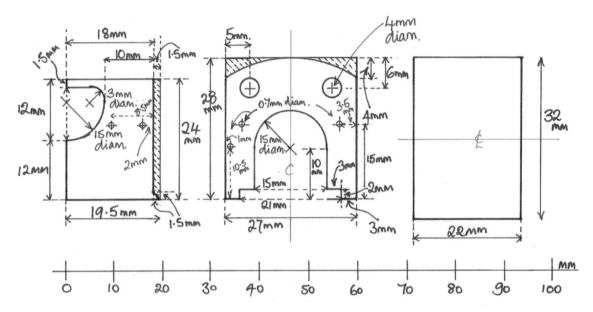

The cab roof, sides and front.

The cab front and sides: these are nice chunky bits of metal to cut out from a sheet of 0.015in nickel-silver.

and they can be cut from the fret using a very sharp scalpel, gently scoring as close to the rim as you can so as to avoid having any tags to file off. Once they're cut, hold them in place on the cab front with the knife blade, and sweat solder with a clean, tinned iron.

Drill the holes for details, and the handrails that run the length of the boiler (which will help you position them later). When you have all three pieces nicely shaped and cleaned, it's time for the exciting part:

- Tack solder the cab front on to the footplate first. Position the cab front by scribing a line on

I use a French curve to transfer the curves from the diagram to the blanks for the cab sides.

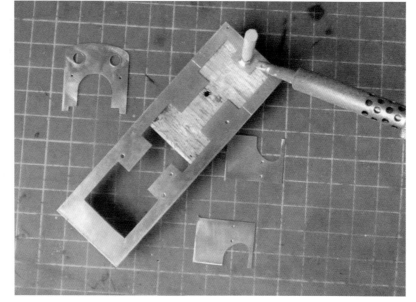

A short bamboo skewer can be screwed into the nut to keep the thread clear of solder.

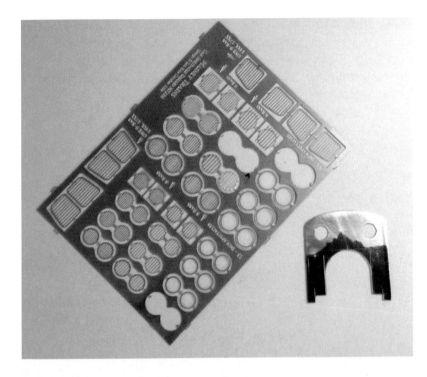

The cab front and spectacle plate fret.

the footplate in the correct position, as shown on the diagram. Also scribe a line down either side, making sure everything is parallel; these lines will centralize the front. Check that it really is central.

• Check carefully with the square that the cab front is upright and at 90 degrees to the sides of the footplate.

If you've marked it out accurately, all should be well; if it isn't, unsolder and start again. Don't put up with it being nearly right because it will throw everything else out later. You can tweak it slightly if it is not quite 90 degrees by very gently bending at the tack joint, although this will weaken the joint.

If you have to re-solder you might get lumpy solder in the way of where you want to put things

Sweat soldering the cab spectacle plates.

Check carefully with the square that the cab front is upright and at 90 degrees to the sides of the footplate.

If you're careful not to touch it, Blu-tak is great to hold things in place while you do your first tack.

back. You can scrape it off, or spread it out thinly where it won't be seen or get in the way. The following is a good way to remove excess solder: hold a piece of fluxed scrap brass up against the edge of your work, and with the iron, spread the solder on to the scrap.

When you're completely satisfied, seam the joint and relax. Then check it again.

The sides go on in just the same manner, locating on to the cab front edges flush with its face. Do one at a time: position them, tack them to the footplate and the cab front, and then seam.

Hold the second side in place with a lolly stick as you solder.

The first side is easier as you have more space to operate in – though by now you are becoming an experienced wielder of the soldering iron and will hopefully be enjoying yourself.

Inspect everything for squareness and centrality again, and when satisfied, seam up and you will have a lovely little cab sitting securely on your footplate. Clean it up with a bit of a brush, and wash and dry it. Then admire your fantastic bit of work.

SPLASHERS

Splashers are still quite complex, and it's particularly important that they sit upright and parallel. Here's your chance to make a few mistakes and perhaps add to your reject pile – they did that with the real thing as well, you know.

The J15 centre splashers are one-piece castings with an integral flange that is used to fix them to the footplate. We can replicate the look by building up simple shapes from flat metal. The front splashers are a more complicated shape as they incorporate the sand-boxes, which are full of sand used to stop the wheels spinning in unfavourable rail conditions. For the J15 I used brass to make the splasher tops – it looks pretty, and I find brass bends more easily than nickel.

CENTRE SPLASHERS

To make the centre splashers, proceed as follows:

- Centre-pop a piece of 0.015in brass to locate your dividers, and scribe a circle to 22mm diameter, which is fractionally larger than that of the wheels. Saw or cut roughly with a pair of tin snips, and file to shape. This takes some patience.
- You should be able to make both of the centre pair of splasher faces from one circle. Measure the length of cut-out in your footplate with the dividers, and mark to the edge of the circle. Scribe a straight line between the marks and saw across. Repeat for the other splasher.

I like to add the splasher tops to the faces before attaching them to the footplate.

- For the centre splashers take a strip of 0.005in brass, 4mm across. Curve it gently by using a

Centre splasher.

The front splashers.

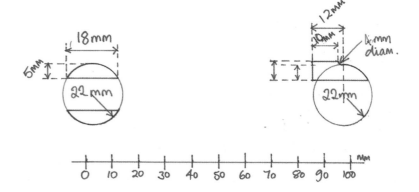

WORKING OUT THE SPLASHER DIMENSIONS

Splasher dimensions.

piece of tubing like a rolling pin, supporting the strip on your thigh or a mouse mat (thigh is easier but more painful).

- When you've got a curve slightly smaller in diameter than the splasher face, you can easily solder it with 180°C solder to the face supported on the bench. Tack and seam as usual on the inside.
- Trim the ends so they are very slightly too long, and then file carefully to match the edges of the face at 90 degrees. Final shaping can be carried out by rubbing the completed splasher on a piece of wet and dry or a sharpening stone. Repeat for both splashers. They should be a good fit over the hole in the footplate and sit upright and parallel. Don't solder them yet.

FRONT SPLASHERS

The front splashers require a curve and a straight top section and end. Draw them directly on to two rectangles of 0.015in brass soldered together. Use a ruler and set square for the straight lines and your circle templates for the curves. Then proceed as follows:

- Check with your card template that the splashers are going to match the front cut-outs in the footplate, and adjust if necessary. Saw and file to a lovely smooth shape, and separate.

- Bend a length of 4mm brass strip around a 3mm rod to produce a small curve at one end. Tack solder the strip beginning at the join between the curved and horizontal sections. Leave a little overhang at the join.
- Form the strip to the curved shape of the splasher face; I used a wood block to press against. Tack solder and then carefully seam.
- Tack solder another piece of strip to the flat top surface of the splasher. Butt it up inside the over-length end of the curved section.
- Bend the strip round the 90-degree corner using round-nosed pliers; tack solder and then seam.
- When satisfied with the shape, hide the middle joint with a fillet of solder and file smooth. Trim the ends very slightly over-length to allow you to smooth to a perfect fit. Rub gently on a sharpening stone or wet and dry paper so that your splasher sits properly at 90 degrees.

When you have two pairs of splashers that you're satisfied with, subtly file and smooth the edges between the tops and the faces to round them off slightly. This gives the pleasing impression that they are castings, as are the real things.

Sit the footplate on to the wheeled chassis and just check, by holding them in place one at a time,

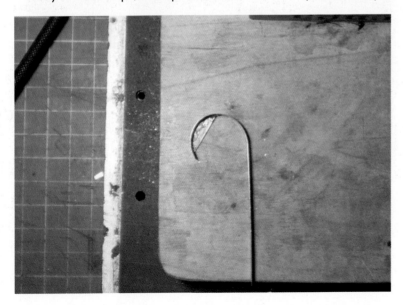

Soldering the centre splasher top to the face.

Saw and file the splashers to a smooth shape, and separate.

Bend and tack solder a length of 4mm brass strip.

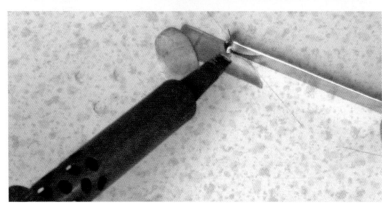

Form the strip to the curved shape of the splasher face.

Tack solder another piece of strip to the flat top surface of the splasher.

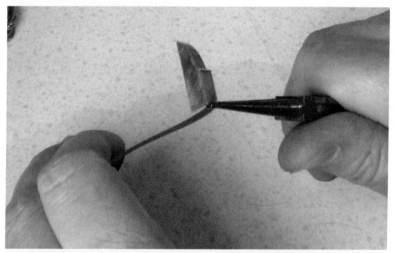

Bend the strip round the 90-degree corner.

Hide the middle joint with a fillet of solder and file smooth.

that the splashers aren't touching the wheels. If you've filed any of them down too much or mismeasured them you might need to make some new ones. Even though this is infuriating, it's better than discovering that they don't fit after you've soldered them all on.

ATTACHING THE SPLASHERS

To attach the splashers, proceed as follows:

- Line up a front splasher with the edges of the footplate cut-outs and scribed lines on the footplate top surface. Hold it steady using a piece of wood to shield your fingers (or hold it in place with Blu-tak), ensuring that it is parallel and square. Tack it from inside with 145°C solder near the centre of the face. Check again.

The tack joint will survive a bit of slight tweaking if things aren't exactly right. Then carefully tack both ends and seam the centre. Work quickly to avoid unsoldering your previous joints. The soldering doesn't have to be pretty, but do make sure to remove any large blobs of solder on the inside that might touch the wheels.

- When the first splasher is fixed, do the same for its opposite partner and then the centre pair; they should all be exactly in line and parallel to each other. It does get easier...

The small sections of the rear splashers that project from the cab front are added later, after the firebox/ boiler assembly has been put in place.

SPLASHER FLANGES

If you want to represent the flanges, you can solder small strips of 0.7mm wide, 0.010in nickel-silver round the edges of the splashers. You want just enough solder to give the impression of a seamless joint between the splasher side and the flange – experience will tell you how much. You can always remove the excess mechanically, or wipe the iron on to a more easily cleaned part of the footplate. This is tricky, and if you'd rather not do it, you can wait until the locomotive is nearly finished and add the flanges using similarly sized plasticard strip.

Tack a front splasher from inside near the centre of the face seam when properly positioned.

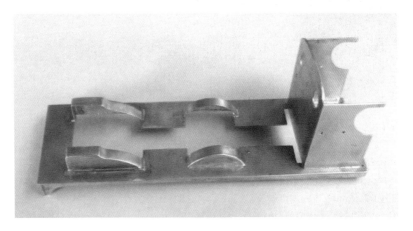

Do the same for its opposite partner and then the centre pair.

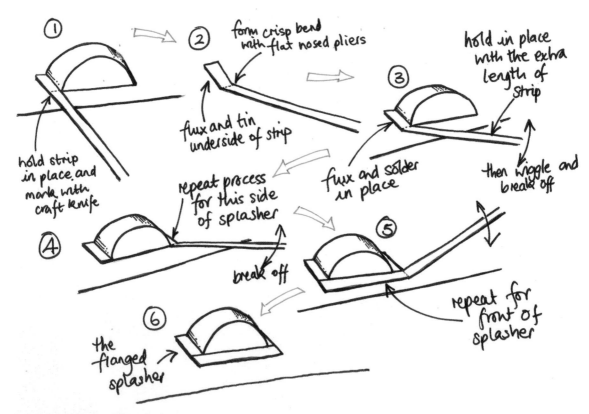

①
hold strip in place and mark with craft knife

② form crisp bend with flat nosed pliers

flux and tin underside of strip

③ hold in place with the extra length of strip

flux and solder in place

then wiggle and break off

④ repeat process for this side of splasher

break off

⑤ repeat for front of splasher

⑥ the flanged splasher

Soldering flanges to the splashers.

To solder the flanges to the splashers, proceed as follows:

- Make sure the model is secure and not going to wander off. Lay the strip along the end of one splasher and mark the width of the splasher end on to the strip with a craft knife.
- Bend the strip slightly along the mark so that you can hold on to the longer end while you position the piece that will act as the flange.
- Tin the underside of your strip with a splash of flux and a smear of 145°C solder so that it already has a thin layer of solder ready to fix it down.
- Lay the strip against the splasher end, add some more flux, apply the tinned iron next to the strip, and it should solder in a flash.
- Break off the excess part of the strip ready for the other end of the splasher.

- Solder a flange across the face of the splasher – and you're fully flanged.

Repeat with all the other splashers, including along the side of the cab. This gives a nice detailed touch to the look of the footplate and is a good exercise in careful, close soldering.

SPLASHER DETAILS
Now you will need to drill a few holes as shown on the sketch. It's a chance to judge the positions and sizes of a few pieces by eye.

There is a prominent cap-like object on the front of each sand-box, which stops up the hole where metal was poured into the mould. These are quickly represented by a small washer and a blob of solder to fill the centre. You can add some rivets later in the 'adding rivets' section. There is also a cap on the top of each sand-box, which allows it to

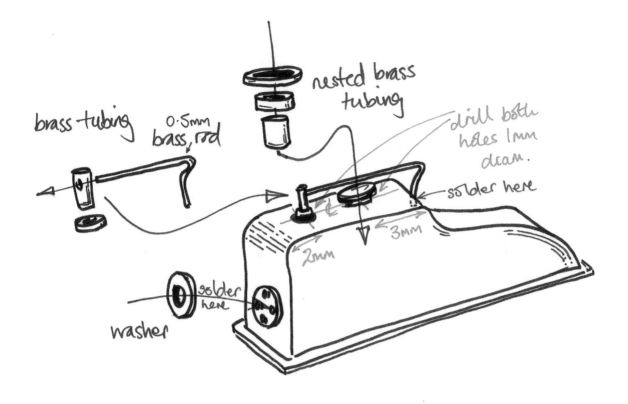

Front splasher details.

be filled with sand – these were made with nested tubes.

To allow sand to drop from the sand-box to the rail in front of the leading driving wheel there is a rod on the left-hand side of the loco body. It is worked all the way from inside the cab, and you can see it emerging from the firebox, running behind the splashers and along the footplate. When it reaches the front splasher it convolutes itself into a lever that twists like a small crank. There must be a connection underneath the smokebox to the other side as that sand-box also needs to do its job – but since we can't see any of that connection we don't have to put it in.

The main lever is made up from 0.5mm brass rod, bent to shape first and then filed flat on the outside. You can't see that it's still round on its inner surface unless you look really closely.

The crank is again a nested tube with a hole drilled in it and a little pool of solder for its nicely rounded base. Everything was held in place with Blu-tack whilst carefully spot soldered from behind with 145°C solder.

Well done. The last task is to clean up and give the model a wash. You now have the beginnings of a locomotive body. Fit the chassis back on and try a little test run. All should be well. Congratulate yourself and look forward to fitting the boiler and the smoke- and fireboxes.

CHAPTER NINE

THE BOILER, SMOKEBOX AND FIREBOX

The boiler, smokebox and firebox comprise a pleasingly large chunk of machinery that can make quick work of completing the major bodywork. They have a great set of names, which, unusually perhaps for locomotive nomenclature, do – in the words of a well known advertisement – 'exactly what they say on the tin'. Nevertheless it is astonishingly easy to mix up which one you are talking about: basically the smokebox is where the smoke comes from, and the firebox has a fire in it. Luckily they are relatively simple shapes which can all be built up from brass tubing. Hurrah!

The smokebox, where the chimney sits, is at the front of the boiler on top of the pistons. The J15

smokebox is slightly larger in diameter than the boiler, with a rather decorative brass ring at the join. The way in which the smokebox is actually connected to the footplate is largely hidden by the front splashers and the base ('piano front') of the smokebox door.

The boiler is where the water is heated up to make steam, and the firebox is situated at the other end of the boiler: it actually protrudes into the cab, and has a hole at its back end that allows coal from the tender to be shovelled directly on to the fire inside. The J15 firebox follows the same shape as the top of the boiler, and simply flares out to the sides.

No. 7564's smokebox, boiler and firebox.

The same view without the decorative cladding and cheery engine crew, or indeed the rest of the locomotive.
KEITH ASHFORD

MAKING THE BOILER ASSEMBLY

THE BOILER AND SMOKEBOX

I used telescopic brass tubing for the boiler assembly. Telescopic tubing consists of a series of tubes that fit snugly one inside the other. It is widely available in 1mm steps and is ideal for the job. It can be cut square quite easily, either with a tube cutter, or with a saw and an old lottery ticket. Using the delightful Alan Gibson-cast smokebox front simplifies this build nicely: it acts as a datum for the choice of boiler size, and positions everything perfectly.

Start with the boiler because it is a simple tube, using a length of 18mm brass tubing. To cut tubing at 90 degrees, first make sure the end of your tube is square by standing it upright on a flat surface against a set square. If it isn't, do that end first. Then proceed as follows:

MAIN COMPONENTS

- Length of 18mm (outside diameter) brass telescopic tubing
- Length of 19mm (outside diameter) brass telescopic tubing
- Alan Gibson J15 smokebox door with piano front
- 1mm square brass wire

- Use a piece of thin card or thick paper with a straight edge (I used to use lottery tickets, though recently they've become a bit plasticky). Wrap the straight edge of the paper round the tube where you want to cut; adjust it carefully so that the edge of the paper overlaps exactly, and stick down with tape. There's your straight edge.

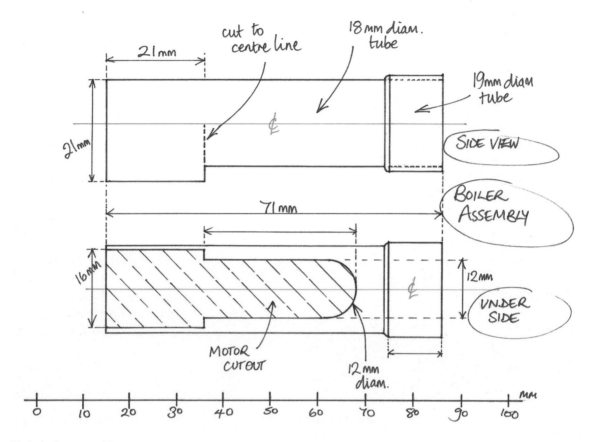

Main boiler assembly.

- Saw lightly just against the paper without pushing it. When you've produced a shallow groove all the way around you can gently start to saw through. I use a piercing saw; you might prefer a razor saw: whatever suits.

Once you've made the boiler, it's a simple matter of cutting a short length (11cm) of 19mm diameter tube for the smokebox.

The smokebox slides securely on to the boiler. If it's a bit stiff, sit it upright on a wood block and gently tap the other end (using another wood block to protect it) with a hammer until the front edges are flush.

THE FIREBOX
The firebox is formed by first cutting a slit along the boiler tube the length of the firebox, and then making another cut at right angles half way through the tube and bending the sides into shape. To do this, proceed as follows:

- Mark the length of the firebox and wrap another lottery ticket round the boiler. Use a set square to mark the long cut on the boiler tube, and saw carefully along it using the piercing saw.

Wrap the straight edge of the paper round the tube where you want to cut.

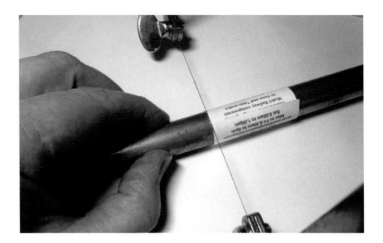

Saw lightly against the paper without pushing it.

- Now you need to saw a line across the tube level, keeping to the edge of the paper to a point half way down on either side. You can mark the half-way point using the calipers set to 9mm.

- It's interesting to see how much tension the cylinder is under, as a certain amount of twanging occurs when the second cut is made.
- Using the flat-nosed pliers, carefully bend each firebox side outwards. Do it a little at a time, and

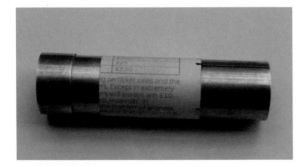

Mark the long cut on the boiler tube and saw carefully along it.

The cylinder is under considerable tension.

Carefully bend each firebox side outwards.

Form the shape of the firebox by eye to start with.

Use a card template of the firebox to produce a symmetrical shape.

Work out how much to trim from the bottom edges.

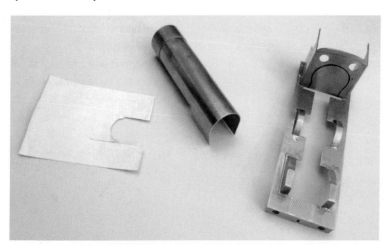

LEFT: **Use the template to trace the firebox outline on to the cab front.**

BELOW LEFT: **Now position your boiler assembly on to the footplate.**

BELOW RIGHT: **Locate the Alan Gibson smokebox door into the front of the boiler assembly.**

try hard not to cause any flat areas by squeezing too hard with the pliers.

- Form the shape of the firebox by eye to start with, using a set square to help keep the edges parallel.
- You can use a card template of the firebox as an aid in producing a symmetrical shape, going very slightly in at the 'waist' and then straight down.
- Use the template and the calipers to work out how much to trim from the bottom edges of the firebox if they are slightly too long; this leaves you with the almost finished stage.
- Use the template to trace the firebox outline on to the cab front, helping to locate the boiler assembly (on the picture I hadn't yet cut the cab front cut-out, which you will have done earlier).
- Now position your boiler assembly on to the footplate using the template outline to help.
- Temporarily locate the Alan Gibson smokebox door into the front of the boiler assembly. This will give you the correct height at the front.
- If necessary, file a little more off the bottom edges of the firebox to allow the boiler assembly to sit parallel with the footplate.

Once everything is fitting nicely, we have one more job to do before joining the boiler assembly to the footplate. A large cut-out has to be removed from the underside of the boiler just forward of the firebox, to allow the motor/gearbox to fit inside the boiler. I have marked the cut-out dimensions on the boiler diagram, but do check for a good fit as you go. The cut-out can be slightly bigger if you wish, as long as you can't see it from the side. The centre splashers hide just about everything.

I would recommend drilling a number of small holes within the waste area, and then use a piercing saw to cut between as many holes as you can. The firebox will get in the way – be careful not to cut into it. You are essentially hacking away at the waste metal. If you have a mini-drill with a dental burr, you can grind away the remaining metal. If you are feeling very adventurous you can use cutting discs in the drill, but I find these difficult to control, and they can fracture spectacularly so always wear eye protection whatever you are doing with the drill. Otherwise use small files. Wash and clean thoroughly to remove any dust and pieces of metal.

Use the mini-drill with a dental burr to shape the boiler cut-out. Notice that I didn't get round to doing this until after I'd soldered the boiler to the footplate. Also notice that I've filed away the foot-plate area within the firebox to accommodate the motor.

Shape the boiler cut-out.

Remove any rough edges to produce a clean cut-out. Test that the motor fits by resting the footplate and the boiler assembly on to the chassis with the motor in place. The motor/gearbox should just fit nicely into the space. File a little more if necessary.

JOINING THE BOILER ASSEMBLY TO THE FOOTPLATE

Any amount of building will almost always involve 'fettling' – a lovely word, which can mean many different things: I like to see it as a mix between fitting and whittling. Unless you're very lucky things won't fit perfectly the first time, but even if they don't, they can almost always be made to do so. Having said that, although little mistakes can be put right, if you make a big enough mistake it's almost always wiser to start again. The adage that 'you can take metal off but you can't put it back on' is good, though not truly accurate: you sometimes can.

After taking a great deal of time fettling the boiler, smokebox and firebox so that it lay central and level, I found it was too short. However, if you find this is the case, all is not lost: I raised mine at the back and lengthened it slightly, which you can do by soldering on some 1mm square-section brass wire. It was easy to shape the wire and solder it with 180-degree solder to the end of the firebox. After a clean-up, you really couldn't see the join. Square wire is marvellous stuff – always have a variety of sizes in stock.

Also, you may find it necessary to file a little away from the inside edge of the front splasher tops to allow the smokebox to sit down between them properly. If you find that your boiler assembly is too long you can file it back.

Make sure you're pleased with the shape of the firebox and the final fit of the whole boiler assembly. It really pays off to make the effort here not to end up with a wonky boiler. When you are completely satisfied, use the mirror for a different perspective,

If your boiler assembly is too short, all is not lost.

Shape the wire and solder it to the end of the firebox.

make a cup of tea, come back and look again. Use the square to check that everything is square, parallel and vertical (in the right places). You can then solder it all together:

- Ensure all the surfaces are clean. Use a craft knife to replace the marked guideline on the cab

front so that you put everything back in the right place (a wipe with meths will clean things up). The boiler is quite a hefty chunk of brass and will disperse heat quickly; I whack up my iron temporarily to 400°C for this.

- Using 145°C solder and plenty of flux, tack the firebox sides to the footplate from underneath,

And there we are. Magnificent.

and to the cab front from inside. The smokebox door will help steady everything at the front. Hold everything carefully with blocks of wood and watch you don't burn your fingers. Check again that all is parallel and in place.

- Tack solder the smokebox piano front on to the footplate, and the smokebox door to the front of the smokebox. These are virtually impossible to do from the inside, so aim for secure joints and be ready to do some heavy duty solder removal afterwards.

- Check once more that everything is correctly in place.

With such large pieces it is not necessary, nor particularly easy, to seam the solder joints; just make sure that you have sufficiently strong tack joints holding everything securely together. Nor is it necessary to solder the boiler to the front splashers.

Finally, remove any excess solder that shows on the outside surfaces, and wash and dry the assembly.

CHAPTER TEN

DETAILING THE LOCOMOTIVE

Detailing the locomotive takes a lot longer than you might have thought. However, it brings the build to glorious life, transforming it into a model locomotive. Some modellers like to have only as much detail as can be easily seen if they were standing watching the locomotive pass through the countryside. Others like to get the number and size of the individual rivets as true to the prototype as they can possibly manage.

As with all models, the detailing process is a mixture of impressions and compromises. Scaling down exactly from the real thing can make parts impossibly small, structurally feeble or virtually invisible. Nevertheless, it is a good idea to know what all the bits and pieces actually do, as it can help you come to a decision whether or not to include them, and if you want your scratch-built models to sit well with your existing stock, then have a look and see what is put on or left off. Can you produce a model to the same character as the rest of your models?

It is quite up to you what you do. I enjoy putting in as much detail as I can in order to give the model the quality that I'm looking for, and I'm quite happy to compromise in size or complexity to achieve that impression.

SOLDER OR GLUE?

As the detailing parts become ever smaller and more fiddly, there is an increasingly strong argument for cooling down the soldering iron and getting out the glues. As it's a really bad idea to mix and match the two you'll need to give a few minutes thought as to the order you're going to do things in.

I've never got on with superglues: the only things I can reliably stick together are my fingers, and I loathe the fumes. Putting a soldering iron anywhere near superglue will produce horribly irritant toxic fumes that can do you no good at all, so any supergluing will have to come last.

Most items you may want to glue are probably going to be very small. The only problem here is that if they are small and easily damaged, such as lamp irons, they are better soldered if at all possible. In fact I will solder anything I can, with the exception of boiler fittings such as chimneys and domes: for these I use a five-minute resin epoxy such as Araldite. These are fairly large chunks of metal, which can be tricky to solder, and the five-minute setting time of the glue gives you plenty of time to adjust them; also any slight irregularities in the fit will be filled with glue. And you can do them right at the end after everything else (if you've not forgotten anything else).

If there is anything you'd rather not solder you'll need to rearrange the order of fitting for yourself. Also there are things you may want to leave off, or extra parts that are particular to your chosen loco. Therefore treat this chapter as a bit of a pick and mix – you might want to make a list before you start. So let's begin.

THE DETAILS

CAB/REAR SPLASHERS

These are a little fiddly, but not too hard. You'll need to curve two pieces to fit the tops of the splashers protruding from the cab sides; proceed as follows:

- Begin with a 6mm wide strip of 0.010in brass. Make sure the end is at 90 degrees, and curve it round a 3mm rod.
- Cut to an approximate shape and size; continue to file and fit until it is just right. This is a good bit of practice for those scratch-building skills.
- Soldering them in from underneath is also quite tricky. A quick splosh of flux and a dab of 145°C solder should do the trick before a good clean-up.

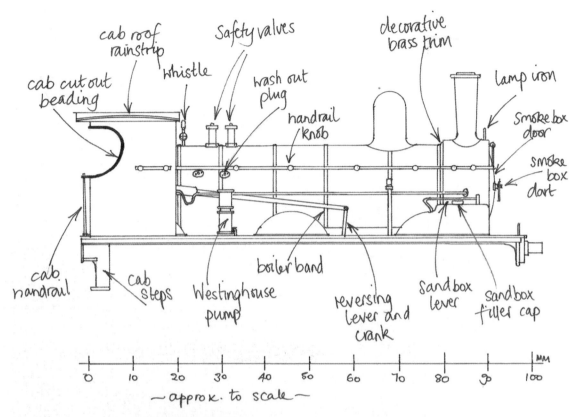

Locomotive body details to approximate scale.

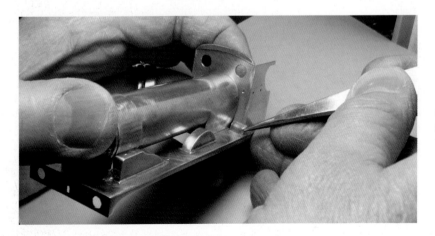

Checking the fit of the cab splasher.

FIREBOX CAB JOINT

To detail the front of the cab where it meets the firebox and hide the joint (if a little ragged), solder a length of 0.7mm square brass wire carefully around the edge of the firebox where it attaches to the cab.

FIREBOX CONDUITS

Firebox conduits are square-section boxes on either side of the firebox where it meets the footplate, which protect small wires or tubing. They need careful filing to fit over the splasher flange and the beginning of its curve. Use 1mm square tubing, if you have it, or 1mm

Firebox conduits and cab splashers.

square wire. Measure the length from the model with the calipers and use the piercing saw to cut it. Solder in place in the same way as the splasher flanges.

THE HANDRAILS

Handrails are one of those details that add enormously to the character of a model, and can be quite a challenge to make. The two important things are to get the handrail knobs (or stanchions) in line with each other and parallel to the boiler and footplate, and then to concentrate on getting the correct curve at the front.

The real thing has the rails to allow the crew to clamber about on the footplate in order to clean

*Front end of the J15
showing the handrails
curving around the
smokebox door.*

things or to access various mechanical bits and pieces without the need for a pair of ladders. The J15 has short knobs on the side of the smokebox and medium-length ones on the boiler sides to match; this is to avoid a kink as the rail follows the sides. Looking at the front again, there is a short knob in the centre and the rail curves round above the smokebox door to allow it to be opened.

The handrails can be represented on the model using 0.5mm brass wire, and you can source turned

This lovely shot through the cab window shows the slight curve of the handrail as it travels along the side of the boiler. It is advisable to make the model handrail straight – in smaller scales the curve shouldn't show.
STEVEN GREENO

handrail from many suppliers such as Markits. Proceed as follows:

- Use the calipers to measure from your drawing the height of the handrail knobs from the footplate. With the inside measuring points of the calipers, mark a line along the boiler.
- Don't worry too much about the mark; keep it light and it'll be hidden beneath the rail and a layer or two of paint. If you're not keen on this method then try making yourself a card template, which is a simple rectangle to the correct height that sits on the footplate and you can scribe or mark with a fine pen along the boiler.

- Take note of where each knob goes from the drawing, and mark with a pen before scribing a short vertical line in each position using the dividers. I did notice that the smokebox has different hole positions on either side.
- Carefully centre-pop each position keeping everything in line, and drill with a small, sharp, 0.5mm drill in a pin-chuck. Open out each hole to the diameter of the knob fixing pin.
- Insert the knobs temporarily, and thread a length of 0.5mm brass rod through them to see whether things are nicely in line. Then remove them, because they will get in the way.
- To enable the handrail to pass through smoothly you may also need to open out the holes in the

Mark along the boiler the height of the handrail knobs from the footplate.

Boiler with handrail knob holes drilled.

knobs themselves with a 0.5mm drill – holding them firmly in your medical forceps.

To form the handrail you'll need to enlist trial and error and quite a bit of patience. Look carefully at the photos to see what shape you need. From the front the rail curves around the top of the smokebox door and then makes a 90-degree bend to run along the sides of the smokebox and boiler before passing through the cab sides. You'll probably need two or three goes at making this. Looking at the sketch, proceed as follows:

- Take a 30cm piece of 0.5mm brass rod; mark the centre with a pen. From the centre, bend it around a brass tube of slightly less diameter than the boiler to form the curve over the smokebox door.
- Now slip a short handrail knob on to the wire at the curved portion as you won't be able to put it on after you've bent all the corners. Hold the curved portion in place against the front of your loco – in between the top of the smokebox door

and the top of the smokebox. Sight along the side of the loco where you can see the line of holes, and mark the positions.

- Take hold of the rod with the round-nosed pliers at this point, and make an upward bend so that the straight portion of the rod is horizontal. Repeat this for the other side of the straight rod.
- When you're satisfied with the front you need to make the 90-degree bends to take the rails down the length of both sides of the boiler. Do this in the same way by holding the rod in place with your thumb, marking the position of the bends and forming with pliers.
- Check for fit by adding the handrail knobs and putting the handrail in place. You may need a few goes at this.

Now, thread the knobs on to the rod – short ones for the smokebox and medium ones for the boiler. Thread the handrail ends through the holes in the cab front and insert all the knobs into their holes. Check that everything fits nicely. If it doesn't,

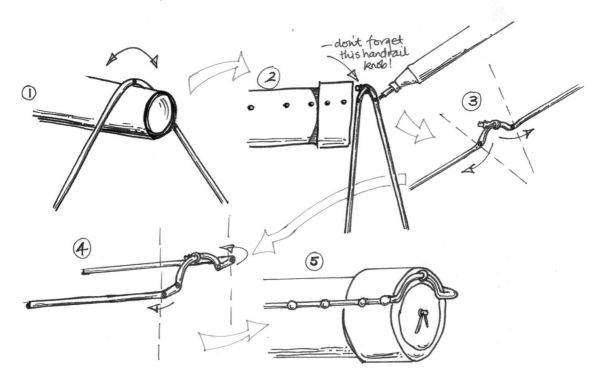

Forming the handrails.

it is better to start again, as trying to change the bends in the rod will create kinks. In this case use this attempt as a model to show where you went wrong.

You may find that the cab front holes aren't in quite the right position and require a bit of re-drilling. If so you can fill the old holes with a blob of solder and re-drill.

Finally, trim the long ends of the rail so that they protrude a few millimetres into the cab – just enough to locate them.

Once you've got a beautifully bent up handrail and all the locating holes in the right place, put it away safely for later as we will be completing other detailing parts first.

WASHOUT PLUGS

The earlier photo of the firebox side with the conduits also shows the washout plugs: these are the oval shapes just beneath the handrail. They allow the boiler to be washed out: a hosepipe is pushed in and water under high pressure sprayed around the inside to give everything a good rinse. Some railway companies liked to hide theirs with little covers in a charmingly Victorian manner, but this is not so with the J15. There are two on each side and they are not symmetrically placed; they are very distinctive.

Washout plugs in model form.

I couldn't find a suitable etch so here's how I made them:

• First I cut small slivers of thin-walled 4mm tubing and slightly flattened them with flat-nosed pliers until I got four good ovals.
• I then marked their positions with the dividers. As the space within the oval boundaries of the plugs was slightly elevated I applied a small smear of solder in approximately the right shape on to the firebox.
• Each oval of tubing was then soldered on. These were carefully filed almost flush with the firebox and excess solder gently removed with a wire brush. I took care not to take off too much, and tried hard not to distort the oval. It's a good example of how you can use solder to add a bit of depth to a detail.
• A 0.5mm hole was drilled in the centre of each, and a small piece of 0.5mm rod soldered in from the inside. Holes were then drilled on both sides diagonally, and all were cleaned up.

This was one of those things that I'd been hanging back from doing as I wasn't entirely sure how to do it, and how difficult it would be. As with most things, it wasn't as hard as I thought, and whilst quite time-consuming, I was very pleased with the result.

REVERSING ROD

I wanted my reversing rod to look as though it worked, so I made sure it went through the footplate. I used a piece of 1.5mm square-section tubing for the little shroud that protects the pipe as it exits the cab front. The shroud is curved at the front and fits diagonally to the cab, so required a little filing, with a tiny file, to fit.

I made the lever with a piece of straight, solid 1mm square-section brass rod. Some of these fittings, like coupling rods, tend to be quite chunky. I soldered the shroud on to one end and drilled a 0.5mm hole in the other before rounding it off with the file. It's easier all round. There is a taper on the lever. It gets thinner towards the crank end so file that carefully, and if it all looks a little chunky thin it down a bit.

On the prototype the reversing rod is connected to the reversing wheel in the cab. At the other end it actuates the reversing gear between the chassis frames. The Westinghouse pump can be seen on the left.

I made the crank with a single piece of 1mm brass strip. In the photos you can see that it is bent in an 'S' shape to transfer the movement to the valve gear and clear the footplate. That's easily done with round-nose pliers after drilling a 0.5mm hole in one end and rounding off. Fit a piece of 0.5mm rod into the two holes to make a joint, and before you solder everything solid, check to see what sort of angle everything should be at. It's a good idea to check it against the model in case of any creeping errors. I find it better

not to cut anything to size if you can avoid it until it's time to fit: it's easier to hold and you might trim it too short.

When you're happy with the angle of the joint between the rod and the crank, give it a quick sizzle with the iron. Solder the crank into the pre-drilled hole in the footplate from underneath and the shroud in place on the firebox side. It is quite strong enough fixed at either end. Remove the excess from the end of the crank where it pokes through the footplate.

WESTINGHOUSE PUMP

This ingenious chunk of machinery encloses an air pump and a series of valves that form part of the vacuum brake system on those J15s that were fitted with it. Check to see if your loco was fitted with one – it's only on the right-hand side. You could quite easily make one up from tubing and wire; sometimes life's too short. There is also a delightful casting available from Alan Gibson, which comes with the fixing bracket.

Carefully clean the firebox side (you won't be able to get behind the cylinder when it's attached). Give the pump casting a good clean with a wire brush to remove any surface coating. Drill the indicated holes about 0.5mm deeper to locate lengths of 0.7mm copper wiring to represent various pipes.

The photo shows the large fixing bracket behind the pump. It is attached solidly to avoid excess vibration that may have prevented it from working properly. Solder the cast bracket in place against the firebox side with 145°C solder.

I was a little wary of soldering the pump to the bracket as it's quite a hefty casting. However, the two pipes, shown in the sketch, can hold it quite securely: one passes through the hole in the cab side near the reversing rod, and the lower right-hand side one through a hole in the footplate. A quick touch of

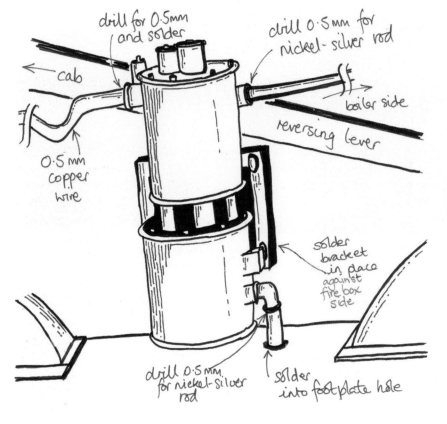

Westinghouse pump fixings.

solder did it. If you're wary, put it on the gluing list for a spot of five-minute epoxy.

OTHER PLUMBING

Next there is a long horizontal pipe from the pump to the mid-centre of the smokebox. It has a number of kinks that follow the shape of the boiler assembly, and I wanted a strong straight line between them. Nickel-silver rod is good for this because it holds its shape, but it is rather tricky to bend. A really helpful trick is to make a pattern from more malleable brass wire by holding it against the loco body and following the shape; then copy it with the nickel-silver rod. You might want to try this approach for the handrail for the front of the loco if you have had trouble shaping it.

This pipe fits into the smokebox via a small oval flange that can be soldered on as you attach the end of the rod into the hole in the smokebox. These details are full of character and can be difficult to make.

I discovered a wonderful etch with many useful flanges and dials from Meridian Models who produce narrow-gauge loco kits. Always look widely for bits and pieces, as many manufacturers of military, aircraft or automobile kits will produce useful detail pieces.

CLACK VALVES

Further piping on the boiler includes the pair of large clack valves – so called because they are valves that go 'clack'. They are actually one-way valves that allow water to flow into the boiler against the pressure of steam trying to get out.

These look good using copper, and are made by soldering a small section of brass tubing to the top of a piece of 1mm copper wire. A further thin slice of larger telescopic tubing is added to make the valve itself. A vertical notch is filed in the side of the narrow tube, and some square brass rod soldered in with a 90-degree bend to act as the piping joining the valve to the boiler (see diagram overleaf).

The valves are fitted into holes drilled in the boiler, and the copper piping passes through the hole in the footplate.

CAB-SIDE HANDRAILS

To make the cab-side handrails, thread two short handrail knobs on to a length of 0.5mm nickel-silver rod. Locate the handrail knobs into the holes in the cab side, and hold in place with some Blu-tack. Solder from the inside, trim the rail to length, and solder to the knobs.

CAB BEADING

Beading is the rather decorative edge around the cut-outs of the cab side. Not only is it good to lean on, it also helps prevent corrosion. To make the beading, proceed as follows:

- Use an over-length 1mm-wide strip of 0.010mm brass, and shape it around the inside of the cut-out with a finger or small piece of thin wooden dowel. Hold everything in place with clamps, pegs and Blu-tack, and support at the back with a piece of card.
- Tack it in the middle of the curve with some 145°C solder. I find it easier to solder on the

Make a template in brass to follow with nickel-silver.

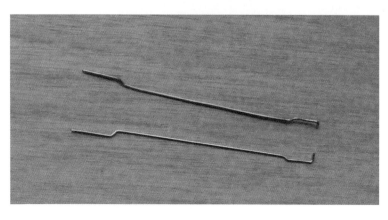

The clack valve is the structure on top of the vertical copper pipe to the left of the front splasher. You can also see the flange on the firebox through which the piping from the Westinghouse pump passes.

outside of the cab; you just have to clean up afterwards. Then it's just a question of tacking and seaming round the edges from the centre outwards till you reach the ends.

• Trim with a slight projection at the top and a longer one at the bottom where the vertical handrail is to join next.

Repeat for the other side, which you'll find easier, and there you are: beaded.

VERTICAL HANDRAILS

The cab handrails are a pleasing tapered shape, which can be easily and excitingly replicated using the mini-drill. Proceed as follows:

• Put a length of 0.7mm brass rod in the chuck of your mini-drill and cut to 18mm; there is excess at the bottom to attach to the cab floor. Hold the rod lengthways down on to a hard wooden block, and run the drill. Using a

Clack valve detail.

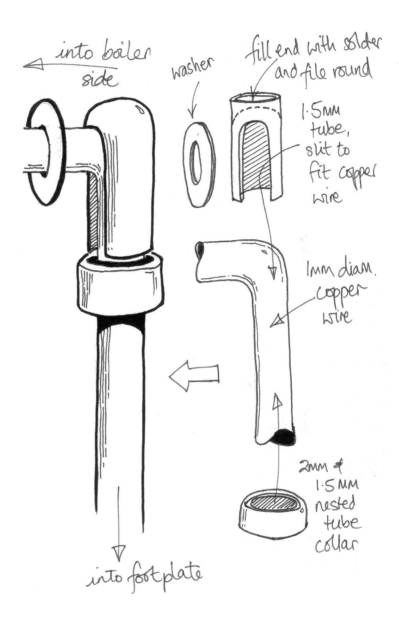

into boiler side

washer

fill end with solder and file round

1.5mm tube, slit to fit copper wire

1mm diam. copper wire

2mm & 1.5mm nested tube collar

into footplate

*BELOW: **Making the cab-side handrails.***

medium-sized flat file, carefully start to taper the rod.

- It's another of those things you do by touch. Run the flat of the file up and down the length of the spinning rod, concentrating more on the unfixed end. *Take great care not to touch the rotating collet with the file.*
- Every now and then stop the drill and use the calipers to check that the top end is becoming

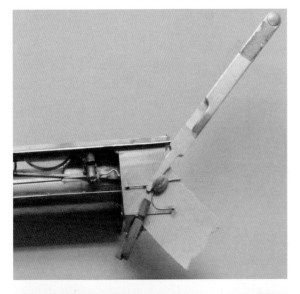

thinner. You only need to go down to 0.5mm at the top.

And that's it, one tapered handrail. Now do another, exactly the same.

I put a little flange of thin tubing on the bottom of the rail just where it goes through the hole in the cab floor. If it's a reasonably tight fit don't bother to solder it until you've got the rail properly adjusted; the solder will be drawn up into the joint when you fix it from under the footplate.

The top of the rail fixes up against the projecting end of the beading. Give it a good blob of solder, and file it to a representation of the shaped end. Snip off any excess at the bottom under the footplate.

*ABOVE LEFT: **Making the beading.***

Prototype cab showing the handrails and beading.

Making the vertical handrails.

SMOKEBOX DOOR HANDLES

Numerous manufacturers make very suitable smoke-box 'darts'. These are handles in the centre of the smokebox: one has a simple lock to close the smoke-box door, and the other a screw thread to tighten it against the boiler pressure inside. The handles are usually positioned somewhere around twenty past eight. I have photos of No. 65447 with them in various positions – take your pick. I soldered mine on; gluing is a definite alternative here.

FRONT BUFFERS

My buffers are Alan Gibson turnings; alternatives are available from other manufacturers. Looking carefully at the real thing shows the circular bases to be chunkier than the ones I had, so I simply cut and soldered some brass tubing to beef them up. They were then soldered on to the buffer beam and cleaned. It's best to keep the buffer heads out of the way until the model has been painted. Store them in a safe place.

TRAIN COUPLING

Now you need to think about your choice of train coupling. There is a wide choice of three-link or screw-link couplings available that are virtually to scale. I have fitted a screw-link coupling: I simply soldered the etched hook of my coupling into the slot in the buffer beam; you can spring it if you want by using a spring and a split pin at the rear of the beam.

Alternatively you can go for any number of different coupling choices. I've fitted a small tension lock coupling (ubiquitous on British ready-to-run stock) to the tender, and you can do the same on the loco. Have a look at the relevant chapter. Any other choices you may make are dependent on your preferences. They may mean that there is less room for the piping that is attached to the buffer beams, so you'll have to be aware of this as you progress. There is a great deal of information available about different sorts of couplings elsewhere.

BRAKE AND STEAM PIPES

Running along the valance on either side of those J15s that were fitted to pull passenger trains are some large pipes. These are set just under the footplate: one is for steam heating, the other for the brake. Check your photos to see if you need either of them.

The brake pipe running along the valance just beneath the footplate has a rather novel shroud covering it – presumably to protect it from damage. In many photos you can see where it has been dented, or in some cases where bits have been broken off, exposing the piping beneath.

I made the shroud simply by gently squashing a 2mm-diameter brass tube and then filing off one side. The peculiar quality whereby metal moves out of the way of the file is quite useful here as you can end up with a D-shaped tube, which aids soldering to the valance.

The rather novel shroud covering the brake pipe, running along the side of the footplate.

The ends are filled with solder and the front is drilled to take a representation of the pipe that leads to the front buffer beam. This is simply a short length of 0.9mm brass rod bent to disappear under the front buffer beam and avoid the end of the chassis frames.

On the left-hand side the pipe is a simple length of 0.9mm brass rod that emerges through a hole in the valance at the back and continues along to the front where it performs a number of right-angled bends to connect up with the front buffer beam.

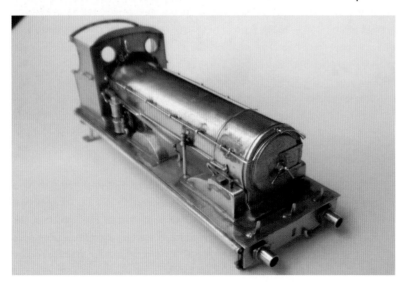

The shroud shown on the model.

The left-hand-side pipe.

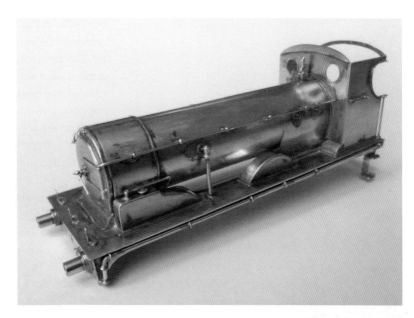

BELOW RIGHT: **The whistle clouded in steam from the safety valves.**

The little brackets that attach it to the valance are simply twists of fine wire soldered on. I soldered the entire thing on at the hole in the back, and on to the valance at the front. It can be simplified to disappear round the back of the buffer beam too if you wish to get it out of the way of your chosen coupling. Copper wire is a good alternative if you have trouble bending the brass in the right places. Try to keep it nice and straight where it should be.

The structures that allow the air and vacuum brakes (and there is another one if you want a steam heating pipe) to be connected along the train are flexible hoses, generally made of wire-reinforced rubber. I bought some lovely cast brass vacuum pipes, which are quite easily soldered into notches in the front buffer beam.

Soldering is much stronger than gluing for these vulnerable details. I connected the vacuum brake pipe to the pipe run with a little sliver of tubing.

THE WHISTLE

The whistle is a multi-tasking work of art. It is very tall and has a small valve wheel on it. I turned some rod and pieces of tube in the mini-drill in a similar way to the clack valves, but it could as easily be made with a shop-bought whistle attached to a piece of tubing.

The wheel is from an etch, and is fitted to a piece of 0.3mm rod soldered into a hole drilled in the whistle tube. Again, all of this could be glued. There's another of those little wheels coming out from the front of the cab: you'd best put that on before the whistle assembly. It all looks great, but do remember it's quite delicate.

Making the whistle.

SOLDERING THE HANDRAIL

You have a choice: solder in the knobs now, or glue them in later. I soldered mine in. You may be able to reach some of them from inside the boiler, but if you do make a mess on the outside, it's quite easy to clean off.

You can buy solder paste, which is a liquid suspension of solder in a flux. It comes in bottles or a handy syringe, and you merely poke a little into the hole before adding the knob and very carefully applying the iron to the side. This is particularly useful for the smallest detailing parts, such as these. Alternatively you can use plenty of flux and the tiniest speck of solder on the iron.

Solder the knobs on both sides. You don't have to solder the front knob as the handrail will keep it in place. Carefully clean any solder off the boiler sides, and wash and dry. (Keep the plug in the sink if you want to catch any loose knobs.)

FOOTSTEPS

To make the step brackets, cut a strip of 0.020mm nickel-silver. Solder together two pieces the correct length, and draw in the cut-out. Then saw and file to shape and separate.

- The treads of the steps are folded up from 0.010in nickel-silver strip. Follow the stages

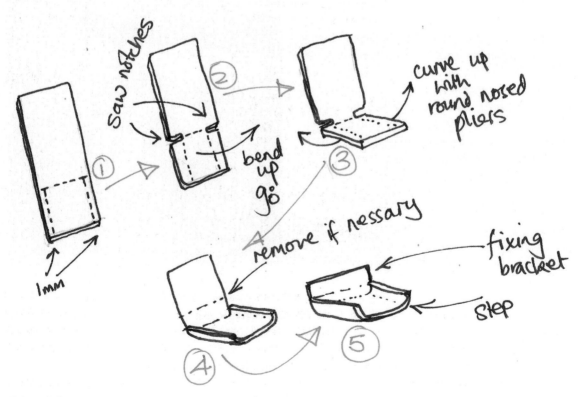

Forming the steps.

An almost complete step tread.

BELOW: *The completed bracket with steps, soldered beneath the cab.*

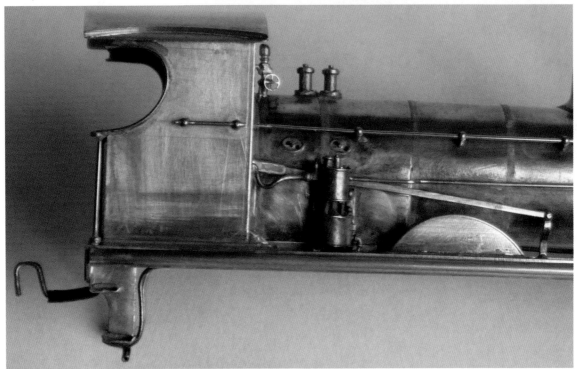

in the diagram using flat-ended and pointed pliers.
- Make four steps and carefully solder two each with 180°C solder to the main step brackets. Hold the steps with tweezers or forceps; pin the brackets to a piece of balsa protected by card.

- Tack solder the completed bracket with 145°C solder to the loco body. Gently support the loco body with a cradle of wood blocks and Blu-tack while you are doing this.
- Make sure the steps line up with the curved cut-outs in the rear buffer beam (they are not right

up against the inside of the valance); adjust if necessary. If your tacked joints are strong enough there's no need to seam; give them a little wiggle to find out.

There are a few more unexplained pipes and so on lurking around. Whatever you can see on your photo and like, go ahead and put them on – you could even do a bit of research and find out what they do. In this spirit I soldered a couple of pieces of copper wire to the back of the valance and the bottom of the steps, and a couple of pieces of hefty

1mm tubing to the back of the steps, peeping out at the bottom.

During this whole detailing process make sure you wash and dry between each session (and use moisturizer, as all this plays havoc with your hands).

You'll have noticed that we haven't fitted the hefty boiler details such as the chimney and dome, nor added any rivets, let alone the cab roof or the excitements that can be found within. Never fear, they are to come.

Meanwhile, admire your workmanship and revel in your skills – and get down to the pub before closing time.

CHAPTER ELEVEN

THE CAB INTERIOR AND ROOF

BUILDING THE BACKHEAD

Well, here we are, with a beautifully detailed locomotive body that has no means of control. The backhead (which has other names) is literally the back end of the boiler assembly. It has a hole that you can shovel coal through, and a set of controls and dials that allow the crew to drive the loco and monitor its condition. Everything is made of big chunks of metal and wood, and it is a work of art in itself. The crew are reasonably comfortably protected by the cab, and have a wooden floor that bucks like a bronco when the loco breaks into a gallop. Everything is hot and dangerous. It really was the job of heroes to drive these locos.

The controls are an interesting set of valves and levers with associated pipes. The coal-hole is generally what it says it is, with a hinged plate that allows it to be closed. Almost all of the loco's functions are controlled from here, including the brakes, speed, direction, whistles, sand from the sand-boxes and frying an egg for breakfast.

Regarding the backhead, you have a choice: there is a lovely little casting from Alan Gibson of a backhead

A delightful study of the J15 cab with crew having a bit of a rest from active heroism. BENJAMIN BOGGIS

that suits the J15 perfectly and can be easily fitted. Or, with your soldering skills honed to perfection, you can fashion your own with a few bits and pieces, time and patience. It's up to you; I've used both in my models.

If you use the casting, you will find it has cut-outs on either side for you to fit the boxes that cover the rear wheels where they protrude into the cab – so take your measurements for those from the casting. Do take time to remove the large casting sprue from the bottom: saw and file it or, faster and more thrilling, grind it off with the mini-drill and dental burr.

There are various wheels, pipes and gauges that you can add from etches or pieces of rod and wire. The casting has a nice deep back, which gives plenty of space for a fly-wheel. You'll probably have so much fun providing all these little finishing touches that you'll want to make the next one yourself: the following notes will help you do that.

MAKING YOUR OWN

As mentioned, the backhead closes off the end of the boiler/firebox and follows the same shape. I bent an overlong piece of 2mm brass tubing around a 14mm diameter wooden rod, and then bowed out the ends with round-nosed pliers to fit inside the same template that I'd used to form the firebox. Solder to a rectangle of 0.015in brass and get a good seam all the way round the inside. Trim the ends of the tube flush with the bottom of the sheet. Then proceed as follows:

- Saw the edges of the brass sheet roughly to match the outline of the tube, and turn over.
- Gently file the brass sheet back to a curved edge, and smooth with some wet and dry. Press and indent firmly with your thumb in the centre of the face – just enough to give an impression

This is what the backhead looks like with all the controls removed – and the crew, and the cab floor. Note its shape as it straightens towards the bottom edge: an excellent opportunity for the modeller to see something normally hidden. KEITH ASHFORD

My backhead.

Brass tubing bent to the shape of the backhead.

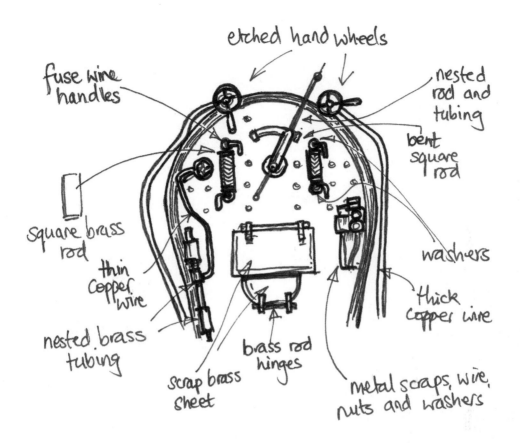

etched hand wheels

fuse wire handles

nested rod and tubing

bent square rod

square brass rod

thin copper wire

nested brass tubing

washers

thick copper wire

scrap brass sheet

brass rod hinges

metal scraps, wire, nuts and washers

CAB FLOOR

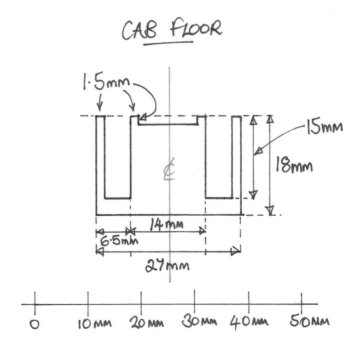

1.5mm

15mm

18mm

14mm

6.5mm

27mm

0   10MM   20MM   30MM   40MM   50MM

Backhead details and cab floor dimensions.

Saw the edges of the brass sheet.

that it is set back slightly behind the rim. Use the dividers to score a line to define the rim.
- To represent the geometric pattern of the bolts and rivets on the front face, mark them out on the rear surface and tap a scriber lightly with a hammer.
- Drill out five large holes and solder washers around them. Cut a circle of thin brass for the coal-hole door, and solder strips of brass curved round a piece of rod for the hinge.
- Cut a rectangle to form the flap that covers the coal-hole door, make hinges for this, and solder everything in position on to the backhead.
- Small pieces of square-section rod act as the water gauges, and various bits of tube and wire represent handles and pipes.
- Any excess solder should be vigorously smoothed with a wire brush, and you do actually get a nice 'all-of-a-piece' finish as the solder blends everything together.

You end up with rather a lovely impression of the whole, and it is pleasing to see what detailed work you can do with a hefty soldering iron.

Now it's time to make a base for the backhead and the cab floor. I made it a tight fit to slide into the cab so that I could remove it for painting. Note the cut-outs to clear the rear wheels: remember to check the dimensions against your model for a good fit. The small cut-out at the front is important as it provides just a little more clearance for the motor.

The floor is slightly raised above the level of the footplate by soldering a folded strip under the floor. The wheel cover/cab seats can be added once you've checked the fit of the base and backhead.

- Using my trusty Jenga block, I soldered the backhead on to the base, from the back, at 90 degrees.
- Slide the base into the cab and check everything fits snugly. Don't worry if it's a little loose – you can glue it in securely once all the painting is done. You may also need to move it back slightly to accommodate the motor.
- When you're happy, build up the wheel covers from strip metal. File some small rounded notches to accommodate the backhead.

Looking back at the prototype photo, decide what other bits and pieces you want add on – perhaps the regulator handle. Everything can be cobbled together with scraps of copper wire, brass tubing and strip; it can be a thoroughly enjoyable exercise, and it'll be up to you to decide where to stop.

THE CAB ROOF

To conclude this part of the build, we need a roof. If it is removable it makes life easier when applying the finishing touches, such as the dials that sit on the inside of the cab above the backhead.

ROOF SUPPORTS
A curved girder supports the roof at the rear and helps to keep everything in shape. It has a number of hooks attached to it – a piece of weatherproof sheeting can be fastened to these – which are a serious modelling challenge. Proceed as follows:

- Cut three rectangles of 0.015in nickel-silver and tack them together. We're going to make three the same: one to fit between the cab sides and two to support the roof. Blacken the front with marker pen. Slide the metal up against the cab front and mark the shape of the top of the curve.

Make a base for the backhead and the cab floor.

Solder the backhead on to the base.

Build up the wheel covers from strip metal.

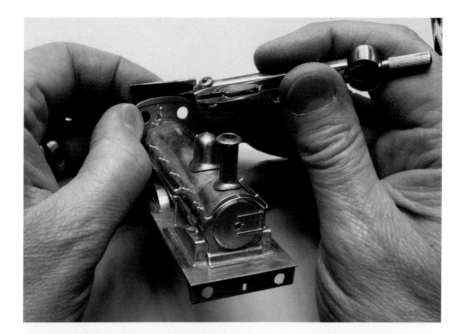

Cut three rectangles of nickel-silver and tack them together. Mark the cab outline.

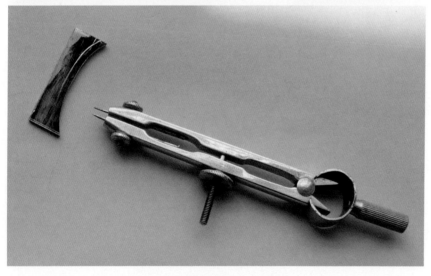

Saw and file to the outline with needle files and trace a parallel curve with the dividers.

- Saw and file to the outline with needle files. Smooth with wet and dry, and re-blacken if necessary. Use the dividers, set to 1.5mm, to trace a parallel curve following the curve you've just made.
- Carefully saw and file off the excess metal. As this becomes increasingly fiddly, use something like the saw table to help support the shape. Try very hard not to bend it. Once you're satisfied, check against your cab front top and very carefully split the three pieces; keep them safe.

If you'd like to include the hooks, here's how to do it:

- Drill a series of 0.3mm holes down the centre of one roof support. Using Blue-tack to steady things, solder in a number of lengths of 0.3mm wire. Bend the wires round a tiny drill and trim with a pair of clippers. File the rear face flush, and smooth with wet and dry.
- Finally, solder between the ends of the cab sides.

Carefully saw and file off the excess metal.

Making the hooks.

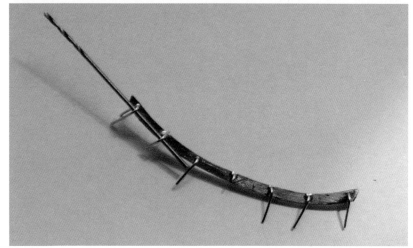

Solder between the projecting ends of the cab sides.

THE CAB ROOF

The roof shape is a large diameter curve and may need very slightly tighter radii at the sides to fit. It took me three attempts to get it right; I'm sure the rejects will come in handy.

Find your cab roof dimensions by making a template from a 23mm wide strip of thin card. Roll the strip over the cab roof support and the cab front, and mark each side along the top of the cab sides. Allow for a 1mm overlap when cutting. Then proceed as follows:

• Use the template to cut a rectangle of 0.010in nickel-silver. Make sure you mark the centre line underneath. Roll the larger diameter curve first with a piece of hefty tubing on a flexible surface such as your thigh.

Curving the rectangle of 0.010in nickel-silver.

Final shaping of the roof.

- Using double-sided sticky tape, stick one edge of the roof to the shank of a hand tool or large drill. Bend gently by eye, pressing into a giving surface such as a balsa block until you have matched the curve of the cab face. Then repeat for the other side.

Test it for a good fit on your cab. Tweak if necessary – though go carefully, because if you do too much tweaking you may need to start again. Once it is close enough, the roof supports that you made earlier will hold it nicely to shape.

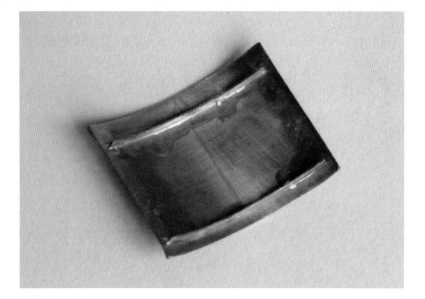

The finished cab roof showing the supports soldered in place.

The finished roof. Splendid.

- Scribe a line 2mm in from one edge of the cab roof with the dividers. Use this to position and tack solder the first support. Make sure it is at 90 degrees, and seam when you are satisfied.
- Put the roof on so that the support you've just soldered fits securely inside the cab front. Then get the sharp point of your dividers up behind the support at the back of the cab and scribe a line that will determine where you solder the final support.
- Take the roof off and tack and seam the other roof support behind the line you have just scored.

This should give you a roof that acts like a lid and fits beautifully. You can either leave it loose to show off your backhead, or fix it permanently once everything else is done.

One last thing: the roofs of rolling stock generally had rain strips which diverted the bucketing water away from the centre of the vehicle to either end, where, if you were unlucky, you could catch a big downpour down your collar. The rain strips on our J15 appear to be L-shaped, and can be represented by soldering a curve of 0.5mm wire on each side of the roof, which gives a good impression.

CHAPTER TWELVE

BUILDING
THE TENDER

The J15 tender.

MAIN COMPONENTS

- Three pairs of Romford 16mm tender wheels for OO gauge
- Three 9.5mm frame spacers
- Markits loco brake gear etch (from loco build)
- 0.030in brass or nickel-silver sheet
- 0.020in nickel-silver sheet
- 0.010in brass or nickel-silver sheet
- Set of Alan Gibson J15 tender axle-box castings
- 0.6mm half-round soft brass wire
- 2mm-diameter fibre washers from Eileen's Emporium

The J15 tender is basically a large water tank on wheels with a well to put coal in and a hole at the front to get the coal out again. There are brakes to stop it from rolling off, and various pipes and connections to the loco. Give or take a few other embellishments, that's basically it. In modelling terms there's less to build than the loco: it's generally simpler, and it doesn't need a motor. It does have some unique features, however – the flares on the sides, for instance – and it offers good practice for your developing scratch-building skills.

THE CHASSIS

The tender wheels, unlike the loco wheels, don't have a simple system to set them back at the right gauge if

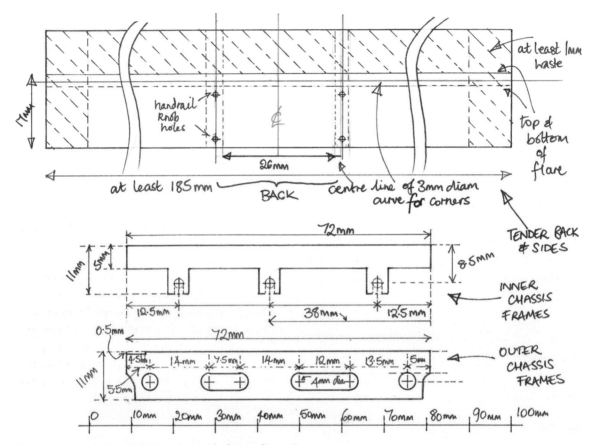

Tender back, sides and inside and outside frame dimensions.

you want to take them off their axles. My solution is to provide a 'false' set of frames inside the real ones with slots instead of circular bearings, and the wheel sets are dropped into these. I used Romford 16mm tender wheels, which are electrically insulated on both sides. They will be converted later to conduct electricity on one side.

INNER CHASSIS FRAMES

- Tack solder two rectangles of 0.030in brass together – much the same as the loco chassis frames. Keeping everything square at the top edge, mark in the bottom frame edge and the centre line for the wheel axle holes. Make absolutely sure these are in a straight line.
- With a set square, mark in the vertical lines for the legs and the axle centres. Centre-pop the axle holes.

- Drill and open out the holes to the same diameter as the wheel axles (check with your calipers – mine were 2mm diameter). Saw and file away the waste area to produce three square legs.
- Drill holes for the brake hangers and brass spacers.
- Using the square, scribe vertical lines down from both sides of each axle hole to the bottom of the leg. This shows you where to cut to make the slots that will form the axle bearing. It's important that the top half of each hole remains circular as it forms the bearing surface. When cutting the slots, make sure you don't widen the holes. File the edges of the slots smooth and parallel.
- Then separate the two pieces and clean up. Bolt them together with the spacers, and slide the wheels in.

The inner chassis frames.

Spend a minute pushing your new chassis along a piece of track. We will be making a keeper plate to stop the wheels from falling out. You can round off the bottom edges of the legs as I have, though this is not essential as they will not be seen.

THE TENDER BODY

THE TENDER BOTTOM AND TOP

Now you'll need to make a base and top for the water tank and coal well. From the sketch, make up two rectangles and tack solder them together. Then proceed as follows:

- Draw in the radii of the rear corners using your circle template, and file to shape.
- Separate and clean the two pieces. On the tank base mark the central waste area, the centre line from back to front, and the two chassis fixing holes. For the tank top, mark the coal-well waste area and the centre line. Remove the waste areas with a piercing saw and file to shape.

The tender tank in all its solitary glory. KEITH ASHFORD

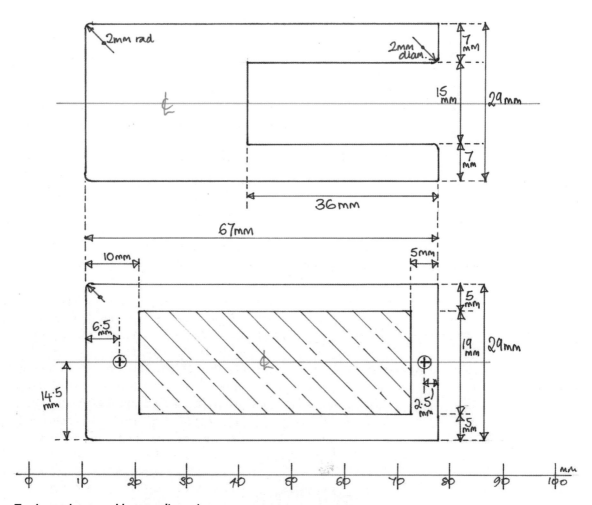

Tender tank top and bottom dimensions.

- Drill the chassis fixing holes with a 0.7mm drill in a pin-chuck, and open out to 2.2mm.

Put these pieces away for later.

THE TENDER SIDES

The tender sides and back, including the flared tops, are produced from a single rectangle of nickel-silver. Forming the flares can be difficult, and you may need to have one or two attempts before you are satisfied with the results. Proceed as follows:

- Break off a rectangle of 0.010in nickel-silver following the dimensions on the diagram. The height is at least 10mm greater than that of the actual sides in order to accommodate the curve of the flare, and to give you a little more to hold on to when you bend the flares (the waste will be removed later).
- Blacken with the marker and, using the diagram, scribe the vertical centre line for the tender back. This will enable you to line up the tank top and base when you come to solder everything together.
- Next scribe the vertical centre lines for the rear corners. Then scribe lines 2mm on either side of the centre lines to help you find the right position for the rod that you will use to form the corners.

Don't forget to mark the positions of the handrail holes (don't drill them yet).

- Turn the rectangle over so that the score lines you have made (on the inside surface of the body) are now face down. Without using the marker pen this time, score a heavy line for the top of the

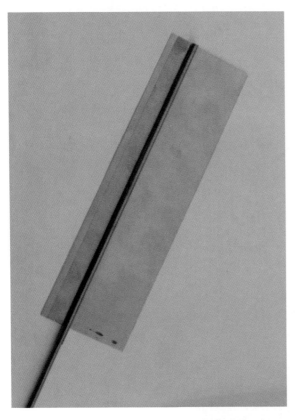

ABOVE: **Sticking down a rod on double-sided tape.**

flare: this will ease the process of breaking off the excess metal after forming the flare.

- Score a line, less heavily, for the bottom of the flare so that you can locate the rod that will act as your curve former.
- Stick double-sided tape over the lines scored for the top and bottom of the flare. You can see the lines through the tape. Then stick a 3mm rod down parallel and exactly between the two lines – the tape keeps it in position.
- Clamp the rod and metal in your bending bars or vice, taking care to line everything up so that it's parallel. The shiny metal side should be on top, the scribed and blackened side underneath.
- Using a straight edge to support the metal, bend it around the rod by 90 degrees to produce the flare. Don't be scared of using your fingers to finish off – pliers can mark the metal. Kinks and wobbles can be ironed out later as the tender body is built up.
- Remove the metal from the bending bars leaving the rod in place. Pressing down on a hard surface, carefully flex at the heavy score line that marks the top of the flare, and bend it back and forth until you can break the excess piece off – it's easier than it sounds.
- Alternatively you can saw off the excess using the score line as a guide, or trim the metal off with tin snips, taking great care not to distort the flare.

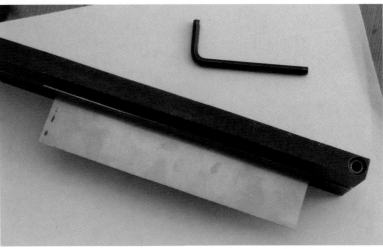

Clamp the rod and metal in your bending bars or vice.

- Finally, remove the rod (carefully, as the double-sided tape can be very sticky). Then peel off the tape – a wipe of meths and gentle scraping with a wooden coffee stirrer can be helpful to remove any residue.
- Smooth the top edge with a small flat file and wet and dry paper. There's your flare.

Before bending the sides and back to make the tender body, the flare needs to be 'relieved' at the corners. Saw three or four little 'fingers' to just below the line marking the bottom edge of the flare. The fingers can be curved and the gaps later filled with solder, then filed and smoothed to produce the complex curves of the prototype.

The next step is to bend the sides and back to make the tender body. Proceed as follows:

- Clean the marker off with meths. Lay the side down on a flat surface with the flare overhanging the edge so that it is not damaged. Place the 3mm diameter rod between the score lines for one of the corners. Supporting it with a straight edge, bend the side around it until it is 90 degrees to the back. You will see the little fingers separating.
- Place the tender base on a flat surface and lay the sides and back up against it to check that the fit is good. The corner you have just formed should match that on the tender base, and the scribed

The flare needs to be 'relieved' at the corners.

Check that the fit of the tender base with the sides and back is good.

centre lines on the tender rear should line up to the centre line on the base.

It is quite easy to accommodate any errors here as the sides were measured intentionally overlength (to be trimmed back later), and the second bend can be made using the tender base as a template. Work out where the bend needs to be by holding the 3mm rod in place at the corner of the base and bending the sides carefully around it. Check in case you need to cut another finger or two to ease the corner. Make sure the sides and back are at 90 degrees to the base.

• Tack solder the back and the sides to the base. Test that everything is nice and flat and doesn't rock. When satisfied that all is good, seam the joints, taking care that no buckling occurs.

ATTACHING THE TENDER BODY TO THE INNER CHASSIS FRAMES

Before attaching the tender tank top we need to consider how to attach the chassis frames to the tender body. The two holes in the tank bottom are fixing holes, which should line up with those in the chassis-frame spacers (you can't see them in some of the photos because I built the tender first and modified the drawings to make the build easier).

If you need to, elongate the holes on the tank base with a round needle file until everything lines up properly. Check that you can pass an 8BA bolt through the holes.

It is possible to solder a nut around the hole on the base – this is called a 'captive nut'. You need to be careful not to get solder in the screw threads of the nut: this can be accomplished by holding the nut in place with a cocktail stick or sharpened wooden dowel (or a roll mop herring stick as previously mentioned) as you solder it. Alternatively you can put a smear of grease or oil on the thread to act as a barrier to the solder.

Another method, which I prefer as it's difficult to stop the oil getting on surfaces that you want to solder, is to 'chemically blacken' or 'gun-blue' the screw thread. This highly toxic substance (don't drink it) produces an interesting colour change in metals, a surface effect that very effectively blocks solder. It's a good illustration of how contaminated surfaces won't solder.

Dip things into the bottle with pair of stainless-steel tweezers and take them out immediately. It's interesting to watch the process occur, as the longer you leave a piece, the blacker it gets. Have a small dish of water to hand to drop the piece into when it's good and black: the water halts the gun-bluing process, and you can rinse and dry the item with a piece of kitchen towel.

Once the nut and bolt are blackened, it's only the threads that you want to be protected, so file one

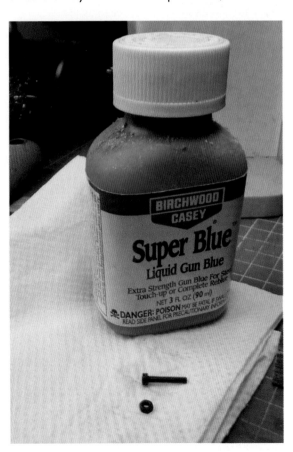

'Gun-bluing' produces an interesting colour change in metals.

Bolt the chassis frame to the tender base.

face of the nut to shine the surface, and polish with a piece of wet and dry. Then proceed as follows:

- Bolt the chassis frame to the tender bases using a blackened nut and bolt at the front and rear. Make sure the shiny face of the nut is in contact with the inside surface of the tender base – firmly, but not too tight. Apply a good splosh of flux, and solder the nut to the base with a generous blob of 145°C solder. Do this for the front and rear nuts.
- Then undo the bolts, and the nuts will stay securely in place. You might want to practise this procedure on some scrap first as it's quite a palaver getting the nut and bolt separated if you've soldered it solid.

THE OUTER CHASSIS FRAMES

Leave the main body for a while and have a look at the prototype photo showing the outer chassis sides. There are two types on the J15: one with upside-down, tea-cup-shaped holes such as those seen on No. 7564, or as on this build, lozenge shapes. The holes save weight, look pretty, and allow you to get at the murky underside of the chassis. (Tenders were swopped around frequently so it's a good bet that whichever loco you choose to model will have had one or the other type at some time.) My diagram

shows the lozenge shapes – you will need to look at your drawings or draw your own if you want the tea cups. To make them, proceed as follows:

- Solder together two strips of 0.015in nickel-silver and mark the centre, top and bottom of the lozenges with the dividers. Centre pop and drill the holes to 0.5mm and gradually open out to 2mm.
- Using the reamer, continue opening out the holes to 4mm. Mark the reamer near 4mm to give you an idea of when you're approaching the right size. Use a 4mm drill or calipers to check the size of the holes. Twiddle a larger drill in the hole to remove the cusps.
- Join the holes with the piercing saw. Make sure you join the right ones – draw some cross-hatching with a marker to show the waste area before you begin.
- Mark and file the small cut-outs at either end and the small rebate at the rear for the end plate of the main tank (shown on the diagram). Tidy up with a file, clean and polish, and you'll have a very pleasing couple of outside frames. Note that they do have a very definite back and front – the shorter lozenge is towards the rear. Label appropriately with a marker.
- Make up the buffer beams from 0.015in nickel-silver strips. I produced the coupling slot in the rear

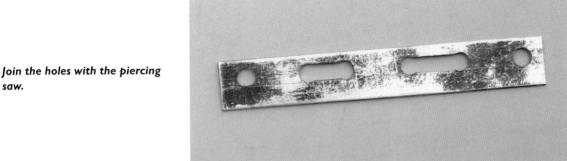

Join the holes with the piercing saw.

Make up the buffer beams from nickel-silver strips.

beam by drilling two 0.7mm holes at either end, and joined them with the piercing saw. The bottom corners of the beam are slightly rounded off.

The front beam – the drag bar – has two small holes for the little buffers between the tender and the loco, and a large lozenge-shaped slot for the draw bar.

COMPLETING THE BODY AND CHASSIS

A TENDER BEHIND

Have a look at the details of the construction of the rear end of the tender. A rectangular plate extends backwards from beneath the tank with a bracket on top that curves around the corners. The rear buffer beam is attached beneath.

Then proceed as follows:

- Solder a small rectangular plate to the tank underside and the buffer beam to that, using the inner chassis gently bolted on to hold things square and steady. The ever-trusty Blu-tack comes in handy here. A piece of card between the frames and the body stops everything else being soldered solid.
- Add a thin strip of nickel-silver, curving around the bottom of the tank, on top of the plate holding the buffer beam, as on the prototype photo. Then solder the outer frames to the underneath of the tender base.
- Use your dividers to score a line 3mm in, along the underside of the tank base as a positioning guide.

Do remember that the shorter lozenge is to the rear, and note that the cut-out at the rear of the frames

The details of the construction of the rear end of the tender.

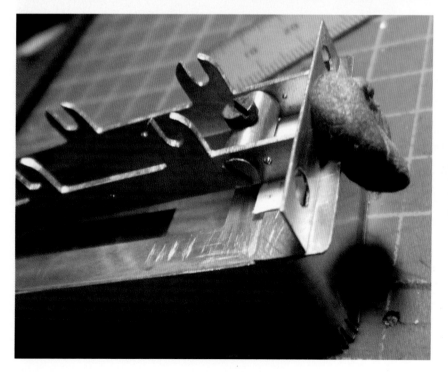

Solder a small rectangular plate to the tank underside and the buffer beam to that.

The outer frames soldered to the underneath of the tender base.

accommodates the little plate above the buffer beam. If it's not sitting properly, give it a bit of a file. Remember to tack solder from inside, then check and seam.

THE TENDER TOP

You can then add the tender top, which fits nicely just below the level of the flares. To do this, proceed as follows:

- Scribe a line with the dividers, using the top of the flare to lead you, giving a parallel guide line for soldering. Tack solder from the inside.
- When you're happy that all is level and in the right place, and you've checked with the mirror and made a cup of tea and come back and checked again, seam it up.

Fitting the tender top.

- Once that's done, use the dividers to scribe a line down the front of the sides as a guide to remove the excess length. Take your measurement from the front of the tank top and base: they should be exactly in line with each other. Saw and file smoothly, trying not to mark the tops of the outside frames.

That's basically it for the main structure; she's already looking very pretty. The front end will come later. Now for a bit of detailing.

THE OUTER FRAME DETAILS

Alan Gibson does some beautiful tender axle-box castings for the J15. There are other makes available; these look so good I couldn't resist them.

The castings need to be carefully sawn from the fret and cleaned up. Give them a light tweak with pliers to straighten them out if they've become distorted. They have no mechanical function on the model: all you need to do is make sure they lie flat and are clean and smooth. I rubbed them on a large fine file to ensure the backs were flat.

Now you get the chance to 'sweat' the castings on to the frame. Mark lightly where they're going to sit, centrally between the lozenge-shaped cut-outs; check your drawing:

- Apply flux and then a thin layer of 145°C solder to the outside surface of the frames. Hold the

casting in the correct position with a piece of card as a spacer and a lolly stick that won't transmit the heat to your fingers, and flux liberally again; then apply the tinned iron to the rear of the frames just behind the casting. Watch the solder make the joint, and remove the iron.

Repeat for each casting; get all six of them on, and then stand back and admire your handiwork.

To finish off the sides at the front you need to carefully file the curve that sweeps from the top of the flare to the front edge. Use the drawing or photographs to help produce a card template. Begin the curve by eye, filing with a square needle file. File off a little at a time and keep checking against the template. When you're satisfied with one side, do the other so that it matches. The template comes in useful later on, so keep it.

THE COAL WELL

We need to make a curved plate for the front of the coal well, which follows the shape of the tank top. With reference to the sketch opposite, proceed as follows:

- Take a rectangle of 0.020in nickel-silver. Drill two small holes at the level of the coal hole, and join them with the piercing saw. Then saw down from the centre of that line to the centre of the bottom edge of the rectangle.

Sweating the axle-box castings to the outside frames.

Using a card template to help produce the front curve.

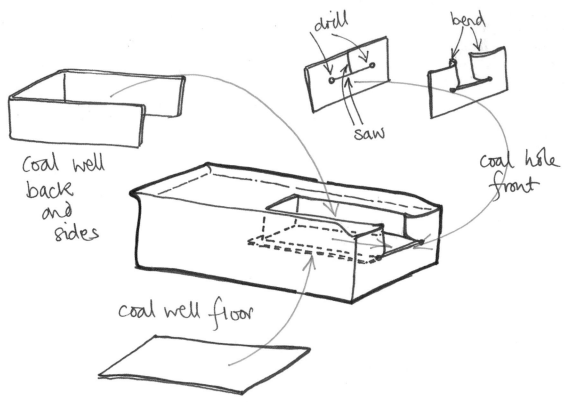

drill

bend

saw

Coal well
back
and
sides

coal hole
front

coal well floor

Forming the coal well.

- Bend the two resulting rectangles to 90 degrees around a 3mm rod (to suit the radius of the tank top front) and check for a good fit, sitting within the space at the tender front. The sides should fit just between the ends of the tender front, and the curved corners should fit flush beneath the curves of the tender top. If necessary, file to fit snugly.
- Tack and seam carefully to the front space. File and smooth the joints for a good finish; any small gaps can be filled with solder before finishing off.

You can also see in the photo (below) the plate at the front that holds back the majority of the coal – this is called the coal hole. It is decorated with beading and a pair of holes. To make this, and to complete the coal well, proceed as follows:

- Use a rectangle of 0.015in nickel-silver cut to fit the space between the curved front that you've just installed. Use the inside measuring blades of your calipers to determine the exact measurement. Saw out the rounded opening and add the beading using copper wire and Blu-tack in the same way that you did for the loco cab sides. It will very usefully hide the join between the curved front and the rest of the inner sides of the coal well. Don't solder it in place yet.
- The inner sides of the coal well are made by bending up a single strip of 0.015in nickel-silver that will fit flush beneath the edges of the cut-out in the tender top. It's probably easier to solder this to the tender top from the outside of the joint; there isn't much space to get your soldering iron inside the tender body, and a lot of this work will eventually be covered by a generous pile of coal.
- When the sides are on, cut a rectangle of 0.010in nickel-silver for the coal well floor slightly larger than the coal well, reaching all the way to the front. You can slide it into the slots

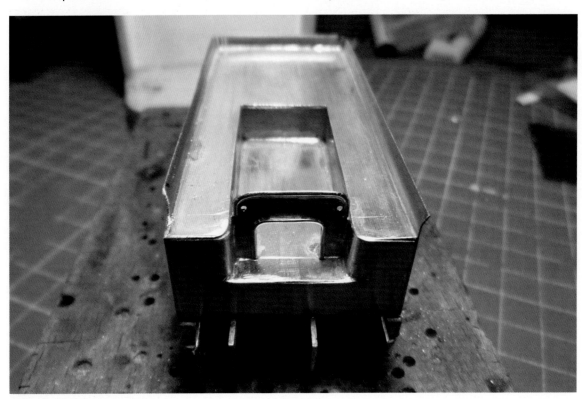

The completed coal well.

where the front curves begin and solder it to the sides.

- Finally solder the coal-hole plate in place.

With the coal well completed, most of the main tender parts have been constructed.

BEADING THE FLARES

This sounds like some sort of exotic 1970s fashion experience: it actually refers to adding the decorative metal edge, or beading, to the top of the tender sides, which looks good and helps prevent corrosion. Beading also gives extra strength and shape to the flared tender corners on the model, and with care, is a very pleasing soldering exercise.

I used 0.6mm half-round 'soft' brass wire from Eileen's Emporium – or some prefer copper or fuse wire. Half-round gives a very good approximation of the shape of the real beading, and has a flat surface that is helpful when soldering it in place. As long as it's soft, it's much easier than trying to do it with something stiff and springy; the only thing you don't want is kinks. If necessary, straighten the wire by clamping one end of a suitable length in a vice, and pulling the other with a pair of pliers until you feel it 'give'. Then proceed as follows:

- Start at the middle of the tender back edge and tack with tiny amounts of 145°C solder using plenty of flux. Lay the wire on the outside edge of the flare with a small amount projecting upwards to make a rebate; this comes in handy when adding the tender side extensions.
- Carefully bend the wire around the flared fingers of the first corner; tidy up the curve a little if it needs it. Encourage the solder to flow into the spaces between the fingers.
- Continue around the side and finish off following the front curve. Snip off the excess and file smooth.

You will want to avoid lingering with the iron, or going back to soldering in the middle between two soldered joints, as the brass may expand and distort. Again, you might want to practise this technique on some scrap.

Once you've done one side, return to the middle of the back and solder round to the front curve on the other side. Carefully clean off any excess solder and shape the filled-in rear curves using wet and dry paper.

You can then return you attention to the flared corners at the back of the tender. The cut fingers should be full of solder and you can shape and smooth them with wet and dry.

Finally wash, dry and admire.

SIDE EXTENSION PLATES

The original tenders of these locos were beefed up to increase their coal-carrying capacity by adding extension plates on top of the flares; these can be

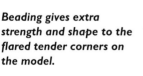

Beading gives extra strength and shape to the flared tender corners on the model.

seen clearly on the prototype photos. To make the extensions, proceed as follows:

- Tack solder two strips of 0.015 nickel-silver together and use the templates you made earlier for the curved fronts of the tender sides. If you cut through the line of the curve on the template with your craft knife you can use the cut edge to mark identical curves at the back and front of the extensions. Flip the template over to produce the mirror image curves at the back.
- Cut and file the curves to shape and very gently separate the two pieces before cleaning up.
- Solder the extension plates carefully to the rebates at the top of the beading on the tender sides.
- Add the beading to the top edge of the extension plates. Start with the front curve and move

towards the other end, holding things steady with a lump of Blu-tack and using a stirring stick to press the wire into place.

As long as you don't go back on yourself you shouldn't have too much of a problem with expansion. I gently rub the soft wire with the stirring stick to coax it into shape as I go along. Try hard not to form any kinks as they're very difficult to get rid of; a bit of solder and some filing will remove any sign of smaller ones.

- Clean up. Wash and dry. Admire some more.

FRONT DRAG BEAM

You can now finish off at the front by soldering in place the forward extension to the tender footplate.

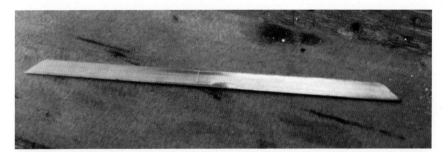

Cut and file the curves to shape.

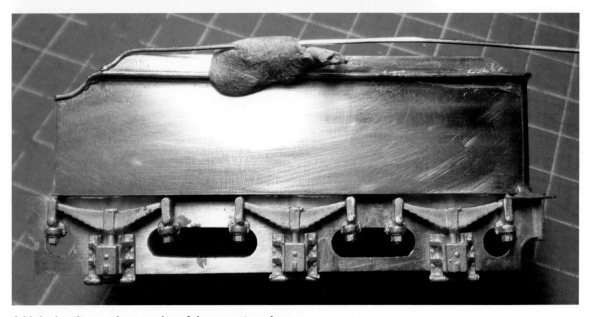

Add the beading to the top edge of the extension plates.

Front drag beam area.

This is a simple rectangle of 0.015in nickel-silver with a hole drilled for the brake standard and a slightly chamfered front edge, perhaps for negotiating very tight corners.

The drag beam has a slot (connect two drill holes with the piercing saw) bordered by two small plates which have holes drilled for the small buffers that prevent the tender and loco from coming into direct contact with each other.

Solder on the drag beam beneath the lip of the floor plate.

THE TENDER STEPS

You can buy etches of generic steps from Mainly Trains, which certainly save time, or you can stretch your modelling skills and build your own. There are three different widths of step on the tender. The small upper steps at the front fit in close to the spring hangers of the axle box springs; they appear to be part of a large riveted plate, which makes it easier to solder the step on to the frame. The lower front step has a much smaller folded bracket. The

rear step is a slightly smaller version of the large front step.

The steps are made in the same way as the loco steps. Cut suitable width strips of 0.015in nickel-silver a little overlength, and saw 1mm notches where the steps fold, as with the loco. Fold up the curved sides and then the step itself.

For the small front steps you have to make the side plate thinner and file a notch in it; this is so that it can fit satisfyingly into its little recess between the back of the tender drag beam and the spring hanger of the axle-box casting. File a little at a time, and test for a good fit. When it fits nicely, tin the back and front of the bracket with 145°C solder, and flux the frame side. Hold the bracket in place with forceps or tweezers, and touch the front of it with the iron to make the joint.

The larger steps have only a 1mm fold-up to attach them. Score horizontal lines in the correct places on the frames to help you locate the steps. The prominent rivets will be added later: they are curiously large and flat-headed – perhaps so as not to trap the toes?

Steps at the front of the tender and the rear of the locomotive.

DETAILS

TENDER TOP DETAILS

There are many details in the tender top that can be added. If we have photos of the prototype that show everything, what do we leave out? It's up to you. Some of the details can be obscured by coal and may not be necessary. You could solder in place small pieces of t-section tubing, or add the pieces from thin plasticard to give a good impression of these details. I built mine up from small soldered pieces of nickel-silver.

Practise your scratch-building skills by forming items from tube and sheet, taking measurements from sketches and drawings, or judging by eye from the photographs. I really enjoy this aspect of scratch building, and completing the tender provides a good opportunity for this. The details I added include the plate at the rear of the tender top that protects the water-filler cap from the coal. I made the water-filler cap from brass tube and scraps of sheet nickel-silver. A tool storage partition takes up most of the middle of the left-hand tender top, along with the lovely little toolbox; both were bent up from thin brass strip.

The distinctive brake standard at the front can be purchased as a casting from a number of manufacturers. It can be made by tapering the outer tube of the brake standard in a mini-drill before filing the oval slots and adding the handle and inner tube from soldered brass rod.

FINISHING DETAILS

It is a good idea to add these details last as they are vulnerable to damage. The front handrails were formed in the same fashion as those on the locomotive with small pieces of strip for the brackets. The rear handrails are merely shaped lengths of 0.5mm brass rod soldered in place. The little buffers can be made from brass pins.

There is a series of ribs on the inside of the tender side extensions which strengthen and connect them to the flares.

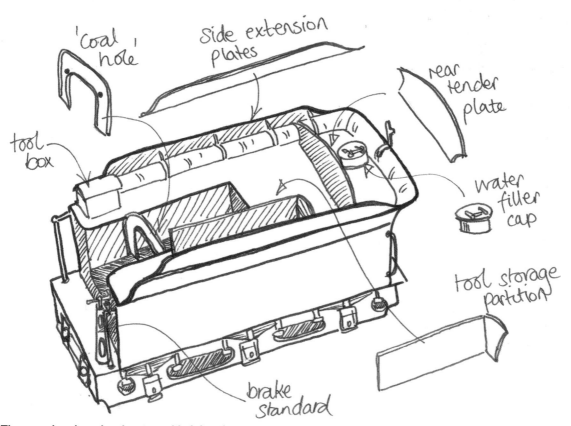

The completed tender showing added details.

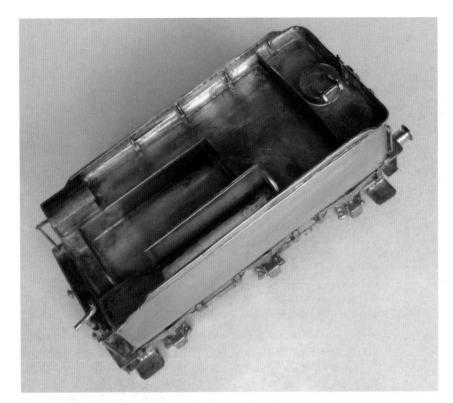

A view of the details of the tender top.

I soldered a coupling hook into the slot in the buffer beam; then it doesn't get in the way of the tension-lock coupling, which will be added later. The buffers are the same as those on the loco front, including the added 1mm collar of brass tube to beef them up a bit.

There is a pair of prominent bars hanging beneath the rear buffer beam: these are guard irons that clear obstacles from the track as the loco runs tender first. I built them from 2mm L-section brass strip, filing most of one side away except for where it forms the bracket connecting the iron to the buffer beam. The irons themselves are filed to shape and formed with the straight-nosed pliers.

The lamp irons are taken from the same etch as those on the loco and are soldered on; you could glue them if you wish when all the soldering is done. The lamp iron at the top of the tender rear is vulnerable: you might want to leave it off altogether or accept that you may need to keep fixing it back on.

Finally, the vacuum hoses match those on the loco front and are soldered into slots filed in the projecting base plate.

There are a few other bits and pieces that I keep noticing and haven't put on yet, or might just leave off. As I said, it's your model and it's up to you to decide.

CHASSIS COMPLETION

There are a few details and some mechanical additions necessary to complete the chassis.

The wheels on one side need to be adapted to pick up electrical current from the track. They are insulated at the little collar that separates the metal wheel casting from the metal wheel tyre. All that is necessary is for this gap to be bridged. The easiest method is to paint over the rear of the wheel with electro-conductive paint. This is usually used to repair things such as car window heating grids, and is suitable for the sorts of currents used in OO modelling. Paint the back of one wheel on each axle, coating the whole surface from the rim to the axle. Use two or three coats, letting the paint dry between each.

To prevent the paint from being worn away, fit 2mm fibre washers on either side of the axle. They

Wheels painted with conductive paint and fitted with fibre washers.

are simple enough to get on without removing the wheels. To do this, slice through the washer on one side with a sharp knife. Flex the washer on either side of the cut enough to slip it over the axle. It will regain its shape and can be fixed to the back of the wheel disc with a spot of Superglue. This protects the paint, and the washers act as packing to restrict the sideways travel of the wheels in the bearings (more washers can be added if needed).

If you're not keen on the paint, or you'd like something tougher, it's quite easy to twist a loop of 0.5mm-diameter copper wire tightly round the axle and push it up against the inside face of the wheel. You can then poke the twisted end of the wire into a 0.7mm hole drilled into the back face of the wheel tyre. It's easier than it sounds. The hole doesn't have to come out of the front of the wheel face, and it's quite easy to clip

the wire to the right length. It can be hidden behind a spoke and secured in place with a spot of Superglue. A fibre washer will protect it in the same way as the paint.

KEEPER PLATE, BRAKES AND COUPLINGS

There are several methods of stopping the wheel sets from dropping out of their slotted bearings when the tender is turned the right way up. Some of these are quite fiddly and involve soldering very near the wheels. I made a keeper plate from a rectangle of 0.010in nickel-silver that bolts to the frame spacer at each end, using the bolts that hold the chassis to the body. It fits snugly between the legs of the inner chassis.

Cut 3mm-length pieces of 3mm-diameter brass tubing as spacers. The wheels are held in when the

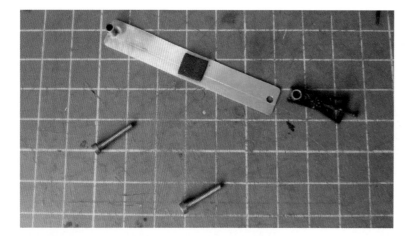

Keeper plate and coupling.

The completed tender.

tender is picked up, and are kept in place by the bearing surfaces of the inner chassis when the tender is running. If there is too much downward movement of the wheels on points or dodgy trackwork, some rudimentary springing can be provided by sticking thin pads of high-density foam rubber to the underside of the keeper plate with double-sided sticky tape.

The brakes can be added in a similar manner to those on the loco: 0.7mm brass rod is soldered through the brake rigging holes in the inner chassis, and brakes from the brake etch are soldered in place. After you've soldered the brake rigging rods through the bottom holes of the brake blocks you can tweak them to avoid touching the wheel treads.

If you are worried about short circuits occurring between the wheel rims and the brake blocks, a good dodge is to smear a thin layer of five-minute epoxy on the brake blocks before you paint them.

I added a tidy little ready-to-run tension lock coupling simply by gluing its rear end to the rear keeper plate spacer. Check that it is the correct height for the rest of your stock.

Rivet detail was added using Super Steel Epoxy Weld, as described in the next chapter. Add as many rivets as you want, and wait for them to set hard.

Your tender is ready to roll.

CHAPTER THIRTEEN

FINISHING OFF

Once you've finished putting everything on that's not going to come off too easily, test this by giving the model a good scrub with a toothbrush. You might want to try a bit of Bar Keeper's Friend or some other cleaner to give it a shiny finish. If you use washing-up liquid, do make sure that you get rid of any residue.

You also need to get rid of any unsightly lumps of solder, as they will show up under paint. In fact, any imperfections become just that – painted imperfections, so a bit more scraping and smoothing may be needed. Equally, if there are gaps and holes that shouldn't be there you can fill them, either with more solder or later on with some form of plastic filler.

The last things to be done are firstly the ash pan, etched axle springs and brake rigging on the chassis, and then the body details, which are some of the most delicate.

CHASSIS DETAILS

ASH PAN

The ash pan is there to collect the ash from the coal burnt in the firebox, and its sides can be seen between the chassis frames underneath the firebox.

Taking measurements from your drawing, it can be simply produced by soldering two shaped pieces of 0.010in nickel-silver in place inside the frame. There are a few small pipe details that can be made from wire and tubing.

BRAKE RIGGING

To make the brake rigging, proceed as follows:

- Solder 2.5mm lengths of 0.7mm brass rod through the brake hanger holes in the chassis; leave them over-length for now. Then solder 2mm lengths of fine tubing over the ends of the brass rod up to the sides of the chassis – these act as spacers.
- Solder the brake blocks to the brake hangers. Then solder them in pairs, 16mm apart, to a length of 0.7mm brass rod. They need to line up with each other.

Make three sets of blocks and hangers. Solder each pair in place holding a piece of card up against the wheel rim with the brake block resting on the other side of the card. This gives the correct spacing, allows you to take the wheels off when necessary, and

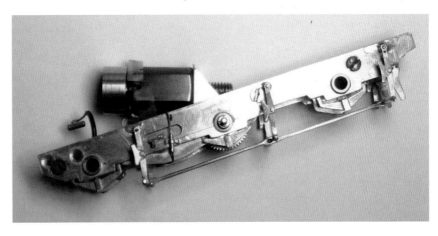

Loco chassis details showing the ash pan, etched axle springs and brake rigging.

Ash pan and brake details.

protects the wheels while you are soldering. For the faint-hearted, check the spacing and take the wheel off before soldering. The hanger rods can be tweaked to get the positioning right.

- Trim the projecting ends of the hanger rods in case they are in the way of the coupling rods.

Repeat a similar procedure for the tender brakes.

CHASSIS FIXING LUG

Bend up a rectangle of 0.015in brass to act as a chassis fixing lug at the front of the loco: see the photo for the proportion. This is soldered centrally to the front underside of the footplate up against the rear

Brake block soldering with card spacer.

Chassis fixing lug.

of the buffer beam, and locates the chassis by trapping the front brake hanger rod as it is slid in. The chassis frames fit on each side of the lug.

GUARD IRONS

These are lengths of metal positioned at the front of the chassis to remove any small obstructions on the track. They are shaped from 0.015in brass and soldered to the frames. There are similar guard irons on the rear of the tender chassis shaped from 2mm L-section brass tube.

LOCO BODY DETAILS

LAMP IRONS

These are small projections on to which the all-important safety lamps can be securely slid when necessary; however, in model form they are vulnerable to damage. You can use a nicely etched lamp iron cut from a fret, reinforced with a spot of solder in the joint, and soldered in place.

Just be careful when you handle the model: the irons on the footplate are generally safe, but the ones on the smokebox top and the back of the tender are always getting bashed about. You can leave them off the smaller scales as they will be barely noticeable, or disguise them by gluing a lamp permanently in place.

BOILER BANDS

Boiler bands cover the joins in the outer boiler cladding. They are generally only a fraction of an inch wide

and can look clumsy and over-scale if you're not careful. I used Scotch Magic Tape, which is easily applied, durable, and looks good. Proceed as follows:

- Cut 0.75mm strips of tape on your cutting board. Starting from underneath the boiler, stick down one end and apply the strip, threading it using tweezers through other boiler features until you reach the starting end.

You may find it easier to remove the handrails first. It is very important that the bands are parallel; you can gently mark the boiler using your dividers. Check carefully before you smooth the tape down – I use a blunt cocktail stick: if you make a mistake, it is easy to remove and apply a new piece of tape.

RIVETS

The J15 has fewer rivets than many locomotives: there are some charismatic lines of rivets on the firebox, and the rest are mainly dotted around seemingly rather at random. Look at the photos and decide which are visible and worth putting on. In some lights you can see rows of small indents that appear to hold the cab sides together – they are tiny and unobtrusive and I haven't put them on. There is also a line following the curve of the rebuilt cab roof and I like those, so on they went. They're all over the tender, too.

I've used two methods for the model: transfer rivets and epoxy rivets.

Apply Scotch Magic Tape to make a boiler band.

Transfer Rivet Sheets

These are great, quite expensive, but you get a lot on the sheet. They consist of 'printed' resin dots on a backing film, and are applied, just like any other transfer, to a clean, grease-free surface; they come pre-spaced so you can cut them into strips and put them straight on. I found it very easy to apply them to the smokebox, and gently bent a strip in a curve around the cab front. A setting solution such as Microsol is recommended to help them sit. You can also use them for single rivets and blocks.

Epoxy Rivets

Another method of cosmetic rivet application is to add them individually (this is particularly useful in hard-to-get-at places). I use Super Steel Epoxy Weld, which gives a lovely small blob effect, just like a round-headed rivet; applied in this way they are very effective.

It takes a bit of practice to produce consistent sizes: use a cocktail stick to dab them into place; apply by eye, or mark the positions in first with the dividers. They dry in five minutes and you have to be quite quick. If misplaced or the wrong size they can be removed easily, after letting them dry for ten minutes or so. Take care not to let them touch each other or the side of a component as they will run instead of producing a distinct blob.

CHIMNEYS, DOMES AND SAFETY VALVES

The large and decorative castings that adorn the boiler assembly need to be carefully prepared to get their fit just right. There's nothing worse than a wonky chimney. Castings may have chunks of metal from the casting proces, which need to be removed: I find a dental burr in the mini-drill invaluable; take it slowly and carefully to avoid damaging the edge of the flare.

The next job is to file and smooth off any imperfections on the outside surface – there may be moulding

Transfer rivets.

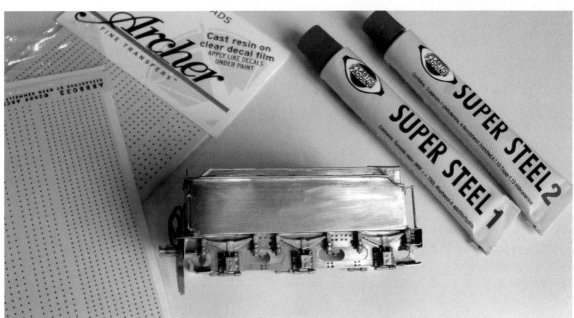

Epoxy rivets and Archer transfers.

seam lines, which can take a bit of shifting. Take your time until you're really satisfied with the look, particularly on domes. Polishing can be achieved either with a thin strip of wet and dry rubbed back and forth, or a buffing wheel in the mini-drill (holding the casting gingerly in a vice).

The dome or chimney needs to be seated properly so that the rim has the same curvature as the boiler.

To do this, find a tube the same diameter as the boiler, or carefully use the actual boiler, and patiently rub the casting along a wide strip of wet and dry placed between the two. Start with quite coarse paper and progress to finer grades until you have a really good fit.

You can fix your boiler fittings in place by gluing, soldering or bolting. I generally glue with epoxy adhe-

Seating the dome or chimney.

BELOW: Fixing boiler fittings in place by gluing.

sive such as Araldite Rapid, and this provides a strong bond without having to solder. However, you can't get the fitting off again easily once the glue has set solid, though you do have plenty of time to adjust everything before it does.

This is a job for the mirrors and squares again: make sure the loco body is properly upright and that your boiler fittings are sitting comfortably. Mix your glue carefully: too much is better, as you are more likely to get the proportions correct. Then proceed as follows:

- Apply glue sparingly to the underside of the fitting and place it on the boiler. View it from all angles using the mirror; placing a square on each side really helps too. You have at least five minutes for fine adjustments, so take your time.

Any spare glue that escapes from underneath can be easily peeled away when it's about fifteen minutes dry. If you leave it a bit later, you'll be able to cut it away. An added bonus of glue is that it will fill any small gaps.

DRAG BAR

The function of the drag bar is to keep the loco and tender connected whilst they are moving. A number of pipes and other connections run be-

tween the two vehicles as well, and you can have a good time working out how you might portray those if you wish. The drag bar on this model has to keep the locomotive and tender electrically separated as well as physically connected. I thought it

The drag bar secured with epoxy resin.

would make things simpler to have the electrical connection running through it too. I made it as follows:

- I stripped a length of insulation from some quite thick wiring and fitted it on to a length of 0.7mm nickel-silver rod. I then bent it to the shape shown in the photo. It has to clear the chassis fixing bolt, loop beneath the loco drag beam and then form a hook to connect up with the tender, looping under the tender drag beam. I put in an extra loop to push against the tender chassis so that the two vehicles couldn't touch, which would cause a short circuit.

You'll have to experiment with the distance you want between the tender and the loco, depending on the curvature of your track work. Make sure the rear hook doesn't lift the front wheels of the tender off the track: I think it took me about five goes to get this right. Keep trying until it works.

The power is connected from the tender body to the motor in the loco by a tube 'plug' soldered to the motor lead, which slips over the uninsulated end of the drag bar. The whole thing was epoxied securely beneath the loco cab floor.

If you want to disguise the gap between the loco and tender it's easy to make up a small rectangle of 0.030in plasticard to represent the hinged 'fall plate' that covers the gap on the real thing. Score it to represent planking, and notch it to clear the base of the brake standard. It can be held down with a little Blu-tack. Make sure it doesn't cause derailments when negotiating curves.

WEIGHT

For good running, the loco and tender need a bit of ballast. An easy way to add weight is to use rolled up or flattened lead sheeting (don't lick it: the Romans did, and look what happened to them). Proceed as follows:

- Blu-tack or tape the lead to the inside of the tender, and pack round with some high density foam sheet to suppress noise. A roll of lead can be inserted in the boiler of the loco and kept in place with Blu-tack. Take care to keep the loco and tender well balanced.

And that's it, you're done. The loco looks fantastic, and it would almost be a shame to paint it – almost. (In fact painting is a whole subject in itself, and there are many fine books available, so we're not going to describe it here.)

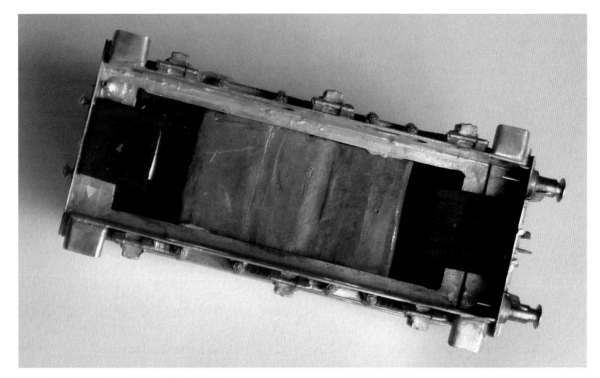

Weight and sound-proofing inside the tender.

RUNNING IN: A MATTER OF DETECTIVE WORK

MOTOR MOUNT AND WIRING

Make sure you have a pair of wires soldered securely to the motor terminals, if you haven't already. Take extra care when soldering so close to the motor, and don't just wind the wires round the terminals and hope they don't drop off, because they will. Proceed as follows:

- Strip about 0.5mm of the insulation off the end of each wire, and pre-tin with a wisp of 145°C solder. Then loop through the motor tags and touch fleetingly with the iron.
- The wire should ideally be flexible, a different colour for each terminal, and just the right length not to get in the way or be too short (which will strain and weaken the joints). You can tape them safely to the motor casing with a little Magic Tape to stop the joints being pulled.

- In fact the motor can then be held in place against its tendency to rise up under power by wrapping a wire around one of the brake rigging wires.

That's all the motor mounting that you're going to need unless you want to seat it in a small lump of Blue-tack too.

- I connected one wire to the chassis by soldering the end to a small bent-up clip of phosphor-bronze, which fits neatly into a section of tubing soldered to the inside surface of one of the chassis frames.
- If you're fitting a fly wheel and it doesn't have a grub screw to attach it to the rear axle of the motor, then now might be the time to apply a tiny drop of Loctite to secure it.

My wiring is very straightforward; please feel free to come up with your own solutions here. My knowledge of the subject is that electricity runs in a loop through wires, and that usually does it for me.

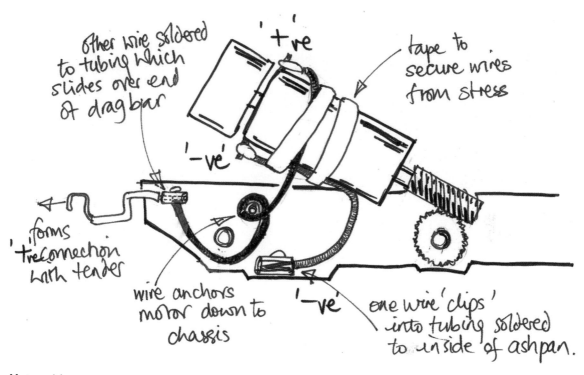

Other wire soldered to tubing which slides over end of drag bar

'+ve'

tape to secure wires from stress

'-ve'

forms the connection with tender

wire anchors motor down to chassis

'-ve'

one wire 'clips' into tubing soldered to inside of ashpan.

Motor wiring.

FAULT FINDING

Once the loco body is on, the wiring in place and the tender coupled, everything should run sweetly, though I'm not boasting when I say that everything did ... for a while.

This can be one of the most aggravating aspects of scratch-building. Right at the end when you've got such a beautiful model, you've enjoyed building it, are pleased with your patience and perseverance, and are justifiably proud of the result – and it won't run. Well, now is the time to do some detective work. Really take note of what is going on: look and listen – you can sometimes even smell out the problems.

I found that the loco and tender chassis both ran beautifully, but when I put the tender body on there was a peculiar scraping noise and it then didn't ride as well. It sounded as though the tops of the wheels were rubbing against the underside of the tank. I put a couple of thin foam pads in between the chassis and body, raising the body by about 0.5mm – and the problem was solved.

However, when I put the loco body on everything became very jolty with a lot of stopping and starting. This could be a sign of intermittent electrical shorts or loose connections. I thought it was because the fly wheel was rubbing against the top of the firebox, although when I took out the backhead I could see it wasn't. Then I realized that the wire at the top of the motor was shorting against the underside of the firebox, and a bit of magic tape insulation solved that.

Also, there was a peculiar smell from the cab. This turned out to be the insulation on the drawbar melting from a short circuit caused by a gap, which was sparking against the underside of the cab. I had to replace the drawbar, again, as I had nicked the insulation when I was bending it.

If you do discover any places where short circuits are occurring – such as on the brake blocks or the wheels rubbing inside the splashers – a smear of Araldite can form an effective insulating barrier. Alternatively, lifting the body by 0.5mm on card packing or pads of high density foam should do the trick.

The completed model.

After quite a lot more detective work, I got everything running beautifully smoothly. The point is that it takes time and patience, lots of it. Keep looking and trying things out. Back track and start again. Go for a walk and think about it. Ask someone else.

Don't blame yourself or give up: it's worth it in the end.

AND FINALLY...

Sit back and admire your model, summon your loved ones and enjoy their compliments. Congratulations, it's a scratch-built locomotive – and it's yours. And like the best Shakespeare, there are a few more endings to come and a little more food for thought. So read on.

CHAPTER FOURTEEN

EM-GAUGE CHASSIS

This book has so far described the building of a 4mm-gauge loco, which I chose to be to OO gauge as a lot of people model in that gauge. It also has a 'rigid' chassis that uses a system of current pick-up requiring no form of contact with the wheels.

In this chapter I will describe an alternative build of an EM (18mm gauge) chassis that will fit just as well as the OO-gauge chassis, although I would recommend that you check the splasher/wheel clearance. (And this build could just as easily be in ScaleFour – I just happened to have some EM axles.)

I could just as happily have gone for P4 (18.83mm gauge), except I already had the axles from Alan Gibson whose lovely driving wheels I use for this project. As with all the more fine-scale gauges, I would recommend you research the standards used and join the relevant society. Both the EM Gauge Society and the Scalefour Society will welcome you happily, and their members' forums and society magazines are absolutely bursting with information that will be invaluable if you wish to pursue fine-scale modelling.

EM CHASSIS REQUIREMENTS

This chapter includes brief descriptions of the following:

- Continuous springy beams (CSBs)
- Horn-blocks
- Articulated coupling rods
- Soldered, etched spacer construction to EM gauge
- Alan Gibson wheels and quartering
- Wheel-bearing electrical pick-up

CONTINUOUS SPRINGY BEAMS

I particularly like continuous springy beams (CSBs): they are elegant and quite simple in practice; they give a satisfyingly smooth ride and a nice sense of momentum; and they provide an air of mysterious engineering processes – and all for a few handrail knobs threaded through with some guitar string. If you want to find out more about the theory and maths there is plenty of information on such websites as CLAG (Central London Group) and the Scalefour Society.

A continuous springy beam is provided, in this case, by a guitar string that works across all the axles on each side of the chassis. As each of the wheels moves up or down in response to changing levels in the track, that movement is compensated for by the other wheels all connected on the same spring. The wheels are different distances apart, and in order to get an equal amount of springiness you have to space the spring attachments correctly (here I use handrail knobs as the attachments). Luckily, an erudite gentleman called Russ Elliot provides the measurements that we need for the J15 on the CLAG website.

All that needs to be done is to solder short handrail knobs into holes drilled in the chassis frames.

HORN-BLOCKS

Horn-blocks are structures in which the wheel bearings are able to move up and down. Model horn-blocks, like their prototype counterparts, are sited in rectangular apertures on the chassis, so instead of a set of drilled holes we need to cut out rectangles (and we need to be just as precise).

Model horn-blocks.

There are many excellent horn-blocks available. I use ones from High Level Models that allow the easy use of CSBs, taking almost all the hard work (but not the fun) out of the whole process. There is plenty of useful advice on their website. They also produce a set of tags that solder to the bearings, setting the ride height of the wheels, along with a jig to help set everything up. I highly recommend them (other systems are available).

ARTICULATED COUPLING RODS

On this chassis the wheels are free to move up and down, and so the coupling rods need to be articulated in order to allow them to do so. They are arranged to articulate about the crankpin of the middle wheel (whereas the real things have a special joint just forward of the crankpin). The coupling rods are

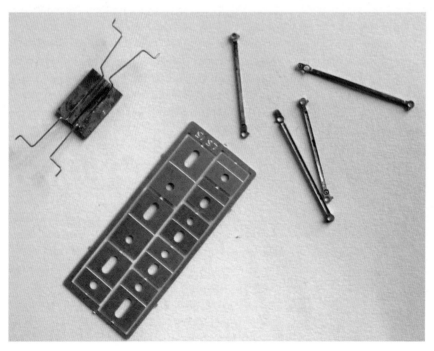

Alan Gibson universal coupling rods etch, a spacer etch and soldered up wiper contacts.

used later to determine the soldered position of the horn-blocks.

I used an Alan Gibson universal coupling rods etch that allows you to build up a set of rods for any loco with a choice of fluted or solid. The photo also shows a spacer etch and soldered up wiper contacts.

SOLDERING THE SPACERS

Soldered rectangular spacers are traditionally used in scratch-building and in etched kits. You can make your own easily enough from a carefully measured and drilled strip of 0.015in nickel-silver or brass, or you can buy a lovely little etch where everything's been done for you. It is generally thought that folded, rectangular, soldered spacers give a more rigid, controlled shape to the chassis due to the greater surface area in contact with the chassis sides, and a more permanent fixing than bolts.

It is even more important to work out your spacer position before you solder them in, because they are much more irksome to shift if they get in the way of subsequent additions. You can use screwed spacers to hold everything square before removing them and soldering in the etched spacers.

If using CSBs, make sure you file a square notch in the sides of the spacers to accommodate the wire beam; it should be able to move 0.5mm up and down easily.

Then proceed as follows:

- Bolt the frames together firmly using your pillar spacers, and check that the top edges are parallel and level on your favoured flat surface. Tweak if you need to. When soldering, take care not to get any solder near the pillars unless you want to leave them in as well.
- Solder one end spacer to one chassis frame side, and then do the same at the other end, except solder it to the opposite frame. Then solder in the centre spacer on one side only: this helps to avoid the frames buckling. Check that your chassis sides haven't buckled, and one by one solder the remaining sides of the etched spacers.
- Undo the bolts, remove the pillars and keep them safe, ready for your next build.

ATTACHING THE HORN-BLOCKS

First you need to solder in just one horn-block to act as a datum – I chose a centre axle to start with. The top of the cut-out in the frame will position the horn-block – just make sure it's square. Use hair-clips to hold everything securely, and don't get solder on the block's inner surfaces.

You need to think about the relationship between each horn-block. The second one should be exactly

Screwed spacers can be used to hold everything square.

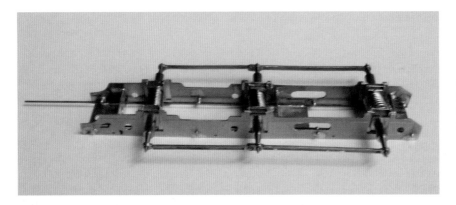

A widely used jig system is a set of three turned rods that fit inside the bearings.

opposite and parallel to the first. There are a number of ways of doing this, and a number of chassis jigs that you can buy to help you. A simple, widely used jig system is a set of three turned rods that fit inside the bearings. They have tapered ends that the coupling rods can be fitted to, ensuring the wheelbase is exact. The horn-blocks can be held in position by springs fitted on the jig axles, and the tops of the frame cut-outs keep everything to the correct height.

Take care that you don't get things at a slight angle. Use a square to check that the axles are at 90 degrees to the frames, or sit the whole thing on some graph paper. Carefully solder the horn-blocks into the frame, and then remove the jig axles.

SETTING THE CSB

When all the horn-blocks are secure, check that the bearings slide easily into them: they may need the lightest of polishes with some wet and dry for a smooth fit. Lock them in place with a wire 'staple' through the holes provided; there is no need to solder. You can then fit the CSB, which is very exciting.

Gauge 14 guitar strings seem to be the spring *du jour*, as discussed on various websites. (I would recommend that you try a few different steel wires from Eileen's Emporium if you can't easily source guitar strings.) Cut a couple of pieces over-length (you can trim them later) and thread them through both the handrail knobs and bearing tags – tweezers and good light are needed for this task. At last you'll have everything in place in all its springy glory. Well done.

ALAN GIBSON WHEELS

There is no reason why you shouldn't use Romford wheels, but Gibson's are considered a step up from them and I wanted to introduce them here. They have a more delicate look to them than the robust Romfords, and have a number of significant differences.

The wheels are a push fit on to the axles. Support the wheel on a flat surface and gently push the axle into the hole – you'll feel it give. There seems to be no harm in repeated removal of the axles, though I would avoid doing it too often.

As the axles are not 'shouldered' like the Romfords there is no way of telling if you've got the wheel 'back-to-back' distance right without a gauge or, usefully, the vernier calipers, set to the correct measurement. Also, the wheel sets won't be automatically 'quartered' as are the Romfords, and this takes some careful adjusting.

Proceed as follows:

- Firstly, the crankpins need to be sorted. The small bolts that are provided with the wheels are gently screwed into the hole in the crank from the back. It's better that the head of the bolt is flush to the wheel back, so very carefully recess the hole with a 2mm drill.
- The bolt is then screwed in and acts as a crank-pin. A crank-pin collar is then screwed on to the projecting bolt. The coupling rods fit over these collars.
- A small circular cap is then screwed on to secure the coupling rod. (If you don't want to keep

Fitting the crankpins.

unscrewing the cap, a small length of model wiring insulation can be used as a temporary measure.)

Once all the wheels are in place on the chassis, quarter the front wheels so the right-hand wheel is a quarter turn ahead of the left. Try to match the quartering with the middle wheels, and then connect the two sets with the front sections of the coupling rods. Then it is just trial and error, gently twisting one set of wheels and lining up the rods by eye until you achieve smooth running. Sighting through the spokes and lining them up can help.

Once that is done, attach the rear sections of the coupling rods and, only twisting the rear wheels, adjust their quartering until smooth running is achieved again. Don't try to adjust the already quartered wheels. This takes some practice.

PICK-UPS

The majority of 4mm model railway locomotives pick up current from the rails via some physical contact with the wheel. This usually consists of a metal strip or wire sprung against the rim. If this is carefully

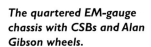

The quartered EM-gauge chassis with CSBs and Alan Gibson wheels.

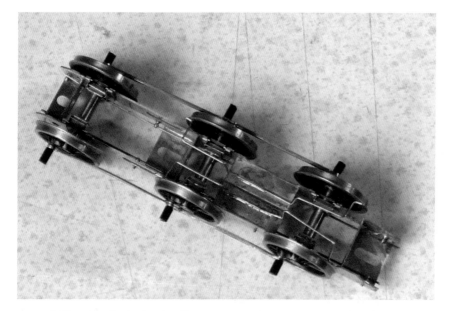

Phosphor-bronze wires bent and soldered to the pad of a printed circuit board.

adjusted it can be very effective and is quite easy to set up – and there are as many preferred ways of doing it as there are railway modellers. I made mine as follows:

- I soldered lengths of phosphor-bronze wire to a rectangle of printed circuit board. A saw cut is made across the copper surface of the board to isolate each side electrically. The longer the wire, the springier it becomes and the less friction it causes against the wheel rims. I have bent mine up in a series of right angles so it clears the axles and is hidden behind the wheels. Some people like to produce beautiful little coils of wire.
- Adjust the wires to bear against the backs of the wheel rims before attaching the PCB to the chassis frames. It can be glued, soldered or bolted to a spacer if you want to remove it easily for maintenance.
- You would be advised to make one set of pick-ups for two pairs of wheels and another for the single pair to enable you to pick up from all the available wheels (if you want, you could do the same for the tender). Take care that the pick-up wires don't short out on the chassis frames.
- Simply connect the motor of your choice by soldering a wire to either side of the PCB.

For more excellent information on pick-ups (as for many subjects touched on in this book), see the ScaleFour Society website.

CHAPTER FIFTEEN

DIESEL BUILD

DIESEL BUILD REQUIREMENTS

This chapter includes brief descriptions of the following:

- 7mm/O gauge
- Compensated chassis
- 'Back-scratcher' pick-ups
- Rivet detail methods
- Finding details
- Dingham auto-couplers

I chose a steam loco for the main subject of this book, partly because there is a much wider choice of prototype available. In N and OO gauge (and increasingly in O gauge) virtually all the common British diesel types are available ready to run – and the not-so-common classes are catching up. Many of these lovely models can be converted quite easily to the finer scale gauges, and a large number of detailing parts and accessories are available for creating your favourite locos.

Although diesels are often thought of as 'boxes' – presumably by their detractors – they are far more than that. Their subtle shapes and curves are tricky to get right, and they're covered with a wide variety of grilles and louvres – but if you can buy them with all that work already done for you, you might ask, why scratch build? Well, it doesn't stop some people from greatly enjoying themselves doing just that, and there are lovely examples of unusual diesel locomotives just crying out to be built. If you leaf through a copy of a book showing the diesel-fuelled products of, for example, the Armstrong Whitworth Locomotive Works, there are some absolute delights.

I will highlight a few challenges that are particular to this build, and also describe some other ideas that you might want to consider as alternatives to those described so far for the J15.

MY DIESEL CHOICE

My diesel choice is the Armstrong Whitworth 0-4-0 diesel electric locomotive, *The Lady Armstrong*, in 7mm/O gauge. This diminutive and charismatic shunting locomotive makes an ideal scratch-building project, particularly in 7mm/O gauge (there is a very nice kit available in 4mm). It's small, it *is* quite boxy, and it has a reasonably simple chassis with the added challenge of a jackshaft drive. It has some lovely detailing work, and a nice big space to put the motor in. This one, bought and run, rather erratically, by the North Sunderland Railway, was named *The Lady Armstrong* after Lord Armstrong's wife (presumably).

There is a great deal of information available about the NSR with plenty of photographs and a good drawing of *The Lady Armstrong* in the Oakwood Press book, *The North Sunderland Railway*. There is also a preserved example on the Tanfield railway that you can go and visit. It's a lovely little loco and the railway staff are helpful and friendly, so there is no excuse needed for you to go and enjoy yourself.

These attractive locos had a diesel engine at the front under the bonnet, which produced electricity to drive the hefty electric motor located at the rear of the cab – hence 'diesel electric'. The motor drove a jackshaft, which then drove the front wheels via the long coupling rod. There were numerous bits and pieces on the running plate that are great to model, and lots of little boxes, catches, handles and grilles – marvellous. *The Lady Armstrong* has an attractive nameplate, lights and horn: it's a glorious thing to model.

Armstrong Whitworth 0-4-0 Diesel Electric Locomotive, No. 2 on the Tanfield Railway. PAUL WINSKILL

7mm/O gauge modelling is very satisfying: you can encrust your models with as many details as you wish, and the bits and pieces are nice and chunky. Furthermore, with a small locomotive like this you can squeeze your layout into a manageable space.

THE COMPENSATED CHASSIS

Whilst this is called an 0-4-0 locomotive because of its four driving wheels, it is actually a bit of an 0-6-0 because the jackshaft has two wheels connected to them via a coupling rod. The jackshaft is the arrangement by which the motor drives the coupled wheels; I attached the motor to one of the wheeled axles.

The most commonly used wheels in 7mm are made by Slaters, and they will supply you with the moulded centre of the disc wheels, suitable for the loco, which can easily be converted to form the basis of the jackshaft.

As usual, it's the coupling rods to start with, and these I made through the 'cut and shut' method. They were soldered together using small headless nails in a wood block to act as a jig to fix their lengths. It is

important to stagger the joints for strength; once the rods were cleaned and polished the joins were almost invisible. They could just as easily be made in the manner of the solid rods for the J15; I just had a spare fret of etched rods that came to hand. Two sets were needed: one short pair for the driving wheels, and the other for the drive from the jack-shaft.

The rods act as jigs for the axle holes in the chassis, which was rather a pleasing little box-like structure. I used L-shaped spacers soldered in using a chassis jig. The front axle is driven by a nice chunky motor/gearbox and flywheel.

COMPENSATION SYSTEM

This loco has a very simple compensated system. Basically, compensation turns a rigid chassis into a three-legged stool-like structure. One axle is rigid and the other can move slightly up and down so that all the wheels are always touching the track, providing a smoother ride and helping with current pick-up.

The driven wheels are kept rigid and the other driving wheels' bearing holes are elongated up and down by 1mm with a round file. Mark above and

The diesel chassis with small coupling rods fitted.

below, and take great care not to drift sideways as you don't want any horizontal movement. The bearings are trapped into the holes when the wheels are in position.

Holes were pre-drilled into the spacers positioned on either side of the compensated axle, matching the position of the centre line of the axle holes. These hold a piece of brass tube that acts as the compensation beam: it bears down across the centre of the wheeled axle, which merely pivots about the beam, moving up and down in the slots – very simple and very effective.

The jackshaft is unaffected by this movement as its coupling rod is connected to the driven axle. The left-hand 'jack-wheel' is modified by cutting the main disc

away with the piercing saw, leaving the axle mounting and the balance weight.

The chassis ran very sweetly first time and was most pleasing. There is a brilliant little book by Mike Sharman, which tells you everything you need to know about compensation – and of course the internet is full of information.

BACK-SCRATCHER PICK-UPS

These are great, I use them all the time when I'm not using split axles. They are simple to make, cheap, almost invisible, and bear lightly against the backs of the wheels – hence the name. These are less commonly used as the wiper contact pick-ups used on our EM

The chassis showing back-scratcher pick-ups and simple compensation beam.

chassis, and I think they are well worth considering as an alternative.

By drawing around the wheel when it's in place you can work out where to position the bearers, which are simply lengths of phosphor-bronze strip. They are set up so as to bear half way down on the back of the wheel rim.

A 2mm slot is filed in the top of the chassis frame directly above the marked position, and short strips of printed circuit board (PCB) are araldited to the inside frames where they won't interfere with the motor and gearbox. A piece of insulating tape is then stuck over the slot and the front and back of the frames, leaving enough of the PCB on which to solder the phosphor-bronze strip and the wiring for the motor. And that's it, they work beautifully. Take care not to catch your fingers on them before the wheels go on.

RIVET DETAIL METHODS

The body was built in the conventional manner: footplate and cut-outs first with a simple valance from square brass rod. The buffer beams are a pleasant shape with a few small rivets.

This might be a good time to mention riveting methods other than those we've already used. Rivet-embossing machines are rather wonderful: they mostly consist of a punch and an anvil that impress a rivet shape into materials without causing distortion.

If you pay more you can get a variety of labour-saving measuring devices that allow you to emboss lots of rivets quickly and accurately in a selection of different sizes. If you are keen to continue scratch building and you enjoy a good bit of riveting, one of these would be a thoroughly useful addition to your tool kit. All of the rivets on the *Lady* were pressed into the metal using a rivet-embossing machine.

FOOTPLATE AND CAB

The loco can be split simply into sections: chassis, footplate, cab and bonnet. The footplate has a single cut-out for the motor, and the cab sides, front and back, are all produced easily.

I used a clever method (not mine) to make the rather beautiful brass window frames. Before cutting out the apertures, the frames are first made as single blank rectangles of thick 0.040in brass. I used the riveter to impress the rivets round the edge. These frames are then soldered on to the cab in the correct places, and the frames marked, drilled and sawn – and there you are, pre-framed windows. You can use this method whenever you want some fine framing all in one piece.

The cab is soldered on to the footplate; I built up the little control desk and floor before adding the back. I tested that all was well with the running at this point. I also added the electric motor casing, which has some nice strapping and ventilators.

THE BONNET

This was interesting: looking at the real thing, the bonnet is obviously made up of a number of panels and pieces, and I wanted to build it up like that.

I'm always impressed by how chunky old machinery is, and the radiator at the front is a glorious hunk of metal. This was built up as a front and sides, soldered together with a lot of solder on the inside; then the edges were rounded with a file and polished.

The rods that I used to bend the sides round became part of the structure, soldered to a radiator-shaped blank at the back. Everything is kept in shape with a false bottom, including a cut-out for the motor. Various panels were beaded with brass wire and individually soldered on to the frame.

The buffer beams went on last as they overlap the body components. The buffers are ingeniously sprung internally using a system described to me by a gentleman called Nick Baines, who has an inspirational website detailing his beautiful scratch-built O-gauge models.

FINDING DETAILS

There are numerous miscellaneous electrical bits and pieces on the right-hand footplate. While no one specifically manufactures these, you can have fun making them up yourself. White metal castings left over from kits are great for sawing and filing; scraps of tube and plasticard, and in this case, parts of toy motorcycle

Loco showing internally sprung buffers and various details.

models bought for pennies second-hand are particularly good for peculiar shapes and engine parts.

DINGHAM COUPLINGS

These are another of the many different coupling systems available in 7mm and other scales. I like

them because they are robust, quite easy to build from the etch, and simple to set up; and they don't look bad, either. They can be operated by magnets set into the base-board allowing automatic uncoupling. In the photos they can be seen attached to the buffer beams.

Incidentally, diesel models do lend themselves to be driven by commercially available motor bogies

Rear of loco showing jackshaft and Dingham coupling.

Ready-to-run motor bogies for scratch-built diesels.

that are all set up and running nicely. If you're not keen on the mechanical side of things, then these may be a good introduction for you. I have used old Lima motor bogies in a scratch-built O-gauge BR Clayton type 17 diesel, and am looking forward to building a 3mm-scale Fell Diesel using a great little motor bogie supplied especially to my requirements.

CHAPTER SIXTEEN

ONGOING PROJECTS: OTHER SCALES AND TECHNIQUES

I couldn't finish this book without revisiting some of the other scales I mention at the beginning, and to repeat that although 4mm OO gauge is the most popular scale, scratch-building allows us to stretch our wings into some more esoteric shapes and sizes. One of the problems – or blessings – is that you can become a little distracted. So here are some of my ongoing projects to introduce a few more thoughts and ideas.

S SCALE

This Furness 4-4-2 tank loco in S Scale that I mentioned previously is being built in plasticard as an exercise and introduction to a different scale and material. Plasticard is cheaper than metal and easier to work: it requires no soldering and can be welded with solvents, and it certainly won't cause short circuits. Shaping is easy, and tubes and curves can be produced through controlled heating with hot water, and tighter curves through laminating and filing. Everything is a lot quicker when building with it.

You do, however, get a lot of mess, and the fumes and dust can be unpleasant. The addition of weight is very important if you want your loco to be able to pull anything at all. Models can be fragile and prone to warping, and there is a possibility of the plastic

S-scale Furness 4-4-2 tank locomotive in plasticard.

becoming brittle after prolonged exposure to sunlight, particularly if left unpainted.

I built the chassis with plasticard too, as a challenge to myself to see if it would work. The driving wheels are proper S scale, with larger 4mm ones with lengthened axles for the carrying wheels.

I've made a collection of 4mm and 7mm scale bits and pieces that are just right or can be modified for the boiler fittings and detail parts. Other parts and track components are available from the S Scale Society and can be commissioned from various sources. There is no barrier to building in S scale, and the society that promotes it will help you out with anything you may need.

I look forward to constructing a few more Furness locos and stock for a minimum space layout, rather like the lovely *St Juliot* that I'm seen helping to operate at the beginning of the book.

2MM SCALE

2mm scale, the fine-scale version of the popular N gauge, is a thriving and fascinating subject. Its smaller size opens up vast opportunities, and has produced a set of standards all its own. Electrical pick-up, for instance, is generally built around the 'split chassis' idea, rather like the American system that I used for the J15. This avoids the need for physical contact pick-up,

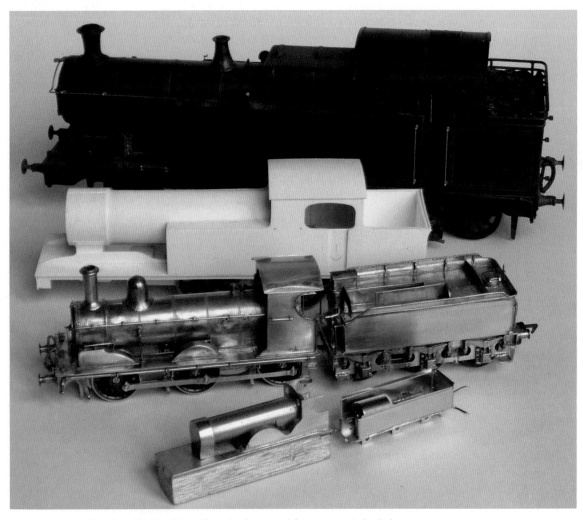

A comparison of scales showing 7mm, S-scale, 4mm and 2mm scratch-built locomotives.

The LSWR X6 locomotive footplate, cab and splasher sides in 2mm scale.

The boiler assembly, cab and splashers of the X6.

A selection of 2mm-scale wheels to be used with the X6.

which potentially produces much more of a braking force at this size.

The wheels are provided with the axles coming in two halves joined by a strong plastic muff giving an insulated centre. Pick-up is directly through the chassis frames, which are also insulated from each other, and quite often built in phosphor-bronze with gapped PCB spacers.

Motors can be small and are quite often situated in the tender, driving the loco wheels through a flexible shaft attached to a gearbox in the loco body.

I'm building an LSWR X6 4-4-0 passenger loco, another beautiful Victorian design. Metalwork in this scale is no different to larger scales, and can even be quicker. The magnifier does come in handy.

The 2mm Society has some magnificent publications and a fantastic shop for all those small additions you might need.

CONCLUSION

I hope you have been inspired to make a start in scratch-building: it is extremely enjoyable, overcoming the obstacles is all part of the fun, and the sense of achievement and the opportunity to learn something new is extremely worthwhile. However, there is a warning that comes with it: it can become addictive. As soon as your modelling friends get to know you're a scratch-builder you'll start receiving photos like the one shown here, with the question, 'I don't suppose you'd be interested, but…'

A very unusual prototype – is this my next project? DAVID COASBY

The end.

FURTHER READING
AND RESOURCES

BOOKS AND PUBLICATIONS

Modelling how-to books:

Ahern, John H. *Miniature Locomotive Construction*

Holt, Geoff *Locomotive Modelling From Scratch and Etched Kits, Part One*

Holt, Geoff *Locomotive Modelling From Scratch and Etched Kits, Part Two*

Rice, Iain *Etched Loco Construction*

Rice, Iain *Locomotive Kit Chassis Construction in 4mm*

Roche, F. J. & Templer, G. G. revised by Stevens-Stratten, S. W. *Building Model Locomotives*

Sharman, Mike *A Guide to Locomotive Building: From Prototype to Small Scale Models*

Sharman, Mike *Flexichas: A Way to Build Fully Compensated Model Locomotive Chassis*

Williams, R. Guy *Model Locomotive Construction in 4mm Scale*

Williams, R. Guy *The 4mm Engine: A Scratchbuilder's Guide*

Williams, R. Guy *More 4mm Engines*

Books on finishing models:

Rathbone, Ian *A Modeller's Handbook of Painting and Lining*

Welch, Martyn *The Art of Weathering*

Books on operating and running locomotives:

Hill, Jim *Buckjumpers, Gobblers and Clauds: A Lifetime on Great Eastern and LNER Footplates*

Semmens, P. W. B. & Goldfinch, A. J. *How Steam Locomotives Really Work*

Topping, Brian *The Engine Driver's Manual: How to Prepare, Fire and Drive a Steam Locomotive*

Specific publication on J15 class:

Yeardon's Register of LNER Locomotives: Vol 35: Class J14 & J15

Fine-scale modelling journal:
Model Railway Journal

Inspirational books on creativity, working with your hands and getting things wrong:

Crawford, Matthew *The Case for Working with your Hands, or why office work is bad for us and fixing things feels good*

Robinson, Ken *Out of our Minds: Learning to be Creative*

Shulz, Kathryn *Being Wrong: Adventures in the Margin of Error*

LIBRARY AND
ARCHIVE CENTRE

National Railway Museum Search Engine
www.nrm.org.uk/ResearchAndArchive.aspx

MODELLING PARTS
AND TOOLS SUPPLIERS

Alan Gibson Model Railway Products
www.alangibsonworkshop.com

Connoisseur Models
www.jimmcgeown.com

Eileen's Emporium
www.eileensemporium.com

Four Track Models
www.fourtrack.co.uk

High Level Models
www.highlevelkits.co.uk

Hobby Holidays
www.hobbyholidays.co.uk

Isinglass Models
www.isinglass-models.co.uk

Mainly Trains
www.mainlytrains.co.uk

Markits
www.markits.com

MODELLING SOCIETIES

The Central London Area Group of the Scalefour
Society
www.clag.org.uk

Gauge O Guild
www.gauge0guild.com

The Model Railway Club
www.themodelrailwayclub.org

RM web
www.rmweb.co.uk

The Scalefour Society
www.scalefour.org

S Scale Model Railway Society
www.s-scale.org.uk

The 2mm Scale Association
www.2mm.org.uk

RAILWAY SOCIETIES

The Great Eastern Railway Society
www.gersociety.org.uk

Gloucestershire Warwickshire Railway
www.gwsr.com

The Midland and Great Northern Joint Railway
Society
www.mandgn.co.uk

North Norfolk Railway
www.nnrailway.co.uk

LOCOMOTIVE MODELLERS

Nick Baines Model Engineering
www.nickbaines.me.uk

Raymond Walley – 7mm:1ft – O Gauge Railway Modelling
www.raymondwalley.com

Simon Bolton Artful Engineering
www.artfulengineering.co.uk

INDEX

easy knitting
Chic

easy knitting
Chic

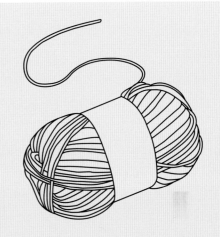

30 projects to make and wear

Consultant: Nikki Trench

KP CRAFT
Cincinnati, Ohio

Easy Knitting Chic
30 Projects to Make and Wear

First published in Great Britain in 2013 by Hamlyn.
Text and photography © Hachette Patchworks Ltd 2013
Design and layout Copyright © Octopus Publishing Group

Published by KP Craft, an imprint of F+W Media, Inc.,
10151 Carver Road, Suite 200, Blue Ash, Ohio 45242.
(800) 289-0963

media
www.fwmedia.com

18 17 16 15 14   5 4 3 2 1

DISTRIBUTED IN CANADA BY FRASER DIRECT
100 Armstrong Avenue
Georgetown, ON, Canada L7G 5S4
Tel: (905) 877-4411

SRN: T2885
ISBN-13: 978-1-4402-4173-4

Contents

Introduction

If you can knit a few basic stitches, you can create stylish knitted items to wear, use to decorate your home and give as gifts for friends and family.

Whether you are a relative beginner, a confident convert or a long-term aficionado, there are projects here to delight. While your first attempts may be a bit uneven, a little practice and experimentation will ensure you soon improve. None of the projects here is beyond the scope of even those fairly new to the hobby.

Knitting has justifyably lost its fusty image – with the right patterns you can create some really chic clothing and smart accessories for you and your home. Whatever your tastes and experience, there is much to choose from here, from cardigans and scarves to bags and cushions/pillows. All would make charming, unique gifts.

Knitting essentials

All you really need to get knitting is a pair of needles and some yarn. For some projects, that's it; for others additional items are required, most of which can be found in a fairly basic sewing kit. All measurements are given in metric and imperial. Choose which to work in and stick with it since conversions may not be exact.

- **Needles** These come in metric (mm), British and US sizes and are made from different materials, all of which affect the weight and 'feel' of the needles – which you choose is down to personal preference. Circular and double-pointed needles are sometimes used as well.
- **Yarns** Specific yarns are listed for each project, but full details of the yarn's composition and the ball lengths are given so that you can choose alternatives, either from online sources or from your local supplier, many of whom have very knowledgeable staff. Do keep any leftover yarns (not forgetting the ball bands, since these contain vital information) to use for future projects.
- **Additional items**: Some projects require making up and finishing, and need further materials or equipment, such as sewing needles, buttons and other accessories. These are detailed in each project's Getting Started box.

What is in this book

All projects are illustrated with several photographs to show you the detail of the work – both inspirational and useful for reference. A full summary of each project is given in the Getting Started box so you can see exactly what's involved. Here, projects are graded from one ball of yarn (straightforward, suitable for beginners) through two (more challenging) to three balls (for knitters with more confidence and experience).

Also in the Getting Started box is the size of each finished item, yarn(s), needles and additional items needed, and what tension/gauge the project is worked in. Finally, a breakdown of the steps involved is given so you know exactly what the project entails before you start.

At the beginning of the pattern instructions is a key to all abbreviations that are used in that project, while occasional notes expand on the pattern instructions where necessary.

Metric	British	US
2 mm	14	0
2.5 mm	13	1
2.75 mm	12	2
3mm	11	n/a
3.25 mm	10	3
3.5 mm	n/a	4
3.75 mm	9	5
4 mm	8	6
4.5 mm	7	7
5 mm	6	8
5.5 mm	5	9
6 mm	4	10
6.5 mm	3	10.5
7 mm	2	n/a
7.5 mm	1	n/a
8 mm	0	11
9 mm	0	13
10 mm	0	15

Wrap-around cardigan

Worked in a soft yarn and lightly textured stitch, this wrap-around jacket will keep you snug on chilly days.

The front of this soft and cuddly unstructured jacket can be left to hang loose or can be fastened with a pin or brooch.

GETTING STARTED

 *Fronts and back worked in one piece with cast/bound-off and cast-on stitches for armhole openings. The sleeves are shaped with simple increases*

Size:

To fit bust: *76–81[81–86:91–97:102–107]cm/ 30–32[32–34:36–38:40–42]in*

Actual size bust (with front overlapped): *85[96.5:108:120]cm/33½[38:42½:47¼]in*

Length (including collar): *55.5[60.5:65:70] cm/22[24:25½:27½]in*

Sleeve seam (with cuff turned back): *48cm (19in)*

Note: *Figures in square brackets [ ] refer to larger sizes; where there is only one set of figures, it applies to all sizes*

How much yarn:

4[5:6:7] x 50g (2oz) balls of Rowan Kid Classic, approx 140m (153 yards) per ball

Needles:

Pair of 5mm (no. 6/US 8) needles

Tension/gauge:

17 stitches and 24 rows to 10cm (4in) over moss stitch on 5mm (no. 6/US 8) needles.
IT IS ESSENTIAL TO WORK TO THE STATED TENSION/ GAUGE TO ACHIEVE SUCCESS

What you have to do:

Cast on. Work in moss/seed stitch. Cast on and cast/ bind off stitches for armhole openings. Shape sleeves with simple increases. Cast/bind off.

Note: *This very simple jacket is worked sideways. The fronts and back are all in one piece with openings left for the armholes, while the sleeves are added afterwards.*

The Yarn

Rowan Kid Classic is a perfect blend of lambswool and 26% kid mohair so the finished fabric is very soft and cuddly. There are a range of muted and neutral shades and some subtle pastels.

Instructions

Abbreviations:

alt = alternate;

cm = centimetre(s)

cont = continue;

foll = following;

inc = increase;

k = knit;

kfb = k into front and back of st;

p = purl; **patt** = pattern;

rep = repeat;

RS = right side;

st(s) = stitch(es);

WS = wrong side

FRONTS AND BACK:

Cast on 95[103:111:119] sts for right front.

1st row: (RS) P1, (k1, p1) to end.

Rep this row to form moss/seed st patt.

Cont in moss/seed st, work 77[83:89:95] more rows.

Shape right armhole:

Next row: (RS) Patt 21[23:25:27] sts, cast/bind off next 33[37:41:45] sts loosely, patt to end.

Cont on last set of 41[43:45:47] sts for underarm. Work 10[14:18:22] rows moss/seed st.

Next row: (WS) Patt 41[43:45:47] sts, cast on 33[37:41:45] sts, patt to end. 95[103:111:119] sts.

Back:

Work 92[102:112:122] rows in moss/seed st.

Shape left armhole:

Work as given for right armhole.

Left front:

Work 77[83:89:95] rows in moss/seed st, ending with a RS row. Cast/bind off in moss/seed st.

SLEEVES: (Make 2)

Cast on 41[45:49:53] sts. Work 44[40:38:44] rows in moss/seed st.

Next row: (inc row – RS) Kfb, patt to last 2 sts, kfb, k1. 43[47:51:55] sts.

Keeping patt correct, inc in this way at each end of every foll 10th[10th:8th:6th] row until there are 57[61:69:77] sts. Patt 3 rows.

Inc one st at each end of next and every foll alt row until there are 67[75:83:91] sts. Work 7[9:11:13] rows without shaping.

Cast/bind off loosely.

Tips

• Cast on for the armholes by looping stitches on with your left thumb. If you give each loop an extra twist before putting it on the right needle, the edge will be flexible but less loopy.

• After sewing up the garment, brush the surface of the knitting lightly with a soft brush to enhance the mohair effect.

Making up

Using backstitch, sew cast/bound-off edge of sleeve to cast/bound-off and cast-on edges of armhole opening, then sew row ends at tops of sleeves to row-ends at underarm. Join sleeve seams, reversing seam for about 5cm (2in) for turn-back cuff.

Peruvian-style hat

With striped ear flaps and a patterned crown, this cosy hat echoes a traditional Peruvian design.

Worked in natural colouring and simple colour patterns, this snug pull-on hat has typical Peruvian styling with a tassel trim, ear flaps and cord ties.

GETTING STARTED

 The fabric is stocking/stockinette stitch but colourwork includes simple stripe and intarsia patterns with yarn carried across the back of the work

Size:
One size to fit average size woman's head
Width around head: *55cm (21½in)*

How much yarn:
1 x 50g (2oz) ball of Wendy Mode DK Pure New Wool, approx 142m (155 yards) per ball, in each of four colours A, B, C and D

Needles:
Pair of 3.75mm (no. 9/US 5) knitting needles
Pair of 4mm (no. 8/US 6) knitting needles
Pair of 4.5mm (no. 7/US 7) knitting needles
Spare 3.75mm (no. 9/US 5) knitting needle

Tension/gauge:
22 sts and 30 rows measure 10 cm (4in) square over st st on 4mm (no. 8/US 6) needles
IT IS ESSENTIAL TO WORK TO THE STATED TENSION/GAUGE TO ACHIEVE SUCCESS

What you have to do:
Work in stocking/stockinette stitch and garter stitch. Shape work with invisible increases (making a stitch) and working two stitches together to decrease. Work stripes. Pick up stitches and work edgings. Work colour patterns, carrying yarn not in use across back of work. Make twisted cords.

The Yarn

The pure wool content and graded natural colourings of Peruvian-style designs can easily be sourced from the Mode DK range by Wendy. In addition, a project knitted in this yarn can be machine washed on a wool cycle and even tumble-dried on a low setting.

 # Instructions

Abbreviations:
alt = alternate; **beg** = beginning; **cont** =continue; **dec** = decrease(ing); **foll** = following; **g st** = garter stitch (every row k); **k** = knit; **m l k** = make a stitch by picking up horizontal loop lying before next stitch and knitting into back of it; **m l p** = make a stitch by picking up horizontal loop lying before next stitch and purling into back of it; **p** = purl; **patt** = pattern; **rem** = remain(ing); **rep** = repeat; **RS** = right side; **st(s)** = stitch(es); **st st** = stocking/stockinette stitch; **tog** = together; **WS** = wrong side

Note: When working 3rd–8th , 11th–14th and 21st and 22nd rows of pattern on Hat, strand yarn not in use loosely across WS of work over not more than 3 sts at a time to keep fabric elastic.

EAR FLAPS: (Make 2)
With 4mm (no. 8/US 6) needles and A, cast on 3 sts.
1st row: (RS) K to end.
2nd row: P1, m l p, p1, m l p, p1. 5 sts.
3rd row: K1, m l k, k3, m l k, k1. 7 sts.
4th row: P to end. Cut off A and join in B.
5th row: With B, k1, m l k, k to last st, m l k, k1.
6th row: P to end.
7th row: As 5th row. 11 sts. Cut off B and join in C.
8th row: With C, p to end.
9th row: With C, as 5th row. 13 sts.
10th row: P to end. Cut off C and join in A.
11th row: With A, as 5th row. 15 sts.
12th row: P to end.
13th row: As 11th row. 17 sts. Cut off A and join in B.
14th row: With B, p to end.
15th row: As 5th row. 19 sts.

16th row: P to end. Cut off B and join in C.
17th row: With C, k to end.
18th row: With C, p1, m1p, p to last st, m1p, p1. 21 sts.
19th row: K to end. Cut off C and join in A.
20th–22nd rows: As 14th–16th rows, but using A instead of B. 23 sts. Cut off A and join in B.
23rd–25th rows: As 17th–19th rows, but using B instead of C. 25 sts. Cut off B and join in C.
26th–28th rows: As 14th–16th rows, but using C instead of B. 27 sts. Joining in and cutting off colours as required and beg with a k row, cont in st st and stripes as foll: Work 3 rows each in A, B, C and A, ending with a WS row. Cast/bind off.

Left side edging:
With 3.75mm (no. 9/US 5) needles, D and RS facing, beg at cast/bound-off edge of left side of first Ear Flap and pick up and k35 sts along shaped row-ends to centre of cast-on edge. Cast/bind off knitways.

Right side edging:
With 3.75mm (no. 9/US 5) needles, D and RS facing, beg at centre of cast-on edge of first Ear Flap and pick up and k35 sts along right side of shaped row-ends to cast/bound-off edge. Cast/bind off knitways.

Top edging:
With 3.75mm (no. 9/US 5) needles, D and RS facing, pick up and k27 sts across cast/bound-off edge of first Ear Flap.
K1 row. Cut off yarn and leave these sts on a holder.
Work Left side edging, Right side edging and Top edging in same way on second Ear Flap.

HAT:
With spare 3.75mm (no. 9/US 5) needle and D, cast on 14 sts, cut off yarn, then on same needle and with D, cast on 39 sts, cut off yarn. With 3.75mm (no. 9/US 5) needles and D, cast on 14 sts, k these 14 sts, with RS facing, k across 27 sts of first Ear Flap, k39 sts from spare needle, k across 27 sts of second Ear Flap, then k14 sts from spare needle.
121 sts. Work in 5 rows in g st, ending with a WS row. Cut off D. Change to 4mm (no. 8/US 6) needles. Joining in and cutting off colours as required, cont in patt as foll:
1st row: (RS) With B, k to end.
2nd row: With B, p to end.
Change to 4.5mm (no. 7/US 7) needles.
3rd row: K1 C, * 6 A, 2 C, rep from * to end.
4th row: *P3 C, 5 A, rep from * to last st, 1 C.
5th row: K1 C, *4 A, 4 C, rep from * to end.

6th row: P3 C, *2 C, 6 A, rep from * to last 6 sts, 2 C, 4 A.
7th row: K3 C, *3 C, 5A, rep from * to last 6 sts, 3 C, 3 A.
8th row: P3 A, *4 C, 4 A, rep from * to last 6 sts, 4 C, 2 A.
Change to 4mm (no. 8/US 6) needles.
9th row: With D, k to end.
10th row: With D, p to end.
Change to 4.5mm (no. 7/US 7) needles.
11th row: K4 B, *1 C, 7 B, rep from * to last 5 sts, 1 C, 4 B.
12th row: P3 B, *3 C, 5 B, rep from * to last 6 sts, 3 C, 3 B.
13th row: K2 B, *5 C, 3 B, rep from * to last 7 sts, 5 C, 2 B.
14th row: P1 B, *7 C, 1 B, rep from * to end.
Change to 4mm (no. 8/US 6) needles.
15th–18th rows: With A, work 4 rows in st st.
19th row: With D, k to end.
20th row: With D, p19, p2tog, (p38, p2tog) twice, p20. 118 sts. Change to 4.5mm (no. 7/US 7) needles.
21st row: K2 B, *2 D, 2 B, rep from * to end.
22nd row: P2 B, *2 D, 2 B, rep from * to end.
Change to 4mm (no. 8/US 6) needles.
23rd –24th rows: With C, work 2 rows in st st.
25th row: With A, k to end.
26th row: With A, p6, p2tog, (p11, p2tog) 8 times, p6. 109 sts.
27th–28th rows: With D, work 2 rows in st st.
Shape crown:
1st row: (RS) With B, k to end.
2nd row: With B, p1, (p2tog, p7) 12 times. 97 sts.
3rd row: With C, k to end.
4th row: With C, p1, (p2tog, p6) 12 times. 85 sts.
5th row: With A, k to end.
6th row: With A, p1, (p2tog, p5) 12 times. 73 sts.
Cont in this way, dec 12 sts on every foll alt row, until 25 sts rem and working in stripes of 2 rows each A, D, B and C.
15th row: With C, (k2tog) 12 times, k1. 13 sts.
Cut off yarn, thread through rem sts, pull up tightly and fasten off securely.

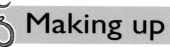

Making up

Press carefully, following instructions on ball band. Join back seam.
Using 4 strands of D, make 2 twisted cords 25cm (10in) long and attach one to pointed end of each Ear Flap.
Using 4 strands of D, make a twisted cord 8cm (3in) long.
Using D, make a tassel 10cm (4in) long and attach to end of twisted cord. Thread other end of twisted cord through top of hat and sew securely in place.

HOW TO
MAKE A TASSEL

Tassels can be used to decorate all kinds of knitted items – but remember they use a lot of yarn.

1 Decide on the length of tassel you want and then cut a piece of stiff card to the same dimension. Wrap the yarn around the card until you have approximately the right quantity for the finished tassel. Cut off the yarn at the end of the cardboard.

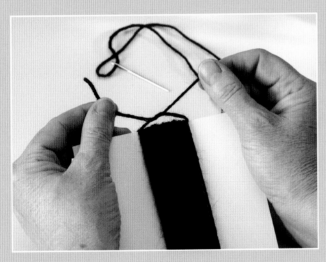

2 Thread another piece of yarn onto a blunt-ended needle and pass the needle under the yarn at the top of the card. Tie the yarn in a knot, leaving a long length of yarn.

3 Cut along the yarn at the bottom edge of the cardboard and remove the cardboard. Push the needle threaded with the length of yarn down into the centre of the tassel from the top.

4 Bring the needle out of the tassel and wrap the yarn around the tassel about 4.5cm (1½in) from the top. Continue wrapping until you have created a band of yarn around the tassel.

5 Thread the needle through the top of the tassel and trim the yarn, leaving enough to attach the tassel. Trim the bottom edges of the tassel to ensure they are even.

Laptop bag

Knitted and then felted, this useful over-the-shoulder bag is practical and looks good, too.

Carry your laptop around in this funky, felted fabric holdall featuring distinctive intarsia stripes.

GETTING STARTED

Simple stocking/stockinette stitch fabric but stripes are knitted in, using the intarsia method

Size:
Bag is 36cm wide x 24cm high x 4cm deep (14in x 9½in x 1½in)

How much yarn:
3 x 50g (2oz) balls of Rowan Kid Classic, approx 140m (153 yards) per ball, in main colour M
1 ball in contrasting colour C

Needles:
Pair of 5mm (no. 6/US 8) knitting needles

Additional items:
Open-ended zip fastener to fit opening
Buckle to fit strap 4cm (1½in) wide
2.5m (2¾ yards) of grosgrain ribbon 4cm (1½in) wide

Tension/gauge:
19 sts and 25 rows measure 10cm (4in) square over st st on 5mm (no. 6/US 8) needles before felting
25 sts and 33 rows measure 10cm (4in) square over st st on 5mm (no. 6/US 8) needles after felting
IT IS ESSENTIAL TO WORK TO THE STATED TENSION/ GAUGE TO ACHIEVE SUCCESS

What you have to do:
Cast on with main colour and also contrast colour for vertical stripes. Work in stocking/stockinette stitch. Twisting yarns together at back of work when changing colour for vertical stripes to prevent a hole forming. Wash fabric to felt it.

The Yarn
Rowan Kid Classic is a combination of lambswool and kid mohair. Its brushed appearance, with a shorter pile than is usual for most mohairs, makes it ideal for felting. When washed, the brushed fibres matt together giving the fabric its characteristic felted appearance.

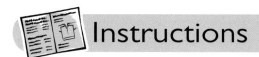 Instructions

Abbreviations:

beg = beginning;
cm = centimetre(s);
cont = continue;
dec = decrease;
foll = following;
k = knit; **p** = purl;
rem = remain;
rep = repeat;
st(s) = stitch(es);
tog = together

THE BAG: (Worked in one piece)

With M, cast on 10 sts; using shade C, cast on 4 sts; using shade M, cast on 62 sts; using shade C, cast on 4 sts; using shade M, cast on 10 sts.

1st row: K10 shade M, k4 shade C, k62 shade M, k4 shade C, k10 shade M.

2nd row: P10 shade M, p4 shade C, p 62 shade M, p4 shade C, p10 shade M.

Rep last 2 rows 34 times more. (70 rows)

With shade C, work 5 rows st st, then work 2nd row again. Rep 1st and 2nd rows 17 times, then work 1st row again. With shade C, work 5 rows st st. (116 rows) Now rep 1st and 2nd rows 35 times. 186 rows. Cast/bind off, keeping colours as set.

STRAP FOR BUCKLE:

With M, cast on 20 sts. Beg with a k row, work 12 rows st st. With shade C, work 5 rows st st. With shade M and beg with a p row, cont in st st until strap measures 82cm (32in) from beg. Cast/bind off.

SHOULDER STRAP:

With M, cast on 20 sts. Beg with a k row, work 12 rows st st. With shade C, work 5 rows st st. With shade M and beg with a p row, cont in st st until strap measures 166cm (65in) from beg, ending with a p row.

Shape end:

Dec 1 st at each end of every row until 2 sts rem. Work 2 tog and fasten off.

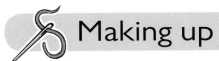

Making up

FELTING:

Place pieces in a washing machine and wash on a short cycle at 40°C (104°F) degrees. Smooth out main piece to measure about 56cm x 36cm (22in x 14in) and straps to measure 4cm (1½in) wide. Allow to dry flat.

ASSEMBLING:

Pin the grosgrain ribbon down the wrong side of one long side of both straps and catch in place with herringbone stitches. Fold straps in half with right sides facing and join long seams using backstitch. Turn straps right side out. Fold the bag in half lengthways and mark centre of base at side seams. With right sides facing, match the centre of cast-on edge of each strap to centre of base. Pin in place, then oversew the bag to the bottom of the straps and continue to join the straps to the side edges, leaving 2cm (¾in) unseamed at top. Pin zip into opening and backstitch in place. Wrap the end of the buckle strap through the buckle and stitch securely. Slot the shoulder strap through buckle, adjust and stitch in place.

HOW TO
JOIN YARN VERTICALLY

1 Knit the row in the first colour until instructed to change to the next colour. Put the right-hand needle into the stitch on the left-hand needle and then loop the new colour around the needle and make the next stitch with the new yarn.

2 At the back of the work, wind the original yarn around the new yarn and keep it tensioned with the fingers of the left hand as you continue knitting using the new yarn.

3 You repeat the same winding procedure when you want to join in the next colour. The technique is the same when working purl rows. Here you can see the white yarn wrapped around the blue yarn before the first white stitch is made.

Rib sweater with lacy panel

This tunic-style sweater is soft, flattering and easy to wear.

Make this lovely sweater with a slightly scooped neckline and raglan sleeves in a silky-feel double knitting (light worsted) yarn. It has an openwork, lacy lower panel that becomes a rib pattern as the work progresses.

GETTING STARTED

Rib pattern is fairly easy but the lacy panel might be a challenge to novices

Size:

To fit bust: *81–86[91–97:102–107]cm/32–34[36–38:40–42]in*

Actual size: *92[102:111]cm/36[40:43¾]in*

Length: *64[65:66]cm/25[25½:26]in*

Sleeve seam: *33[34:35]cm/13[13½:13¾]in*

Note: *Figures in square brackets [ ] refer to larger sizes; where there is only one set of figures, it applies to all sizes*

How much yarn:

13[15:16] x 50g (2oz) balls of Sirdar Flirt DK, approx 95m (104 yards) per ball

Needles:

Pair of 3.25mm (no. 10/US 3) knitting needles
Pair of 4mm (no. 8/US 6/US 6) knitting needles

Tension/gauge:

25 sts and 35 rows, when slightly stretched, measure 10cm (4in) square over rib patt on 4mm (no. 8/US 6) needles

IT IS ESSENTIAL TO WORK TO THE STATED TENSION/ GAUGE TO ACHIEVE SUCCESS

What you have to do:

Work lower panel in two lacy patterns, starting with one pattern and decreasing as instructed. Work top section in rib pattern, shaping raglan armholes and neckline as instructed. Pick up stitches around neckline and knit a few rows.

The Yarn

Sirdar Flirt DK is a blend of 80% bamboo-sourced viscose and 20% wool. It produces a fabric with a soft feel and matt sheen that can be machine washed. There is a good range of contemporary colours to choose from.

Instructions

Abbreviations:

beg = beginning; **cm** = centimetre(s); **cont** = continue; **dec** = decrease; **foll** = follow(s)(ing); **inc** = increasing; **k** = knit; **p** = purl; **patt** = pattern; **psso** = pass slipped stitch over; **pwise** = purlwise; **rem** = remaining; **rep** = repeat; **RS** = right side; **sl** = slip; **st(s)** = stitch(es); **tog** = together; **WS** = wrong side; **yfwd** = yarn forward/yarn over to make a stitch; **ytb** = yarn to back; **ytf** = yarn to front

BACK:

With 4mm (no. 8/US 6) needles cast on 155[171:187] sts. K 1 row. Cont in lace patt A as foll:

1st row: (RS) K2, (yfwd, k2, sl 1, k2tog, psso, k2, yfwd, k1) to last st, k1.

2nd row: P to end.

Rep these 2 rows to form lace patt A until work measures 19cm (7½in) from beg, ending with a RS row.

Dec row: (WS) P3, (p2tog, p1, p2tog, p3) to end. 117[129:141] sts. Cont in lace patt B as foll:

1st row: (RS) K2, (yfwd, k1, sl 1, k2tog, psso, k1, yfwd, k1) to last st, k1.

2nd row: P to end.

Rep these 2 rows to form lace patt B until work measures 32cm (12½in) from beg, ending with a RS row.

Next row: (WS) K1, (p1, k2) to last 2 sts, p1, k1.

Cont in rib patt as foll:

1st row: (RS) P1, (ytb, sl 1 pwise, ytf, p2) to last 2 sts, ytb, sl 1 pwise, ytf, p1.

2nd row: K1, (p1, k2) to last 2 sts, p1, k1. Rep these 2 rows to form rib patt until work measures 42cm (16½in) from beg, ending with a WS row.

Shape raglan armholes:

Keeping patt correct, cast/bind off 4[5:6] sts at beg of next 2 rows. 109[119:129] sts.

Next row: (RS) K1, sl 1, k1, psso, patt to last 3 sts, k2tog, k1.

Next row: P2, patt to last 2 sts, p2.

Next row: K2, patt to last 2 sts, k2.

Next row: P2, patt to last 2 sts, p2.

Rep last 4 rows 11[12:13] times more. 85[93:101] sts.*

Next row: K1, sl 1, k1, psso, patt to last 3 sts, k2tog, k1.

Next row: P2, patt to last 2 sts, p2.

Rep last 2 rows 13 times more. 57[65:73] sts. Cut off yarn and leave rem sts on a st holder.

FRONT:

Work as given for Back to *.

Shape neck:

Next row: (RS) K1, sl 1, k1, psso, patt 25 sts, k2tog, turn and cont on these 28 sts for left front neck.

Next row: Patt to last 2 sts, p2.

Next row: K1, sl 1, k1, psso, patt to last 2 sts, work2tog. Rep last 2 rows 11 times more, ending with a WS row. 4 sts.

Next row: K1, sl 1, k2tog, psso. 2 sts.

Next row: P2.

K2tog and fasten off. Return to sts on holder. With RS of work facing, sl centre 25[33:41] sts on to a holder, join yarn to next st, work2tog, patt to last 3 sts, k2tog, k1.

Complete to match first side of neck, reversing shapings.

SLEEVES:

With 3.25mm (no. 10/US 3) needles cast on 63[69:75] sts. K 4 rows.

Change to 4mm (no. 8/US 6) needles. Cont in rib patt as foll:

1st row: (RS) P1, (ytb, sl 1 pwise, ytf, p2) to last 2 sts, ytb, sl 1 pwise, ytf, p1.

2nd row: K1, (p1, k2) to last 2 sts, p1, k1.

These 2 rows form rib patt. Cont in patt, inc 1 st at each end of next and every foll 8th row, working extra sts into patt, until there are 87[93:99] sts.

Cont straight until work measures 33[34:35] cm/13[13½:13¾]in from beg, ending with a WS row.

Shape raglan top:

Keeping patt correct, cast/bind off 4[5:6] sts at beg of next 2 rows. 79[83:87] sts.

Next row: (RS) K1, sl 1, k1, psso, patt to last 3 sts, k2tog, k1.

Next row: P2, patt to last 2 sts, p2.

Next row: K2, patt to last 2 sts, k2.

Next row: P2, patt to last 2 sts, p2.

Rep last 4 rows 3 times more. 71[75:79] sts.

Next row: K1, sl 1, k1, psso, patt to last 3 sts, k2tog, k1.

Next row: P2, patt to last 2 sts, p2.

Rep last 2 rows 29[31:33] times more. 11 sts. Cut off yarn and leave rem sts on a st holder.

NECK EDGING:

Join front and right back raglan seams.

With 3.25mm (no. 10/US 3) needles and RS facing, pick up and k across 11 sts from left sleeve, pick up and k 21 sts down left front neck, k across 25[33:41] centre front sts, pick up and k 21 sts up right front neck, k across 11 sts from right sleeve and 57[65:73] back neck sts. 146[162:178] sts. K 2 rows. Cast/bind off firmly.

Making up

Join left back raglan and edging seams. Join side and sleeve seams.

Classic beret

Give a contemporary twist to a design classic by knitting this beret in vivid colours.

Back in fashion, this easy-to-wear beret is worked flat and shaped into a circle during the knitting process. The ribbed edge has a narrow stripe in a contrasting colour.

GETTING STARTED

 Fairly large number of stitches, but main fabric is simple stocking/stockinette stitch and shaping is easy

Size:
To fit an average size woman's head

How much yarn:
1 x 50g (2oz) ball of Patons Diploma Gold 4-ply, approx 184m (201 yards) per ball, in main colour M
1 ball in contrast colour C

Needles:
Pair of 2.75mm (no. 12/US 2) knitting needles
Pair of 3.25mm (no. 10/US 3) knitting needles

Tension/gauge:
28 sts and 36 rows measure 10cm (4in) square over st st on 3.25mm (no. 10/US 3) needles
IT IS ESSENTIAL TO WORK TO THE STATED TENSION/GAUGE TO ACHIEVE SUCCESS

What you have to do:
Work single rib in a contrast colour. Use main colour to work in stocking/stockinette stitch. Decrease by knitting two stitches together at regular intervals on shaping rows. Finish off by cutting yarn and threading through small number of remaining stitches.

The Yarn
Patons Diploma Gold 4-ply is a hard-wearing mixture of 55% wool, 25% acrylic and 20% nylon. It is ideal for headwear as it can be machine washed when necessary. You can choose from a large shade range of classic and contemporary colours.

Abbreviations:

alt = alternate;
beg = beginning;
cm = centimetre(s);
cont = continue;
foll = follow(s)(ing);
k = knit;
m1 = make one stitch by picking up strand lying between needles and working into back of it;
p = purl;
rem = remain;
rep = repeat;
RS = right side;
st(s) = stitch(es);
st st = stocking/stockinette stitch;
tog = together;
WS = wrong side

Instructions

BERET:

With 2.75mm (no. 12/US 2) needles and C, cast on 151 sts.

1st rib row: (RS) K1, *p1, k1, rep from * to end.

2nd rib row: P1, *k1, p1, rep from * to end. These 2 rows form rib. Cut off C. Join in M. Work a further 9 rows in rib, ending with a RS row.

Next row: (WS) Rib 2, m1, *(rib 3, m1, rib 4, m1) twice, rib 4, m1, rep from * to last 5 sts, rib 3, m1, rib 2. 193 sts.

Change to 3.25mm (no. 10/US 3) needles. Beg with a k row, cont in st st and work 36 rows, ending with a WS row.

Shape crown:

1st row: (RS) K1, *k2tog, k14, rep from * to end. 181 sts.
Work 3 rows.

5th row: K1, *k2tog, k13, rep from * to end. 169 sts.
Work 3 rows.

9th row: K1, *k2tog, k12, rep from * to end. 157 sts.

Work 3 rows. Cont in this way working 1 st less between each decrease, dec 12 sts on next and every foll 4th row until 109 sts rem. Work 1 row, so ending with a WS row.

Next row: K1, *k2tog, k7, rep from * to end. 97 sts.
Work 1 row.

Next row: K1, *k2tog, k6, rep from * to end. 85 sts.

Cont in this way working 1 st less between each decrease on every foll alt row until 13 sts rem. Cut off yarn, leaving a long end. Thread cut end of yarn through rem sts, draw up tightly and fasten off securely.

STALK:

With 3.25mm (no. 10/US 3) needles and 2 strands of C,
cast on 7 sts.
Cast/bind off knitways.

 Making up

Use long end of yarn to join seam with backstitch. Cut
a circle, approximately 30cm (12in) in diameter, from
white card. Stretch beret over card and cover with a
slightly damp cloth. Leave to dry flat, then remove card.
Sew stalk to centre of crown.

Striped scarf with pompoms

Rainbow stripes and giant pompoms at each end make this a fun scarf to wear.

Worked in stocking/stockinette stitch and multi-coloured stripes, the side edges of this scarf are sewn together to form a double thickness. The ends are then gathered up and trimmed with big pompoms.

GETTING STARTED

Easy stocking/stockinette stitch and stripes but fabric is double width (to be folded in half and sewn up), so working a long scarf may take a little time

Size:
Scarf is 15cm wide x 159cm long (6in x 62½in), excluding pompoms

How much yarn:
1 x 50g (2oz) ball Wendy Mode Emu Superwash DK, approx 110m (120 yards) per ball, in each of 5 colours A, B, C, D and E
2 balls in colour F

Needles:
Pair of 4mm (no. 8/US 6) knitting needles

Tension/gauge:
22 sts and 30 rows measure 10cm (4in) square over st st on 4mm (no. 8/US 6) needles
IT IS ESSENTIAL TO WORK TO THE STATED TENSION/GAUGE TO ACHIEVE SUCCESS

What you have to do:
Work in stocking/stockinette stitch. Follow stripe pattern. Join in and cut off colours as required. Make pompoms to trim ends of scarf.

The Yarn
Emu Superwash DK from Wendy Mode is a classic 100% wool yarn with a practical twist – it can be machine washed. There are over 30 shades to choose from so you can have a lot of fun with choosing the colour combinations for your stripes.

Abbreviations:
beg = beginning;
cont = continue;
cm = centimetre(s);
foll = follows;
k = knit;
patt = pattern;
rep = repeat;
RS = right side;
st(s) = stitch(es);
st st = stocking/
stockinette stitch;
WS = wrong side.

 # Instructions

SCARF:
With 4mm (no. 8/US 6) needles and A, cast on 67 sts. Beg with a k row, cont in st st and stripe patt, joining in and cutting off colours as required as foll:
1st–6th rows: In A.
7th–10th rows: In B.
11th–12th rows: In C.
13th–20th rows: In D.
21st and 22nd rows: In E.
23rd–28th rows: In F.
29th–32nd rows: In A.
33rd and 34th rows: In B.
35th–42nd rows: In C.
43rd and 44th rows: In D.
45th–50th rows: In E.
51st–54th rows: In F.
55th and 56th rows: In A.
57th–64th rows: In B.
65th and 66th rows: In C.
67th–72nd rows: In D.
73rd–76th rows: In E.
77th and 78th rows: In F.
79th–86th rows: In A.
87th and 88th rows: In B.
89th–94th rows: In C.
95th–98th rows: In D.

99th and 100th rows: In E.
101st–108th rows: In F.
109th and 110th rows: In A.
111th–116th rows: In B.
117th–120th rows: In C.
121st and 122nd rows: In D.
123rd–130th rows: In E.
131st and 132nd rows: In F.

These 132 rows form stripe patt. Rep them twice more, then work 1st–50th rows again, ending on WS of stripe in E. Cast/bind off.

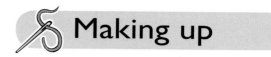 # Making up

Press carefully according to directions on ball band. With RS facing, fold scarf in half and join long seam with backstitch. Turn scarf through to RS, placing seam down centre of one side. Work a row of gathering stitches around cast-on and cast/bound-off edges of scarf, pull up tightly and fasten off securely.
With F, make 2 pompoms, each 10cm (4in) in diameter. Sew a pompom securely to each end of the scarf.

HOW TO
MAKE A POMPOM

Use this technique to make the large pompoms at each end of the scarf.

1 These pompoms are 10cm (4in) in diameter. Cut two circles of thick cardboard that are slightly larger than the diameter of the finished pompom. Cut a circle from the centre of each disc.

4 Using small sharp scissors, cut around the outside edge of the discs, snipping through all the layers of yarn.

2 Thread a large-eyed sewing needle with as many ends of yarn as you can fit through the eye. Each length of yarn should be approximately 1m (1 yard) long.

5 Gently ease the discs apart so that there is a straight section of yarn visible between them. Take a small piece of yarn and tie it firmly around the middle of the pompom, knotting it as tightly as possible.

3 Hold the two discs one on top of the other. Thread the needle through the centre and hold the ends of the yarn with one thumb. Take the needle around the discs and back through the centre. Continue to do this working your way evenly around the discs until the centre hole is full.

6 Ease the discs off the pompom and fluff it up into a round shape. Trim around the pompom, turning it as you work, to give an even shape.

Striped sweater

With a simple shape and a great colour combination for the stripes, this sweater will always look crisp and fresh.

Worked in stocking/stockinette stitch and a two-colour stripe pattern, this classic fitted sweater has a nautical feel. With a scoop neck and set-in sleeves, it looks good worn casually or under a jacket for work.

GETTING STARTED

Simple to work in stocking/stockinette stitch with basic shaping

Size:
To fit bust: 81[86:91:97]cm/32[34:36:38]in
Actual size: 90[96:100:106]cm/35½[37¾:39½:41¾]in
Length to back neck: 54[55:56:57cm/21¼[21¾:22:22½]in
Sleeve seam: 42cm (16½in)
Note: Figures in square brackets [ ] refer to larger sizes; where there is only one set of figures, it applies to all sizes

How much yarn:
3[4:4:5] x 50g (2oz) balls of Sirdar Luxury Soft Cotton DK, approx 95m (104 yards) in colour A
4[5:6:6] balls in colour B

Needles:
Pair of 3.75mm (no. 9/US 5) knitting needles
Pair of 4mm (no. 8/US 6) knitting needles

Tension/gauge:
22 sts and 28 rows measure 10cm (4in) square over st st on 4mm (no. 8/US 6) needles
IT IS ESSENTIAL TO WORK TO THE STATED TENSION/ GAUGE TO ACHIEVE SUCCESS

What you have to do:
Work in stocking/stockinette stitch. Follow stripe pattern, carrying colour not in use up side of work. Work simple decreases and increases to shape sweater. Pick up and knit stitches around neck to work edging.

The Yarn

Sirdar Luxury Soft Cotton DK is 100% cotton with a light twist and subtle sheen. The shade range contains beautiful fashion colours that are perfect for colour work and stripes.

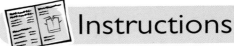 Instructions

STRIPE PATT:
1st–4th rows: Work 4 rows in A.
5th–10th rows: Work 6 rows in B.
11th and 12th rows: Work 2 rows in A.
13th–16th rows: Work 4 rows in B.
17th and 18th rows: Work 2 rows in A.
19th and 20th rows: Work 2 rows in B.
20th and 21st rows: Work 2 rows in A.
23rd–26th rows: Work 4 rows in B.
Rep these 26 rows to form patt.

BACK:
With 4mm (no. 8/US 6) needles and A, cast on 90[96:100:106] sts. K1 row. Beg with a k row, cont in st st

Abbreviations:

alt = alternate;
beg = beginning;
cm = centimetre(s);
cont = continue;
dec = decrease;
foll = follow(s)(ing);
inc = increase; **k** = knit;
patt = pattern;
rem = remaining;
rep = repeat;
RS = right side;
st(s) = stitch(es);
st st = stocking/stockinette
stitch;
WS = wrong side

and stripe patt, AT SAME TIME shape sides by dec 1 st
(2 sts in from edge) at each end of 7th and every foll 10th row to 82[88:92:98] sts. Work 11 rows straight, then inc 1 st (2 sts in from edge) at each end of next and every foll 10th row to 90[96:100:106] sts. Cont straight until work measures about 33cm (13in) from beg, ending on WS with 14th row of patt.

Shape armholes:

Keeping patt correct, cast/bind off 3 sts at beg of next 2 rows.
Dec 1 st at each end of every row to 74[76:80:82] sts, then at each end of every foll alt row to 66[68:70:72] sts.*
Work straight until armholes measure 19[20:21:22]cm/ 7½[8:8¼:8¾]in from beg, ending with a WS row.

Shape shoulders and back neck:

Cast/bind off 5 sts at beg of next 2 rows. 56[58:60:62] sts.
Next row: Cast/bind off 5 sts, k18 (including st on needle after cast/

bind-off), turn and complete this side of neck first.
Cast/bind off 6 sts at beg of next 2 rows.
Cast/bind off rem 6 sts.
With RS of work facing, rejoin yarn to rem sts, cast/bind off centre 10[12:14:16] sts loosely, k to end. Cast/bind off 5 sts at beg of next row, then complete to match first side of neck.

FRONT:

Work as given for Back to *. Cont straight until armholes measure 9[10:11:12]cm/ 3½[4:4½:4¾]in from beg, ending with a WS row.

Shape neck:

Next row: K27[28:29:30], turn and leave rem sts on a spare needle.
Complete this side of neck first. Keeping armhole edge straight, dec 1 st at neck edge on next 4[6:8:10] rows, then on every foll alt row to 16 sts. Work a few rows straight until Front matches Back to shoulder, ending at armhole edge.

Shape shoulder:

Cast/bind off 5 sts at beg of next and foll alt row.
Work 1 row. Cast/bind off rem 6 sts.
With RS of work facing, rejoin yarn to rem sts, cast/bind off centre 12 sts loosely, k to end. Complete to match first side of neck, reversing shaping.

SLEEVES:

With 4mm (no. 8/US 6) needles and A, cast on 46[48:50:52] sts. K1 row. Beg with a k row, cont in st st and stripe patt, inc 1 st (2 sts in from edge) at each end of 9th row and 2 foll 12th rows. Cont to inc at each end of every foll 14th row to 62[64:66:68] sts. Work straight until Sleeve measures about 42cm (16½in) from beg, ending with same patt row as Back at armholes.

Shape top:

Cast/bind off 3 sts at beg of next 2 rows. Dec 1 st at each end of next and every foll 4th row to 46[46:46:48] sts, then at each end of every foll alt row to 34[34:38:38] sts. Dec 1 st at each end of every row to 20 sts.
Cast/bind off evenly.

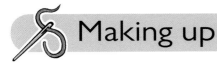

Making up

Press lightly on WS according to directions on ball band. Join right shoulder seam.

Neck edging:

With 3.75mm (no. 9/US 5) needles, A and RS of work facing, pick up and k68[72:74:76] sts evenly around front neck and 32[34:36:38] sts around back neck. 100[106:110:114] sts. K 2 rows. Cast/bind off evenly.
Join left shoulder and neck edging seam.
Sew in sleeves. Join side and sleeve seams.

Envelope clutch bag

Use your knitting skills to make this pretty bag – with your choice of yarn and lining fabric, it will be unique.

Perfect for daily use, this pretty bag in a soft brushed yarn is worked in an easy textured rib pattern. Tuck it under your arm as a clutch purse, or attach a cord and use over your shoulder to keep your hands free.

GETTING STARTED

 Bag is a simple shape and stitch pattern but care must be taken with finishing touches for a neat appearance

Size:
Bag is 25cm wide x 12cm tall (10in x 4¾in)

How much yarn:
1 x 50g (2oz) ball of Orkney Angora 'St Magnus' 50/50 DK, approx 200m (219 yards) per ball

Needles:
Pair of 3.75mm (no. 9/US 5) knitting needles

Additional items:
1 decorative button, about 2cm (¾in) in diameter
1m (1 yard) antique gold cord
Lining fabric in co-ordinating colour
Matching sewing thread
Card for stiffening

Tension/gauge:
21 sts and 32 rows measure 10cm (4in) square over patt on 3.75mm (no. 9/US 5) needles
IT IS ESSENTIAL TO WORK TO THE STATED TENSION/GAUGE TO ACHIEVE SUCCESS

What you have to do:
Work in moss/seed stitch. Work in broken rib pattern. Shape flap by casting/binding off stitches at start of rows. Pick up and knit stitches along flap edge. Sew simple fabric lining.

The Yarn
'St Magnus' 50/50 DK from Orkney Angora is a versatile blend of lambswool with angora that exhibits all the best qualities of both fibres. There are 35 colours to choose from so it is easy to accessorize all your outfits.

Abbreviations:
beg = beginning;
cm = centimetre(s);
cont = continue;
foll = follows; **k** = knit;
p = purl; **patt** = pattern;
rep = repeat;
RS = right side;
st(s) = stitch(es);
WS = wrong side

Instructions

BAG:
Cast on 55 sts.

Next row: K1, *p1, k1, rep from *
to end.

Rep this row 5 times more to form moss/
seed st. Cont in broken rib patt as foll:

Next row: (RS) K to end.

Next row: P1, *k1, p1, rep from * to end.

Rep last 2 rows until work measures 26cm
(10¼ in) from beg, ending with a WS row.

Shape flap:
Next row: Cast/bind off 3 sts knitwise,
k to end.

Next row: Cast/bind off 3 sts purlwise,
patt to end.

Rep these 2 rows 8 times more. Fasten off
last st.

Flap edging:
With RS of work facing, pick up and k59 sts
along shaped edges of flap.

BROKEN RIB

This is the main stitch used to make the bag. It makes a textured rib pattern with columns of flat knit stitch interspersed with recessed columns of purl stitches with a twisted effect.

1 The pattern is worked over two rows. Knit the first and every alternate row.

2 Begin the second row with a purl stitch and then work a knit one, purl one sequence to the end of the row.

Next row: P1, *k1, p1, rep from * to end.
Cast/bind off.

Making up

Press lightly using a warm iron over a dry cloth.
Using knitted piece as a template, cut out lining fabric, allowing 5mm (¼in) seam allowance all round. Fold seam allowance to WS and press in place.
Fold knitted piece, with RS together, so that cast-on edge is 2cm (¾in) below the flap and join side seams. Turn right side out. Make up lining fabric in the same way but leave WS out. Cut a piece of card to fit inside back of bag. Place lining in bag, then slide card in place between bag and lining. Slip stitch lining neatly in place all around opening and flap.
Make a button loop with 20cm (8in) of cord. Make a loop in the centre and secure with a knot. Tie the ends into a bow. Sew the button to the bag front, just below point of flap. Sew the cord bow to the

flap so that loop fits neatly over the button.
Measure rest of cord to required length for strap, allowing 10cm (4in) extra at each end. Make a loop at each end and tie securely. Sew a loop to the top of each side seam.

Candyfloss scarf

Practise your openwork stitch with this easy-to-knit scarf that's light as a feather.

This soft and pretty scarf is perfect to tuck in the neck of a jacket. Extra-large needles and fine brushed yarn combine to give a frothy concoction with openwork stitch panels and broken rib borders.

GETTING STARTED

Straight piece of knitting with easy lace pattern and simple broken rib

Size:
Scarf is 18cm wide x 112cm long (7in x 44in)

How much yarn:
2 x 25g (1oz) balls of Sublime Kid Mohair, approx 112m (122 yards) per ball

Needles:
Pair of 6mm (no. 4/US 10) knitting needles

Tension/gauge:
16 sts and 20 rows measure 10cm (4in) square over broken rib patt on 6mm (no. 4/US 10) needles
IT IS ESSENTIAL TO WORK TO THE STATED TENSION/GAUGE TO ACHIEVE SUCCESS

What you have to do:
Work in broken rib pattern by knitting one row, then working one row in single rib. Work simple decorative increases and decreases for lace pattern.

The Yarn
Sublime Kid Mohair is a luxurious yarn spun from 60% of the very softest quality of kid mohair blended with 35% nylon and a 5% touch of merino wool. It is amazingly light and comes in eight misty, feminine colours.

Instructions

Abbreviations:

cm = centimetre(s); **cont** = continue;

foll = following; **k** = knit;

p = purl; **rep** = repeat;

RS = right side;

st(s) = stitch(es);

tog = together;

WS = wrong side;

yo = yarn over needle to make a decorative increase

SCARF:

Cast on 29 sts.

Work rib patt for edging as foll:

1st row: (WS) K1, *p1, k1, rep from * to end.

2nd row: K to end.

Rep these 2 rows 3 times more, then work 1st row again.

Cont in lace patt with ribbed edges as foll:

1st row: (RS) K to end.

2nd row: (K1, p1) twice, k1, *yo, k2tog, rep from * to last 6 sts, k2, (p1, k1) twice.

3rd row: K to end.

4th row: (K1, p1) twice, k2, *yo, k2tog, rep from * to last 5 sts, k1, (p1, k1) twice.

Rep these 4 rows 5 times more (24 rows in total).

Work rib patt as foll:

1st row: (RS) K to end.

2nd row: K1, *p1, k1, rep from * to end.

Rep these 2 rows 4 times more (10 rows in total).

Alternating lace and rib patts, rep them 4 times more, then work 24 rows in lace patt, until Scarf measures approximately 108cm (42½in), ending with a WS row.

Work 8 rows in rib patt for edging. Cast/bind off knitwise.

Making up

Pin out to given measurements. Steam gently to straighten side edges and raise the pile.

HOW TO
CREATE THE OPENWORK STITCH

Mohair yarn worked with large needles creates large airy stitches that show off the fine-spun yarn to its best advantage.

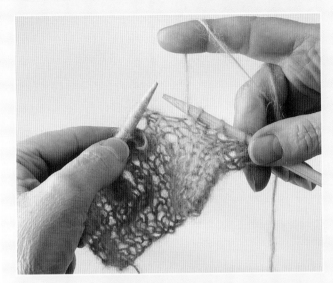

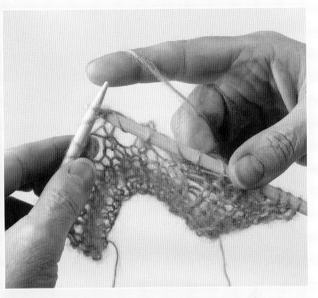

1 The openwork stitch is created by a combination of yarn-over increases and knit-two-together decreases. Begin the second row of the lace pattern by working the broken rib edge, then knit one. Bring the yarn to the front of the work and take it over the right-hand needle to the back to create a yarn-over increase (yo).

3 Working each wrong-side row with yarn-over increases and knit-two-together decreases, and then knitting each right-side row creates a pattern of interlinked 'holes' and gives the lacy effect to this openwork stitch.

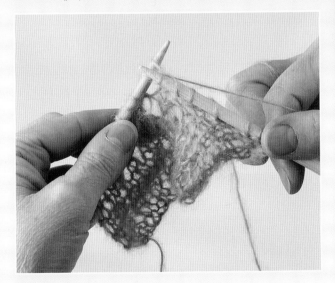

2 Knit the next two stitches together to decrease a stitch. Continue with this yarn-over, knit-two-together sequence to the last six stitches. Knit two and then work the broken rib edge.

Skinny Fair Isle scarf

Combine Fair Isle techniques with straightforward stocking/ stockinette stitch for this stylish scarf.

Worked in stocking/stockinette stitch with moss/seed stitch edgings, this fine wool scarf has panels of distinctive graphic Fair Isle patterns at each end.

The Yarn

Debbie Bliss Rialto 4-ply is 100% extra fine merino wool. It gives good stitch definition for stocking/stockinette stitch fabrics and can be machine washed at a low temperature. There are plenty of beautiful contemporary shades to choose from for original colour work.

GETTING STARTED

 Fair Isle techniques for patterned panels will take some practice

Size:
Scarf is 20cm wide x 148.5cm long (8in x 58½in)

How much yarn:
3 x 50g (2oz) balls of Debbie Bliss Rialto 4-ply, approx 180m (197 yards) per ball, in main colour A
1 ball in each of four contrast colours B, C, D and E

Needles:
Pair of 3.25mm (no. 10/US 3) knitting needles

Tension/gauge:
28 sts and 36 rows measure 10cm (4in) square over st st on 3.25mm (no. 10/US 3) needles
IT IS ESSENTIAL TO WORK TO THE STATED TENSION/GAUGE TO ACHIEVE SUCCESS

What you have to do:
Work borders in moss/seed stitch and main fabric in stocking/stockinette stitch. At each end of scarf work Fair Isle pattern panel from a chart. Use Fair Isle techniques of stranding yarn not in use loosely across wrong side of work.

Abbreviations:

beg = beginning
cm = centimetre(s)
cont = continue
foll = follows;
k = knit
p = purl;
patt = pattern
rep = repeat
RS = right side
st(s) = stitch(es)
st st = stocking/
stockinette stitch
WS = wrong side

 # Instructions

SCARF:
With B, cast on 57 sts.
1st row: K1, (p1, k1) to end.
Rep this row to form moss/seed st. Work
3 more rows in moss/seed st.
Change to A and cont as foll:
1st row: (RS) Moss/seed st 3, k to last 3
sts, moss/seed st 3.
2nd row: Moss/seed st 3, p to last 3 sts,
moss/seed st 3.
Cont in st st with 3 sts in moss/seed st at
each end as set, work 2 more rows in A,
4 rows in B and 4 rows in A.
Place chart 1:
Next row: (RS) Moss/seed st 3 A, k
across 51 sts of chart 1 stranding yarn
not in use loosely across WS of work,
moss/seed st 3 A.
Next row: Moss/seed st 3 A, p across
51 sts of 1st row of chart 1, moss/seed
st 3 A.
Keeping edge sts correct, cont in st st
and Fair Isle patt from chart 1 until

25 rows have been completed.
Now cont in A only until work measures
137cm (54in) from beg, ending with a
WS row.
Place chart 2:
Next row: (RS) Moss/seed st 3 A,
k across 51 sts of 1st row of chart 2
stranding yarn not in use loosely across
WS of work, moss/seed st 3 A.
Next row: Moss/seed st 3 A, p across
51 sts of 2nd row of chart 2, moss/seed
st 3 A.
Keeping edge sts correct, cont in st st
and Fair Isle patt from chart 2 until 25
rows have been completed.
Cont in A only, work 3 rows, then 4
rows in B and 4 rows in A. Cut off A.
With B, work 4 rows in moss/seed st.
Cast/bind off in moss/seed st.

Making up

Sew in all ends. Press lightly according to directions on ball band.

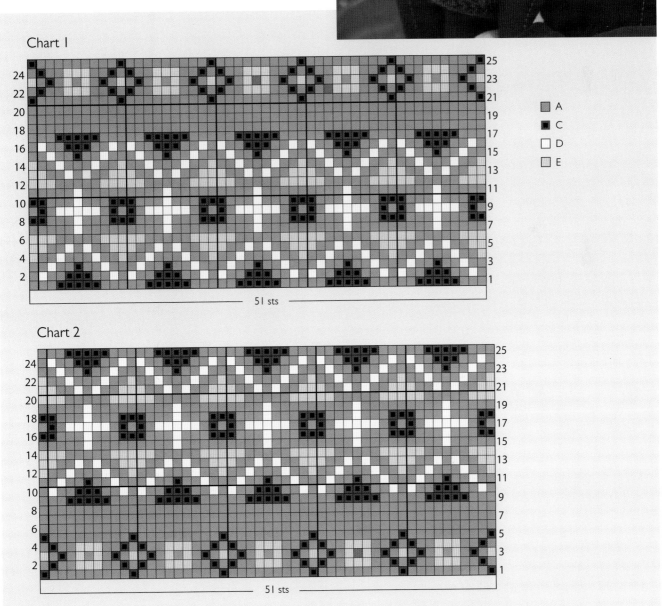

Chart 1

Chart 2

A
C
D
E

51 sts

Soft cable sweater

This sweater has classic elegant lines; knitted in soft angora, it's a romantic masterpiece.

Cuddle up in this timeless sweater with set-in sleeves and round neck. Knitted in the softest angora blend, it features a simple, yet stylish cable panel on the front.

GETTING STARTED

 The cable panel may seem daunting, but it is formed with the simplest rope cables

Size:

To fit bust: 76–81[86–91:97–102]cm/30–32[34–36:38–40]in

Actual size: 87[95:103.5]cm/34¼[37½:40¾]in

Length: 50[53:56]cm/19¾[21:22]in

Sleeve seam: 45[46:47]cm/17¾[18:18½]in

Note: Figures in square brackets [ ] refer to larger sizes; where there is only one set of figures, it applies to all sizes

How much yarn:

4[5:6] x 50g (2oz) balls of Orkney Angora 'St Magnus' 50/50 DK, approx 200m (219 yards) per ball

Needles:

Pair of 3.75mm (no. 9/US 5) knitting needles

Pair of 4.5mm (no. 7/US 7) knitting needles

Cable needle

Additional items:

Two stitch holders

Tension/gauge:

22 sts and 28 rows measure 10cm (4in) square over st st worked on 4.5mm (no. 7/US 7) needles. Cable panel (49 sts) measures 14cm (5½in) across

IT IS ESSENTIAL TO WORK TO THE STATED TENSION/ GAUGE TO ACHIEVE SUCCESS

What you have to do:

Work welt in single (k1, p1) rib. Work back in stocking/ stockinette stitch. Work front in stocking/stockinette stitch with central cable pattern panel. Make simple rope cables. Work simple decreases and increases to shape sweater. Pick up stitches around neckline to work neckband in single rib.

The Yarn

Orkney Angora 'St Magnus' 50/50 DK is a blend of unbrushed, finest grade angora and best-quality lambswool. This soft yarn (it becomes slightly fluffy with handling, washing and wearing) is extremely versatile for accessories and garments, and is available in 35 superb shades.

Instructions

Abbreviations:

alt = alternate;
beg = beginning;
cm = centimetre(s);
cont = continue;
C6B = slip next 3 sts on to cable needle and leave at back of work, k3, then k3 sts from cable needle;
C6F = slip next 3 sts on to cable needle and leave at front of work, k3, then k 3 sts from cable needle;
dec = decrease(ing);
foll = follow(s)(ing);
inc = increase(ing);
k = knit;
kfb = knit into front and back of stitch; **p** = purl;
patt = pattern;
pfb = purl into front and back of stitch;
psso = pass slipped stitch over;
rem = remaining;
rep = repeat;
RS = right side; **sl** = slip;
st(s) = stitch(es);
st st = stocking/stockinette stitch;
tbl = through back of loops; **tog** = together;
WS = wrong side

BACK:

With 3.75mm (no. 9/US 5) needles cast on 95[105:115] sts.

1st row: (RS) K1, *p1, k1, rep from * to end.

2nd row: P1, *k1, p1, rep from * to end. Rep these 2 rows twice more.

Change to 4.5mm (no. 7/US 7) needles. Beg with a k row, work 86[90:94] rows in st st, ending with a p row.

Shape armholes:

Cast/bind off 3[4:5] sts at beg of next 2 rows.

Next row: K1, sl 1, k1, psso, k to last 3 sts, k2tog, k1.

Next row: P to end.

Rep last 2 rows 4[5:6] times more, then work first of them again. 77[83:89] sts. Work 39[41:43] rows straight, ending with a p row.

Shape shoulders:

Cast/bind off 8[9:10] sts at beg of next 4 rows. Cut off yarn. Leave rem 45[47:49] sts on a holder.

FRONT:

With 3.75mm (no. 9/US 5) needles cast on 103[111:119] sts. Rib 5 rows as given for Back.

Inc row: (WS) Rib 33[37:41], (kfb, rib 2, pfb, rib 2, kfb, rib 3) 3 times, kfb, rib 2, pfb, rib 2, kfb, rib 33[37:41]. 115[123:131] sts. Change to 4.5mm (no. 7) needles. Work in

cable panel patt as foll:

1st row: (RS) K33[37:41], (p2, k6, p2, k3) 3 times, p2, k6, p2, k33[37:41].

2nd row: P33[37:41], (k2, p6, k2, p3) 3 times, k2, p6, k2, p33[37:41].

3rd–6th rows: Rep 1st and 2nd rows twice.

7th row: K33[37:41], (p2, C6B, p2, k3) twice, p2, C6F, p2, k3, p2, C6F, p2, k33[37:41].

8th row: As 2nd row.

The last 8 rows form cable panel patt. Patt 78[82:86] rows more, ending with a 6th[2nd:6th] patt row.

Shape armholes:

Cast/bind off 3[4:5] sts at beg of next 2 rows.

Next row: K1, sl 1, k1, psso, patt to last 3 sts, k2tog, k1.

Next row: Patt to end.

Rep last 2 rows 4[5:6] times more, then work first of them again. 97[101:105] sts. Patt 31[33:35] rows straight, ending with a 2nd patt row.

Shape neck:

Next row: (RS) K21[23:25], k2tog, k1, turn and complete this side of neck first.

Next row: P1, p2tog, p to end.

Cont to dec 1 st at neck edge in this way on next 6 rows. 16[18:20] sts.

Shape shoulder:

Cast/bind off 8[9:10] sts at beg of next row. Work 1 row.

Cast/bind off rem 8[9:10] sts.

With RS of work facing, sl centre 49 sts on to a holder, rejoin yarn to next st, k1, sl 1, k1, psso, k to end.

Next row: P to last 3 sts, p2tog tbl, p1.

Complete as first side of neck, reversing shaping as shown and working 1 row straight before shaping shoulder.

SLEEVES: (Make 2)

With 3.75mm (no. 9/US 5) needles cast on 43[47:51] sts. Rib 6 rows as given for Back. Change to 4.5mm (no. 7/US 7) needles. Beg with a k row, cont in st st, inc 1 st at each end of next and every foll 8th row to 71[77:83] sts. Work 15[11:5] rows straight, ending with a p row.

Shape sleeve top:

Cast/bind off 3[4:5] sts at beg of next 2 rows. Dec 1 st at each end of next and every foll alt row to 39[41:43] sts, then at each end of every row to 21[23:25] sts. Cast/bind off 3 sts at beg of next 4 rows. Cast/bind off rem 9[11:13] sts.

NECKBAND:

Join right shoulder seam.

With 3.75mm (no. 9/US 5) needles and RS of work facing, pick up and k9 sts down left front neck, k across sts on holder as foll: (p2tog, k2, k2tog, k2, p2tog, k3) 3 times, p2tog, k2, k2tog, k2, p2tog, pick up and k9 sts up right front neck, k across 45[47:49] back neck sts. 100[102:104] sts.

Work 5 rows in k1, p1 rib. Cast/bind off in rib.

 Making up

Do not press. Join left shoulder and neckband seam. Sew in sleeves. Join side and sleeve seams.

Boyfriend sweater

You could knit this for your boyfriend, but then there's the hassle of borrowing it back — so why not just treat yourself?

Warm and cuddly in soft Aran (fisherman) yarn, this V-neck sweater is generously sized for relaxed and casual weekend wear.

GETTING STARTED

Some increasing and decreasing, but mostly in straightforward stocking/stockinette stitch

Size:

To fit bust: *86–81[86–91:97–102]cm/ 32–34[34–36:38–40]in*

Actual size: *109[120:131]cm/43[47¼:51½]in*

Length from shoulder: *65[68.5:72]cm/25½[27:28½]in*

Sleeve seam: *47[48.5:50]cm/18½[19:19¾]in*

Note: *Figures in square brackets [ ] refer to larger sizes; where there is only one set of figures, it applies to all sizes*

How much yarn:

15[16:17] x 50g (2oz) balls of Debbie Bliss Rialto Aran, approx 80m (87 yards) per ball

Needles:

Pair of 4.5mm (no. 7/US 7) knitting needles
Pair of 5mm (no. 6/US 8) knitting needles

Tension/gauge:

18 sts and 24 rows measure 10cm (4in) square over st st on 5mm (no. 6/US 8) needles

What you have to do:

Work in stocking/stockinette stitch. Leave stitches on a spare needle or stitch holder to work each side of neck separately. Decrease stitches to shape V-neck. Increase stitches to shape sleeves.

The Yarn

With 55% merino wool, Debbie Bliss Rialto Aran is the perfect yarn to achieve stocking/ stockinette stitch that is smooth and even and to create a fabric that feels soft and luxurious. There is a colour palette of fabulous shades, including jewel brights as well as neutrals and pastels, to suit every taste.

Abbreviations:

alt = alternate;
beg = beginning;
cont = continue;
dec = decrease;
foll = following;
inc = increase(ing);
k = knit; **p** = purl;
rem = remain(ing);
RS = right side;
st(s) = stitch(es);
st st = stocking/
stockinette stitch;
tbl = through back
of loops;
k2tog = knit 2 stitches
together

Instructions

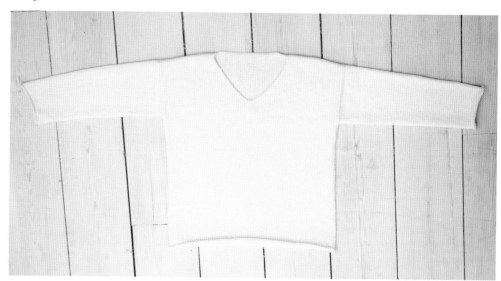

BACK:

With 4.5mm (no. 7/US 7) needles cast on 100[110:120] sts. Beg with a k row, work 4 rows in st st. Change to 5mm (no. 6/US 8) needles.* Work another 152[160:168] rows in st st, ending with a p row.

Shape shoulders:

Cast/bind off 11[12:13] sts at beg of next 6 rows. Cast/bind off rem 34[38:42] sts.

FRONT:

Work as Back to *. Work another 118[122:126] rows in st st, ending with a p row.

Shape neck:

Next row: K47[52:57], k2tog, k1, turn and leave rem sts on a spare needle or stitch holder.

Cont on these 49[54:59] sts for left front. P 1 row.

Dec 1 st at neck edge on next and every foll alt row to 33[36:39] sts, ending with a p row.

Shape shoulder:

Cast/bind off 11[12:13] sts at beg of next and foll alt row. Work 1 row. Cast/bind off rem 11[12:13] sts.

With RS of work facing, rejoin yarn to sts on spare needle or stitch holder, k1, k2tog tbl, k to end. Work to match first side of neck, reversing shapings.

Sleeves: (Make 2)

With 4.5mm (no. 7/US 7) needles cast on 52[58:64] sts. Beg with a k row, work 4 rows in st st. Change to 5mm (no. 6/US 8) needles. Cont in st st, inc 1 st at each end of next and every foll 12th row until there are 70[76:82] sts. Work 11[15:19] rows straight, ending with a p row. Cast/bind off.

Making up

Press the pieces carefully using a warm iron over a clean cloth. Do not press the lower edges of the back, front and sleeves as these should be allowed to roll up.

Joining the seams:

Using backstitch, join shoulder seams. Mark position of underarms about 19[21:23]cm/7½[8¼:9]in down from shoulders on back and front. Matching the centre of top edges of sleeves to shoulder seams, sew in sleeves between markers. Join side and sleeve seams.

HOW TO
USE A STITCH HOLDER

Stitch holders are a useful tool for the knitter and are constructed like a giant safety pin. They come in a variety of lengths and you can select the holder according to the number of stitches that you need to store on it.

3 Open the stitch holder and slide the stitches, one by one, onto the left-hand needle. Again, be careful not to twist the stitches.

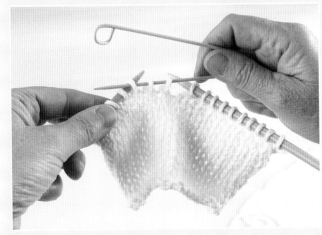

1 Knit to the instructed point in the row. Open the stitch holder and slide the needle end under each stitch on the left-hand needle. Keeping the stitches the right way around, take them onto the holder. Clip the holder shut.

4 Join in the yarn on the right-hand edge and knit the remaining stitches for the instructed length.

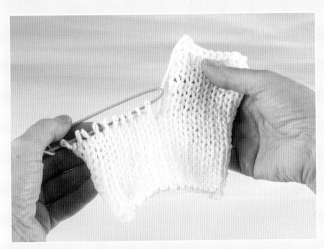

2 Continue knitting the stitches remaining on the right-hand needle for the instructed length and then cast/bind off.

5 This is the effect created by working two sets of stitches separately and in this pattern it is used to create the v-neck.

Soft yoga top

Chill out in this soft, loose, hooded top that is easy to knit and relaxing to wear.

Worked in stocking/stockinette stitch with garter-stitch edgings, this simple top combines style with comfort.

GETTING STARTED

Simple shaping and pattern stitches but care is needed to pick up stitches evenly around the neck

Size:

To fit bust: *81–86[86–91:97–102]cm/ 32–34[34–36:38–40]in*

Actual size: *97.5[104:113]cm/38½[41:44½]in*

Length: *62[64:66]cm/23¾[24½:25¼]in*

Sleeve seam: *40cm (15¾in)*

Note: *Figures in square brackets [ ] refer to larger sizes; where there is only one set of figures, it applies to all sizes*

How much yarn:

14[15:16] x 50g (2oz) balls of Debbie Bliss Cashmerino Aran, approx 90m (98 yards) per ball

Needles:

Pair of 5mm (no. 6/US 8) knitting needles
5mm (no. 6/US 8) circular knitting needle

Additional items:

Stitch holder, stitch marker

Tension/gauge:

18 sts and 24 rows measure 10cm (4in) square over st st on 5mm (no. 6/US 8) needles
IT IS ESSENTIAL TO WORK TO THE STATED TENSION/GAUGE TO ACHIEVE SUCCESS

What you have to do:

Work in stocking/stockinette stitch with garter-stitch edge on side opening, neck opening and hood edges. Work decorative paired shapings on the raglan armholes. Pick up stitches around the neck to work the hood.

The Yarn

Containing a mixture of 55% merino wool with 33% microfibre and 12% cashmere, Debbie Bliss Cashmerino Aran is a luxurious yarn with a slight sheen. Its silky-soft handle is perfect for warmth and comfort, and there is a wide colour palette to choose from, with plenty of subtle fashion shades.

Instructions

Abbreviations:
alt = alternate;
beg = beginning;
cm = centimetre(s);
cont = continue;
dec = decrease(ing);
foll = follow(s)(ing);
inc = increase(ing);
k = knit;
m1 = make 1 stitch by picking up horizontal loop between needles and working into back of it;
p = purl; **patt** = pattern;
rem = remain(ing);
rep = repeat;
RS = right side;
st(s) = stitch(es);
st st = stocking/stockinette stitch;
tbl = through back of loops; **tog** = together;
WS = wrong side

BACK:
With 5mm (no. 6/US 8) needles cast on 88[94:102] sts. K3 rows.
Next row: (RS) K to end.
Next row: K3, p to last 3 sts, k3.
Rep last 2 rows until Back measures 9cm (3½in), ending with a WS row.
Beg with a k row, cont in st st until Back measures 37cm (14½in) from beg, ending with a WS row.
Shape raglan armholes:
Cast/bind off 4 sts at beg of next 2 rows. 80[86:94] sts.
3rd row: K2, k2tog, k to last 4 sts, k2tog tbl, k2.
4th row: P to end.
5th row: K to end.
6th row: P to end.
Rep 3rd–6th rows until 74[78:84] sts rem, then 3rd and 4th rows only until 28[32:36] sts rem. Cast/bind off.

FRONT:
Work as given for Back until 58[64:70] sts rem when shaping raglan armholes, ending with a WS row.
Divide for neck opening:
Next row: K2, k2tog, k25[28:31], turn and leave rem sts on a spare needle. 28[31:34] sts.

Complete this side of neck first.
Next row: K3, p to end.
Next row: K2, k2tog, k to end.
Rep last 2 rows until 14[16:18] sts rem, ending with a WS row. Cut off yarn and leave sts on a holder.
With RS of work facing, rejoin yarn to rem sts, k to last 4 sts, k2tog tbl, k2.
Next row: P to last 3 sts, k3.
Complete to match first side of neck, ending with a WS row, but do not cut off yarn (this will be used for working the hood).

SLEEVES: (Make 2)
With 5mm (no. 6/US 8) needles cast on 46[50:56] sts. K 3 rows. Beg with a k row, cont in st st, inc one st (2 sts in from edge) at each end of 5th and every foll 6th row until there are 68[72:78] sts. Inc one st at each end of every foll 8th row twice. 72[76:82] sts. Work straight until Sleeve measures 40cm (15¾in) from beg, ending with a WS row.
Shape top:
Cast/bind off 4 sts at beg of next 2 rows. 64[68:74] sts. Rep 3rd–6th rows of Back raglan shaping until 56[60:66] sts rem, then rep 3rd and 4th rows only until 14 sts rem, ending with a WS row. Cast/bind off.

Making up

PRESSING:

Following instructions given on ball band, press very lightly on WS, avoiding garter-stitch edges.

Join raglan seams, using backstitch.

HOOD:

With 5mm (no. 6/US 8) circular needle and RS of work facing, return to ball of yarn attached at right front neck and work as foll: k14[16:18] sts from right front neck, pick up and k14 sts from right sleeve, 27[31:35] sts from back neck, 14 sts from left sleeve, then k across 14[16:18] sts from left front neck. 83[91:99] sts. Place a marker on st at centre back neck.

Next row: K3, p to last 3 sts, k3.

Work 2 more rows in st st and edge patt as set.

Shape back of hood:

Increase row: (RS) K to marked st, m1, k marked st, m1, k to end. Work 3 more rows in st st and edge patt as set.

Rep last 4 rows 3 times more, then work inc row again. 93[101:109] sts. Work straight in patt until hood measures 28[29:30]cm/11[11½:11¾]in, ending with a WS row.

Shape top:

Next row: K to within 2 sts of marked st, k2tog, k marked st, k2tog tbl, k to end.

Work 3 rows in st st and patt as set.

Next row: K to within 2 sts of marked st, k2tog, k marked st, k2tog tbl, k to end.

Cont to dec in this way on every foll alt row to 83[91:99] sts, ending with a RS row. Cast/bind off.

Join hood seam. Join sleeve seams and side seams to top of side opening.

Wrap top

This ballerina-style top has been adapted and refined to make a great-looking addition to your wardrobe.

Look elegant in this classic crossover top with set-in sleeves that fastens around the waist with ties. Worked in stocking/stockinette stitch with moss/seed stitch borders, it will be a perennial favourite in your wardrobe.

GETTING STARTED

Easy to knit in stocking/stockinette stitch but pay attention to simultaneous shaping of front and side edges on the fronts

Size:

To fit bust: 81–86[91–97:102–107]cm/32–34[36–38:40–42]in

Actual size: 88[99:110]cm/34½in[39:43½]in

Length: 53[56:59]cm/21[22:23¼]in

Sleeve seam: 44[45:47]cm/17½[17¾:18½]in

Note: Figures in square brackets [ ] refer to larger sizes; where there is only one set of figures, it applies to all sizes

How much yarn:

10[11:11] x 50g (2oz) balls of Sublime Extra Fine Merino Wool DK, approx 116m (127 yards) per ball

Needles:

Pair of 3.25mm (no. 10/US 3) knitting needles
Pair of 4mm (no. 8/US 6) knitting needles

Tension/gauge:

22 sts and 28 rows measure 10cm (4in) square over st st on 4mm (no. 8/US 6) needles
IT IS ESSENTIAL TO WORK TO THE STATED TENSION/ GAUGE TO ACHIEVE SUCCESS

What you have to do:

Work main fabric in stocking/stockinette stitch with integrated moss/seed stitch-borders. Work simple shaping for side, armhole and front edges. Make separate ties and sew on afterwards.

The Yarn

Sublime Extra Fine Merino Wool DK is 100% natural as its name implies. Spun from the finest quality of merino wool, it is a luxuriously smooth yarn giving clear stitch definition. It comes in a colour palette of 20 beautiful subtle shades.

Instructions

Abbreviations:

alt = alternate;
beg = beginning;
cm = centimetre(s);
cont = continue;
dec = decrease;
foll = follow(s)(ing);
inc = increase; **k** = knit;
m1 = make one stitch by picking up horizontal strand lying between needles and working into back of it;
p = purl;
psso = pass slipped stitch over;
rem = remaining;
rep = repeat;
RS = right side; **sl** = slip;
st(s) = stitch(es);
st st = stocking/ stockinette stitch;
tbl = through back of loops;
tog = together;
WS = wrong side

BACK:

With 3.25mm (no. 10/US 3) needles cast on 99[111:123] sts.
1st row: K1, (p1, k1) to end.
Rep this row to form moss/seed st. Work 5 rows more.
Change to 4mm (no. 8/US 6) needles.
Next row: K3, sl 1, k1, psso, k to last 5 sts, k2tog, k3.
Beg with a p row, work 5 rows in st st. Rep last 6 rows 4[5:5] times more, then work dec row again. 87[97:109] sts. Beg with a p row, work 5[3:7] rows straight. Insert markers at each end of last row to indicate waistline.
Next row: K3, m1, k to last 3 sts, m1, k3. Work 5[5:7] rows in st st. Rep last 6[6:8] rows 4[5:5] times more, then work inc row again. 99[111:123] sts. Work 25[21:11] rows straight, ending with a p row.

Shape armholes:

Cast/bind off 6[7:8] sts at beg of next 2 rows. 87[97:107] sts. Dec 1 st at each end of next and foll 8[10:12] alt rows. 69[75:81] sts. Work 35[33:31] rows straight, ending with a p row.

Shape shoulders:

Cast/bind off 16[18:19] sts at beg of next 2 rows.
Change to 3.25mm (no. 10/US 3) needles. Work 4 rows in moss/seed st on rem 37[39:43] sts. Cast/bind off firmly in moss/seed st.

LEFT FRONT:

With 3.25mm (no. 10/US 3) needles cast on 91[103:115] sts. Work 6 rows in moss/seed st.
Change to 4mm (no. 8/US 6) needles.
Next row: K3, sl 1, k1, psso, k to last 3 sts, work 3 sts in moss/seed st for front border.
Next row: Work 3 sts in moss/seed st, p to end.
Work 4 rows straight, keeping border as set. Rep last 6 rows 4[5:5] times more, then work dec row again. 85[96:108] sts. Work 5[3:7] rows straight, ending on WS. Insert markers at each end of last row to indicate waistline.
Next row: K3, m1, k to last 5 sts, k2tog, work 3 sts in moss/seed st.
Next row: Work 3 sts in moss/seed st, p2tog, p to end.
Work 4[4:6] rows more, keeping side edge straight and dec 1 st at front edge on every row as set. Rep last 6[6:8] rows 4[5:5] times more, then work 1st row again. 60[66:66] sts. Work 25[21:11] rows, keeping side edge straight and dec 1 st at front edge on every RS row. 48[56:61] sts.

Shape armhole:

Next row: Cast/bind off 6[7:8] sts, k to last 5 sts, k2tog, work 3 sts in moss/seed st.

Cont to dec as set at front edge, AT SAME TIME dec 1 st at armhole edge on every RS row until 23[26:26] sts rem. Keeping armhole edge straight, cont to dec at front edge only on every foll 4th row until 19[21:22] sts rem. Work 19[13:15] rows straight, ending with a WS row. Cast/bind off.

RIGHT FRONT:

With 3.25mm (no. 10/US 3) needles cast on 91[103:115] sts. Work 6 rows in moss/seed st. Change to 4mm (no. 8/US 6) needles.

Next row: Work 3 sts in moss/seed st, k to last 5 sts, k2tog, k3.

Next row: P to last 3 sts, work 3 sts in moss/seed st. Work 4 rows straight, keeping border as set. Rep last 6 rows 4[5:5] times more, then work dec row again. 85[96:108] sts. Work 5[3:7] rows straight, ending on WS. Insert markers at each end of last row to indicate waistline.

Next row: Work 3 sts in moss/seed st, sl 1, k1, psso, k to last 3 sts, m1, k3.

Next row: P to last 5 sts, p2tog tbl, work 3 sts in moss/seed st.

Work as given for Left front from * to *.

Next row: Work 3 sts in moss/seed st, sl 1, k1, psso, k to end.

Shape armhole:

Next row: Cast/bind off 6[7:8] sts, p to last 3 sts, work 3 sts in moss/seed st.

Complete as given for Left front, noting that 1 more row will be worked before casting/binding off for shoulder.

SLEEVES: (Make 2)

With 3.25mm (no. 10/US 3) needles cast on 47[49:53] sts. Work 6 rows moss/seed st.

Change to 4mm (no. 8/US 6) needles.

Next row: K3, m1, k to last 3 sts, m1, k3.

Beg with a p row, work 9 rows in st st. Rep last 10 rows 10[11:11] times more, then work inc row again. 71[75:79] sts. Work 9[3:7] rows straight, ending with a p row.

Shape top:

Cast/bind off 6[7:8] sts at beg of next 2 rows. Dec 1 st at each end of next row and foll 12[14:16] alt rows, then on every row until 15[17:19] sts rem. Cast/bind off.

TIES: (Make 2)

With 3.25mm (no. 10/US 3) needles cast on 5 sts. Work in moss st until tie measures 56cm (22in). Cast/bind off in moss/seed st.

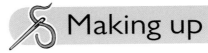

Making up

Join shoulder and neck edging seams. Sew in sleeves. Join sleeve and side seams, leaving a 2cm (¾in) gap at waistline on right side seam for tie. Sew ties to front edges at waistline.

Twist wrap

This clever twist top uses ribbon yarn to great effect to create an elegant fabric with a metallic sheen.

Glamorous enough for any occasion, this wrap with a single twist at the front will not fall off your shoulders. It is knitted in two luxury yarns and a slip-stitch pattern to create a fabulous textured fabric.

The Yarn

Louisa Harding Grace is a blend of 50% silk and 50% merino wool in a double knitting (light worsted) weight. It has a slight pearlised sheen and is available in a small range of colours. Louisa Harding Sari Ribbon is an exotic ribbon yarn containing 90% nylon and 10% metallic. There is a range of variegated colours, each containing a central strip of metallic threads.

GETTING STARTED

 Wrap is a straight piece of fabric but pattern will need some practice first

Size:
Wrap is approximately 38cm wide x 90[96:100]cm long (15in x 35½[37¾:39½]in)

How much yarn:
4 x 50g (2oz) balls of Louisa Harding Grace, approx 100m (100 yards) per ball, in colour A
4 x 100g (3½oz) hanks of Louisa Harding Sari Ribbon, approx 120m (131) yards per hank, in colour B

Needles:
Pair of 5mm (no. 6/US 8) knitting needles
Cable needle

Additional items:
Matching sewing thread and needle

Tension/gauge:
21 sts and 25 rows measure 10cm (4in) square over patt on 5mm (no. 6/US 8) needles
IT IS ESSENTIAL TO WORK TO THE STATED TENSION/GAUGE TO ACHIEVE SUCCESS

What you have to do:
Work a slip-stitch and cable pattern using two yarns and colours. Knit a garter-stitch section in the centre. Work pattern in reverse for second half. Make a single twist in garter-stitch section before sewing ends of wrap together.

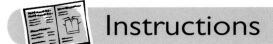 Instructions

WRAP: (Worked in one piece)
With 5mm (no. 6/US 8) needles and A, cast on 80 sts.
Foundation row: (RS) With B, k to end.
Now cont in patt as foll:
1st row: (WS) With B, p1, pw2, p4, *(pw2) twice, p4, rep from * to last 2 sts, pw2, p1.
2nd row: With A, k1, sl 1p allowing extra loop to fall off needle, k4, *sl 2p allowing extra loops to fall off needle, k4, rep from * to last 2 sts, sl 1p allowing extra loop to fall off needle, k1.
3rd row: With A, p1, sl 1p, p4, *sl 2p, p4, rep from * to last 2 sts, sl 1p, p1.
4th row: With A, k1, sl 1p, k4, *sl 2p, k4, rep from * to last 2 sts, sl 1p, k1.
5th row: As 3rd row.
6th row: With B, k1, *c3f, c3b, rep from * to last st, k1.
These 6 rows form patt. Cont in patt until work measures 45[48:50]cm/17¾[19:19¾]in, ending with 6th row. With B only, p 1 row.
Dec row: With A, k3, k2tog, *k4, k2tog, rep from * to last 3 sts, k3. 67 sts. Now cont in g st for 15cm (6in), ending on a WS row.
Inc row: With A, k3, k into front and back of next st,

Abbreviations:

beg = beginning;

cm = centimetre(s);

cont = continue;

c3b = slip next 2 sts on to cable needle and leave at back of work, k1, then k2 from cable needle;

c3f = slip next st on to cable needle and leave at front of work, k2, then k1 from cable needle;

dec = decrease;

foll = follows;

g st = garter stitch (every row knit);

k = knit; **p** = purl;

patt = pattern;

pw2 = purl next stitch wrapping yarn twice around needle;

rep = repeat;

RS = right side;

sl 1(2)p = slip one(two) stitch(es) purlwise;

st(s) = stitch(es);

tog = together;

WS = wrong side;

Note: To join in a new ball of Sari Ribbon, overlap the two ends by 1.5cm (½in) and oversew together securely using matching sewing thread. Cont in patt, knitting the join in when you come to it.

*k4, k into front and back of next st, rep from * to last 3 sts, k3. 80 sts.

Now work patt in reverse as foll:

Next row: (RS) With B, k to end.

Beg with 1st row, cont in patt to match first side before g st panel, ending with 6th row. With B, p 1 row. With A, cast/bind off.

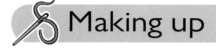

Making up

Make a single twist in the centre of the wrap, through g st panel. Now join cast-on and cast/bound-off edges, with RS of pattern uppermost on both edges.

To finish off raw ends of ribbon yarn, thread through a few stitches on WS. Trim to 1.5cm (½in), fold under raw edge and oversew securely in place using a matching sewing thread.

HOW TO
WORK THE SLIP STITCH AND CABLE PATTERN

The pattern is worked with yarn (A) and ribbon yarn (B).

1 Cast on with yarn A and then work a foundation row of knit stitches with yarn B. Start the first row of the pattern with yarn B. Purl one, then purl the

next stitch wrapping the yarn twice around the needle (abbreviated as pw2 and shown above), purl four. Repeat a sequence of pw2 twice, and purl four to the last two stitches, pw2 and purl one.

2 Pick up yarn A for the second row. Begin with knit one, then slip one purlwise, allowing the extra loop to fall off the left-hand needle

(sl 1p), and knit four. Repeat a sequence of slipping two stitches purlwise, allowing the extra loops to fall off the needle (sl 2p), and knit four to the last two stitches. Slip one purlwise, allowing the extra loop to fall off the needle (sl 1p), and knit one.

3 Still with yarn A, begin the third row with purl one, slip one purlwise and purl four. Repeat a sequence of slip two

purlwise and purl four to the last two stitches. Slip one purlwise and purl one.

4 For the fourth row with yarn A, knit one, slip one purlwise and knit four. Repeat a sequence of slip two

purlwise and knit four to the last two stitches, slip one purlwise and knit one.

5 For the fifth row, still with yarn A, repeat the third row.

6 Change to yarn B for the sixth row. Begin with knit one, then slip the next stitch onto a cable needle and leave at the front of the work. Knit the next two stitches and then knit the

stitch on the cable needle (c3f). Slip the next two stitches onto the cable needle and leave at the back of the work. Knit one and then knit the two stitches from the cable needle (c3b). Repeat a sequence of c3f and c3b to the last stitch, knit one.

7 These six rows form the pattern and are repeated as instructed.

Ruffle and lace sweater

With a lean body and ruffles around the neck and bottom, this stunning sweater looks almost like a pierrot costume.

Intricate and sophisticated, this cotton sweater with its narrow vertical lace panels fits neatly over the body and flares out around the hemline and cuffs, ending in elaborate lace ruffles like the neck.

The Yarn

Rowan Handknit Cotton is 100% cotton. It is soft to handle and machine washable. There is a range of interesting colours to choose from including neutrals, pastels and some deep fashion shades.

GETTING STARTED

Fairly easy main fabric but dealing with large number of stitches for ruffle edges can be tricky

Size:

To fit bust: 81–86[91–97:102–107]cm/32–34[36–38:40–42]in

Actual size: 99[111:124]cm/39[43¾:48¾]in

Length: 68[70:72]cm/26¾[27½:28¼]in

Sleeve seam: 46cm (18in)

Note: Figures in square brackets [ ] refer to larger sizes; where there is only one set of figures, it applies to all sizes

How much yarn:

16[19:22] x 50g (2oz) balls of Rowan Handknit Cotton, approx 85m (92 yards) per ball

Needles:

Pair of 4mm (no. 8/US 6) knitting needles

4mm (no. 8/US 6) circular knitting needle, 80cm (32in) long

Additional items:

2.75mm (no. 12/US C) crochet hook

Tension/gauge:

19 sts and 30 rows measure 10cm (4in) square over st st and lace patt on 4mm (no. 8/US 6) needles

IT IS ESSENTIAL TO WORK TO THE STATED TENSION/GAUGE TO ACHIEVE SUCCESS

What you have to do:

Cast on stitches for shoulders and neck edge and work downwards. Work in stocking/stockinette stitch with lacy panels. Work simple shaping for armholes and side edges. Work ruffles at lower edges in rows on circular needle to cope with large number of stitches. Make a picot cast/bound-off edge using crochet hook. Pick up stitches around neckline. Work ruffle collar in rounds on circular needle.

Instructions

Abbreviations:

alt = alternate; **cont** = continue; **dec** = decrease(ing); **foll** = following; **inc** = increase(ing); **k** = knit; **kfb** = knit into front and back of stitch; **patt** = pattern; **p** = purl; **pfb** = purl into front and back of stitch; **psso** = pass slipped stitch over; **rep** = repeat; **RS** = right side; **sl** = slip; **st(s)** = stitch(es); **st st** = stocking/stockinette stitch; **tog** = together; **WS** = wrong side; **yo** = yarn over needle to make a stitch

Note: The sweater is worked from the top down so the ruffle edging grows out of the lines of lace. If necessary, use the circular needle to contain the amount of stitches when working the lower edge ruffles as well as for working the collar ruffle in the round.

BACK:

Cast on 70[80:90] sts.

1st row: (RS) K6[4:2], (yo, p2tog, k5) 8[10:12] times, yo, p2tog, k6[4:2].

2nd row: P6[4:2], (yo, p2tog, p5) 8[10:12] times, yo, p2tog, p6[4:2]. These 2 rows form st st and lace patt. Cont in patt, work 42[46:50] more rows.

** Shape armholes:

Inc row: (RS) Kfb, patt to last 2 sts, kfb, k1. 72[82:92] sts. Taking incs into patt, inc in this way at each end of next 7[8:9] RS rows. 86[98:110] sts. Work 1 row.

Next row: (RS) Patt to end, do not turn, using left thumb loop on 4 sts. 90[102:114] sts.

Next row: Taking cast-on sts into patt, patt to end, do not turn, using left thumb loop on 4 sts. 94[106:118] sts. Cont in patt with 4[3:2] sts in st st at each side, work 28 rows.

Dec row: (RS) K1, k2tog, patt to last 3 sts, sl 1, k1, psso, k1. 92[104:116] sts. Cont in patt, dec in this way on foll 10th

row. 90[102:114] sts. Work 13 rows straight.
Inc row: (RS) Kfb, patt to last 2 sts, kfb, k1. 92[104:116] sts.
Taking incs into patt, inc in this way at each end of 8[9:10]
foll 6th rows. 108[122:136] sts. Work 29[23:17] rows
straight.

Ruffle edging:
1st row: (RS) K4, (p2tog, k5) 14[16:18] times, p2tog, k4.
93[105:117] sts.
2nd row: P3, (p2tog, yo, p4) 15[17:19] times. 93[105:117] sts.
3rd row: K4, (yo, k1, yo, k5) 14[16:18] times, yo, k1, yo,
k4. 123[139:155] sts.
4th and every WS row: P to end.
5th row: K4, (yo, k3, yo, k5) 14[16:18] times, yo, k3, yo,
k4. 153[173:193] sts.
7th row: K4, (yo, k5, yo, k5) 14[16:18] times, yo, k5, yo,
k4. 183[207:231] sts.
9th row: K4, (yo, k7, yo, k5) 14[16:18] times, yo, k7, yo,
k4. 213[241:269] sts.
11th row: K4, (yo, k9, yo, k5) 14[16:18] times, yo, k9, yo,
k4. 243[275:307] sts.
13th row: K to end.
Picot cast/bound-off row: (WS) Insert crochet hook in
first stitch, pull loop through and drop st off left needle,
* insert hook in next st, pull loop through st and loop on
hook, drop st off left needle, make 3 chain, slip stitch in 3rd
chain from hook, insert hook in next st, pull loop through
st and loop on needle, drop st off left needle, rep from * to
end. Fasten off.

FRONT:
Left side:
Cast on 12[17:22] sts.
1st row: (RS) *1st size* K4, yo, p2tog, k6, *2nd size* k4, yo,
p2tog, k5, yo, p2tog, k4, *3rd size* k4, (yo, p2tog, k5) twice,
yo, p2tog, k2.
2nd row: *1st size* P6, yo, p2tog, p4, *2nd size* p4, yo, p2tog,
p5, yo, p2tog, p4, *3rd size* p2, (yo, p2tog, p5) twice, yo,
p2tog, p4. These 2 rows form st st and lace patt. Work
8[12:16] more rows.
Shape neck:
1st inc row: (RS) Kfb, patt to end. 13[18:23] sts.
Taking incs into patt, inc in this way at beg of next 5 RS
rows. 18[23:28] sts.
2nd inc row: (WS) Patt to last 2 sts, pfb, p1.
19[24:29] sts. Inc in this way at neck edge on next 2 rows.
21[26:31] sts. Cut off yarn and leave sts on a holder.
Right side:
Cast on 12[17:22] sts.

1st row: (RS) *1st size* K6, yo, p2tog, k4, *2nd size* k4, yo,
p2tog, k5, yo, p2tog, k4, *3rd size* k2, (yo, p2tog, k5) twice,
yo, p2tog, k4.
2nd row: *1st size* P4, yo, p2tog, p6, *2nd size* p4, yo, p2tog,
p5, yo, p2tog, p4, *3rd size* p4, (yo, p2tog, p5) twice, yo,
p2tog, p2. These 2 rows form st st and lace patt. Work
8[12:16] more rows.
Shape neck:
1st inc row: (RS) Patt to last 2 sts, kfb, k1.
13[18:23] sts. Taking incs into patt, inc in this way at end of
next 5 RS rows. 18[23:28] sts.
2nd inc row: (WS) Pfb, end. 19[24:29] sts. Inc in this way
at neck edge on next 2 rows. 21[26:31] sts.
Joining row: (RS) Patt 21[26:31] sts of right side of neck,
using left thumb loop on 28 sts, patt 21[26:31] sts of left
side of neck. 70[80:90] sts. Cont in patt, work 19 rows
straight. Complete as given for Back from **.

SLEEVES:
Cast on 21[28:35] sts.
1st row: (RS) K6, (yo, p2tog, k5) 2[3:4] times, k1.
2nd row: P6, (yo, p2tog, p5) 2[3:4] times, p1.
These 2 rows set st st and lace patt.
Shape top:
3rd row: (RS) Kfb, patt to end, using left thumb, loop on 2
sts. 24[31:38] sts.
4th row: Pfb, (yo, p2tog, p5) 3[4:5] times, yo, p2tog, using
left thumb, loop on 2 sts. 27[34:41] sts.
5th row: Kfb, k1, (yo, p2tog, k5) 3[4:5] times, yo, p2tog, k2,
using left thumb, loop on 2 sts. 30[37:44] sts.
6th row: Pfb, p3, (yo, p2tog, p5) 3[4:5] times, yo, p2tog,
p3, using left thumb, loop on 2 sts. 33[40:47] sts.
7th row: Kfb, k4, (yo, p2tog, k5) 4[5:6] times, using left
thumb, loop on 2 sts. 36[43:50] sts.
8th row: Pfb, p6, (yo, p2tog, p5) 4[5:6] times, p1, using left
thumb, loop on 2 sts. 39[46:53] sts.

9th row: Kfb, (yo, p2tog, k5) 5[6:7] times, yo, k3. 41[48:55] sts.
10th row: P2, (yo, p2tog, p5) 5[6:7] times, yo, p2tog, p2.
11th row: Kfb, patt to last 2 sts, kfb, k1. 43[50:57] sts.
Cont in patt, inc in same way as 11th row on next 3 RS rows. 49[56:63] sts. Work 7 rows straight.
Shape armholes:
Inc in same way as 11th row on next row and 7[8:9] foll RS rows. 65[74:83] sts. Work 1 row.
Next row: (RS) Patt to end, do not turn, using left thumb loop on 4 sts. 69[78:87] sts.
Next row: Patt to end, do not turn, using left thumb loop on 4 sts. 73[82:91] sts.
Cont in patt, work 20 rows straight.
Dec row: (RS) K1, k2tog, patt to last 3 sts, sl 1, k1, psso, k1. 71[80:89] sts. Cont in patt, dec in this way on 13[14:15] foll 6th rows. 45[52:59] sts. Work 19[13:7] rows straight.
Ruffle edging:
1st row: (RS) K4, (p2tog, k5) 5[6:7] times, p2tog, k4. 39[45:51] sts.
2nd row: P3, (p2tog, yo, p4) 6[7:8] times. 39[45:51] sts.
3rd row: K4, (yo, k1, yo, k5) 5[6:7] times, yo, k1, yo, k4. 51[59:67] sts.
4th and every WS row: P to end.
5th row: K4, (yo, k3, yo, k5) 5[6:7] times, yo, k3, yo, k4. 63[73:83] sts.
7th row: K4, (yo, k5, yo, k5) 5[6:7] times, yo, k5, yo, k4. 75[87:99] sts.
9th row: K4, (yo, k7, yo, k5) 5[6:7] times, yo, k7, yo, k4. 87[101:115] sts.
11th row: K4, (yo, k9, yo, k5) 5[6:7] times, yo, k9, yo, k4. 99[115:131] sts.
13th row: K to end.
Work picot cast/bound-off as given for Back.

COLLAR:
Matching sts, join shoulder seams.
Using 4mm (no. 8/US 6) circular needle and with WS facing, pick up and k 48 sts across back neck, 18[25:32] sts down right front neck, 28 sts across front neck and 18[25:32] sts up left front neck. 112[126:140] sts.
1st round: (RS) K2, (p2, k5) to last 5 sts, p2, k3.
2nd round: K2, (yo, p2tog, k5) to last 5 sts, yo, p2tog, k3.
3rd round: K2, (k2tog, yo, k5) to last 5 sts, k2tog, yo, k3.
4th round: As 2nd round.
5th round: As 3rd round.
6th round: K2, (p2tog, k5) to last 5 sts, p2tog, k3. 96[108:120] sts.
7th round: K2, (yo, k2tog, k4) to last 4 sts, yo, k2tog, k2.

8th round: K2, (yo, k1, yo, k5) to last 4 sts, yo, k1, yo, k3. 128[144:160] sts.
9th and every alt round: K to end.
10th round: K2, (yo, k3, yo, k5) to last 6 sts, (yo, k3) twice. 160[180:200] sts.
12th round: K2, (yo, k5) to last 3 sts, yo, k3. 192[216:240] sts.
14th round: K2, (yo, k7, yo, k5) to last 10 sts, yo, k7, yo, k3. 224[252:280] sts.
16th round: K2, (yo, k9, yo, k5) to last 12 sts, yo, k9, yo, k3. 256[288:320] sts.
18th round: K2, (yo, k11, yo, k5) to last 14 sts, yo, k11, yo, k3. 288[324:360] sts.
20th round: K2, (yo, k13, yo, k5) to last 16 sts, yo, k13, yo, k3. 320[360:400] sts.
K 2 rounds. Turn, work picot cast/bind-off as given for Back.

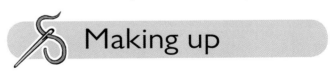

Making up

Press according to directions on ball band. Set in sleeves. Join side and sleeve seams.

Long tubular scarf

Practise knitting in the round and make this striped scarf.

This simple scarf is a long length of tubular stocking/stockinette stitch fabric with a clever use of two colours in stripes of varying widths that reverse at mid-point.

GETTING STARTED

This is a good exercise for working in rounds

Size:

Scarf is approximately 13cm wide x 114cm long (5in x 45in)

How much yarn:

2 x 50g (2oz) balls of Debbie Bliss Baby Cashmerino, approx 125m (137 yards) per ball, in colour A
2 balls in colour B

Needles:

Set of four 3.25mm (no. 10/US 3) double-pointed knitting needles

Tension/gauge:

25 sts and 34 rows measure 10cm (4in) square over st st on 3.25mm (no. 10/US 3) needles
IT IS ESSENTIAL TO WORK TO THE STATED TENSION/ GAUGE TO ACHIEVE SUCCESS

What you have to do:

Cast on all stitches and divide between three needles, using fourth needle of set to work with. Work throughout in rounds of stocking/stockinette stitch to produce a tubular fabric. Follow directions to work two-colour stripes in varying widths.

The Yarn

Debbie Bliss Baby Cashmerino is a soft blend of 55% merino wool, 33% microfibre and 12% cashmere. It can be machine washed at a low temperature and there is a wide choice of fabulous colours for stripes.

Instructions

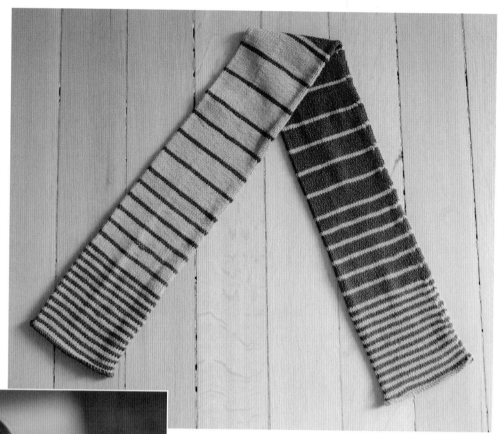

SCARF:

With A, cast on 66 sts. Divide sts evenly between three needles and join into a round. Using fourth needle to work with, k 1 round. Cont throughout in rounds of st st (every round k), working striped sections as foll:

Narrow-stripe section:

(48 rounds)

Work 2 rounds B and 2 rounds A. Rep these 4 rounds 11 times more.

Medium-stripe section:

(48 rounds)

Work 6 rounds B and 2 rounds A. Rep these 8 rounds 5 times more.

Wide-stripe section:

(48 rounds)

Work 10 rounds B and 2 rounds A. Rep these 12 rounds 3 times more.

Very wide stripe section:

(96 rounds)

Work 14 rounds B and 2 rounds A. Rep these 16 rounds twice more.

Work 2 rounds in B and 14 rounds in A. Rep these 16 rounds twice more.

Wide-stripe section:

(48 rounds)

Work 2 rounds B and 10 rounds A. Rep these 12 rounds 3 times more.

Medium-stripe section:

(48 rounds)

Work 2 rounds B and 6 rounds A. Rep these 8 rounds 5 times more.

Narrow-stripe section:

(48 rounds)

Work 2 rounds B and 2 rounds A. Rep these 4 rows 11 times more. Work 2 more rounds in B, then cast/bind off.

Press tubular scarf flat, according to directions on ball band.

Fringed poncho

This poncho is the perfect garment to slip on over a pair of jeans to keep chilly winds at bay.

Knitted in chunky yarn, this trendy poncho will quickly grow before your eyes. It looks great with everything from jeans to summer dresses.

GETTING STARTED

Some increasing and shaping plus eyelet holes for pattern above fringing, but most of the poncho is straightforward

Size:

Length: *50cm (20in), excluding fringe*

Width (at lower edge): *250cm (98½in)*

How much yarn:

6 x 100g (3½oz) balls of Sirdar Denim Chunky, approx 156m (171 yards) per ball

Needles:

Pair of 6.5mm (no. 3/US 10½) knitting needles

Short 6.5mm (no. 3/US 10½) circular needle

Additional items:

Crochet hook for fringing

Tension/gauge:

14 stitches and 19 rows to 10cm (4in) in stocking/ stockinette stitch; 13 stitches to 10cm (4in) and 8 rows measure 5cm (2in) over eyelet pattern, all on 6.5mm (no. 3/US 10½) needles

IT IS ESSENTIAL TO WORK TO THE STATED TENSION/ GAUGE TO ACHIEVE SUCCESS

What you have to do:

Cast on. Work in stocking/stockinette stitch (st st). Increase stitches to shape panels. Make stitches to form eyelet holes. Cast/bind off. Knit collar on circular needle (optional). Make fringing.

Note: The poncho is knitted in four sections, and the collar is worked in the round after the sections have been joined. See page 39 if you prefer to work the collar on two needles.

The Yarn

Sirdar Denim Chunky is a range in which most of the colours are blended so they have a denim appearance. A mix of 60% acrylic, 25% cotton and 15% wool gives it a lovely soft feel.

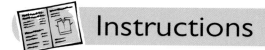

Instructions

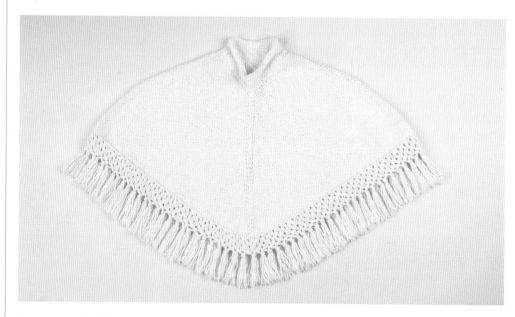

LEFT BACK:
Cast on 15 sts.
1st row: (RS) K1, kfb, k to end. 16 sts.
2nd row: P to end.
3rd row: (inc row) K1, kfb, k to last 3 sts, kfb, k2. 18 sts.
Cont in st st, inc in this way at each end of next 19 RS rows. 56 sts.
** Cont in st st, (inc as before at end of next RS row and at each end of foll RS row) 3 times. 65 sts.
Cont in st st, (inc as before at end of next 2 RS rows and at each end of foll RS row) 3 times. 77 sts.
Cont in st st, inc at end of next 6 RS rows. 83 sts. Work 2 rows in st st.

Edging:
1st row: (WS) K to end.
2nd row: K2, (yo, k2tog, k1) 27 times.
3rd, 5th and 7th rows: P to end.
4th row: K1, (yo, k2tog, k1) 27 times, k1.
6th row: K3, (yo, k2tog, k1) 26 times, yo, k2tog.
8th row: As 2nd row. Cast/bind off knitwise.

RIGHT BACK:
Cast on 15 sts.
1st row: (RS) K to last 3 sts, kfb, k2. 16 sts.

2nd row: P to end.
3rd row: K1, kfb, k to last 3 sts, kfb, k2. 18 sts.
Cont in st st, inc in this way at each end of next 19 RS rows. 56 sts.
** Cont in st st, (inc as before at beg of next RS row and at each end of foll RS row) 3 times. 65 sts.
Cont in st st, (inc as before at beg of next 2 RS rows and at each end of foll RS row) 3 times. 77 sts.
Cont in st st, inc at beg of next 6 RS rows. 83 sts. Work 2 rows in st st.

Edging:
Work as given for Left back edging.

RIGHT FRONT:
Cast on 3 sts.
1st row: (RS) K1, kfb, k1. 4 sts.
2nd row: Pfb, p to end. 5 sts.
3rd row: K1, kfb, k to last 2 sts, kfb, k1. 7 sts. Work last 2 rows 3 more times, then work 2nd row again. 17 sts.
Next row: (RS) K1, kfb, k to last 2 sts, kfb, k1, cast on 7 sts. 26 sts.
P 1 row.
Next row: (RS) K1, kfb, k to last 3 sts, kfb, k2. 28 sts.
Cont in st st, inc in this way at each end

of next 14 RS rows. 56 sts.
Complete as given for Left back from ** to end.

LEFT FRONT:

Cast on 3 sts.
1st row: (RS) K1, kfb, k1. 4 sts.
2nd row: P to last 2 sts, pfb, p1. 5 sts.
3rd row: Kfb, k to last 3 sts, kfb, k2. 7 sts.
Work last 2 rows 4 more times. 19 sts.
Next row: (WS) P19, cast on 7 sts. 26 sts.
Next row: (RS) K1, kfb, k to last 3 sts, kfb, k2.
Cont in st st, inc in this way at each end of next
14 RS rows. 56 sts.
Complete as given for Right back from ** to end.

COLLAR:

Taking one st in from each side, join front, back and side
seams with mattress stitch. Darn in ends. Using circular
needle, and with RS of work facing, pick up and k 26 sts
across back neck, 20 sts down left front neck and 20 sts
up right front neck. 66 sts.
K 14 rounds. Cast/bind off knitwise.
If you prefer to work the collar on two needles, join
back, front and left side seam. With RS of work facing,
pick up and k 27 sts across back neck, 20 sts down
left front neck and 21 sts up right front neck. 68 sts.
Beg with a p row, work 15 rows in st st. Cast/bind off
knitwise. Join right side seam and collar, reversing seam
at rolled edge of collar.

FRINGE:

Cut 432 x 38cm (15in) lengths of yarn. For each tassel,
take 4 lengths of yarn, fold in half, with RS facing, and
proceed as described on the right.

HOW TO
MAKE A FRINGE

1 Take the strands of yarn and fold in half. Put a crochet hook through the eyelet hole and catch the top of the loop of folded strands with the hook.

2 Pull the looped strands up through the eyelet hole.

3 Pass the ends of the strands through the loop from back to front. Pull downwards to tighten the knot formed right up to the fabric.

4 Continue making tassels in this way until you have finished. Comb through the tassels with your fingers. Using sharp scissors, trim the tassels to an even length.

Cardigan with lace bands

With bands of lace and a picot edging, this cardigan is unashamedly pretty.

This cardigan with three-quarter sleeves has bands of openwork lace pattern on a stocking/stockinette stitch background and picot edgings.

The Yarn
Sublime Soya Cotton DK is a blend of 50% soya and 50% cotton. It is a unique natural yarn with a luxurious drape that is very soft next to the skin. There is an unusual palette of some spicy, rich shades and contrasting cool, watery colours.

Instructions

Abbreviations:
alt = alternate; **beg** = beginning; **cm** = centimetre(s); **cont** = continue; **dec** = decrease; **foll** = follow(s)(ing); **inc** = increase; **k** = knit; **p** = purl; **psso** = pass slipped stitch over; **rem** = remain(ing); **rep** = repeat; **RS** = right side; **sl** = slip; **st(s)** = stitch(es); **st st** = stocking/stockinette stitch; **tog** = together; **WS** = wrong side; **yfwd** = yarn forward/yarn over to make a stitch

BACK:
With 3.25mm (no. 10/US 3) needles cast on 99[107:115] sts loosely.
1st row: (RS) K2, (p1, k1) to last st, k1.
2nd row: K1, (p1, k1) to end.
Rep these 2 rows twice more.

GETTING STARTED

Straightforward style although openwork pattern may take some practise

Size:
To fit bust: 86[91:97]cm/34[36:38]in
Actual size: 90[97:104.5]cm/35½[38:41]in
Length: 57[58:60]cm/22½[23:23½]in
Sleeve seam: 26.5cm (10½in)
Note: Figures in square brackets [ ] refer to larger sizes; where there is only one set of figures, it applies to all sizes

How much yarn:
9[9:10] x 50g (2oz) balls of Sublime Soya Cotton DK, approx 110m (120 yards) per ball

Needles:
Pair of 3.25mm (no. 10/US 3) knitting needles
Pair of 4mm (no. 8/US 6) knitting needles

Additional items:
Stitch holder
8 buttons

Tension/gauge:
22 sts and 28 rows measure 10cm (4in) square over st st on 4mm (no. 8/US 6) needles
IT IS ESSENTIAL TO WORK TO THE STATED TENSION/ GAUGE TO ACHIEVE SUCCESS

What you have to do:
Work hems in single (knit one, purl one) rib. Work main fabric in stocking/stockinette stitch with bands of openwork mesh. Use simple shaping for armholes, neck and sleeve tops. Finish edges of ribbed bands with decorative picot cast/bind-off.

Change to 4mm (no. 8/US 6) needles. Beg with a k row, work 15 rows in st st. ** Work mesh lace band as foll:
1st row: (WS) P1, (k1, p3) to last 2 sts, k1, p1.
2nd row: K2, (yfwd, sl 1, k2tog, psso, yfwd, k1) to last st, k1.
3rd row: As 1st row.
4th row: K3, (yfwd, sl 1, k1, psso, k2) to end.
5th–15th rows: Rep 1st–4th rows twice, then 1st–3rd rows again.
Beg with a k row, work 21 rows in st st. **
Rep from ** to ** once more, then work 1st–15th rows of mesh lace band again.***
K 1 row and p 1 row.

Shape armholes:
Cont in st st only, cast/bind off 6[7:8] sts loosely at beg of next 2 rows. Dec 1 st at each end of next 3[3:5] rows, then at each end of every foll alt row until 75[79:85] sts rem. Work straight until armholes measure 18[19:21] cm/7[7½:8¼]in from beg, ending with a p row.

Shape shoulders:
Cast/bind off 6[7:7] sts loosely at beg of next 4 rows and 7[6:8] sts at beg of next 2 rows. Cut off yarn.
Leave rem 37[39:41] sts on a holder.

RIGHT FRONT:
With 3.25mm (no. 10/US 3) needles cast on 47[51:55] sts. Work as given for Back to ***. K 1 row, p 1 row and k 1 row.

**** Shape armhole:
Cont in st st only, cast/bind off 6[7:8] sts loosely at beg of next row. Dec 1 st at armhole edge on next 3[3:5] rows, then on every foll alt row until 35[37:40] sts rem. Work straight until Front measures 11[13:14]cm/4½[5:5½]in from beg of armhole, ending at front edge.

Shape neck:
Cast/bind off 11[12:13] sts loosely at beg of next row. Dec 1 st at neck edge on next 5 rows. 19[20:22] sts. Work straight until Front measures same as Back to shoulder, ending at armhole edge.

Shape shoulder:
Cast/bind off 6[7:7] sts at beg of next and foll alt row. Work 1 row. Cast/bind off rem 7[6:8] sts.

LEFT FRONT:
With 3.25mm (no. 10/US 3) needles cast on 47[51:55] sts. Work as given for Back to ***. K 1 row and p 1 row. Now complete as given for Right front from **** to end.

SLEEVES: (Make 2)
With 3.25mm (no. 10/US 3) needles cast on 51[55:63] sts loosely. Work 6 rows in k1, p1 rib as given for Back. Change to 4mm (no. 8/US 6) needles. Beg with a k row, work 15 rows in st st, inc 1 st at each end of 7th and 13th[1st, 5th, 9th and 13th:1st, 5th, 9th and 13th] rows.

55[63:71] sts.
Now work 1st–15th rows of mesh lace band as given for Back, inc 1 st at each end of 4th and 10th rows. 59[67:75] sts.
Beg with a k row, work 21 rows in st st, inc 1 st at each end of 1st, 7th, 13th and 19th rows. 67[75:83] sts.
Now work 1st–15th rows of mesh lace band again, inc 1 st at each end of 4th and 10th rows. 71[79:87] sts.
K 1 row and p 1 row.

Shape top:
Cont in st st only, cast/bind off 6[7:8] sts loosely at beg of next 2 rows. Dec 1 st at each end of next and every foll alt row until 29[33:35] sts rem, then at each end of every row until 19[23:25] sts rem. Cast/bind off loosely.

NECKBAND:
Join shoulder seams.
With 3.25mm (no. 10/US 3) needles and RS of work facing, pick up and k 29[30:33] sts evenly up right front neck, k across back neck sts on holder and pick up and k 29[30:33] sts evenly down left front neck. 95[99:107] sts.
Beg with a 2nd row, work 6 rows in rib as given for Back.
Cast/bind off to form picot edge as foll: *Cast/bind off 2 sts, sl st on right needle back on to left needle, cast on 2 sts, cast/bind off 2 sts, k2tog, sl 2nd st on right over first st, rep from * to last 2 sts, cast/bind off 2 sts, fasten off.

BUTTON BAND:
With 3.25mm (no. 10/US 3) needles cast on 9 sts. Cont in rib as given for Back until strip, when slightly stretched, fits up Left front to top of neckband. Cast/bind off in rib.
Sew band in place. Mark positions of 8 buttons, the first and last to be in 3rd/4th rows from upper and lower edges, and others evenly spaced between.

BUTTONHOLE BAND:
Work as given for Button band, making buttonholes to correspond with markers as foll:
1st buttonhole row: (RS) Rib 3, cast/bind off 3 sts in rib, rib to end.
2nd buttonhole row: Rib to end, casting on 3 sts over those cast/bound off in previous row. Sew band in place.

PICOT BORDERS:
With 3.25mm (no. 10/US 3) needles and RS of Back facing, k up one st from every rib st at cast-on edge. Work picot cast/bind-off row as given for Neckband. Work similar picot border on lower Front and Sleeve edges.

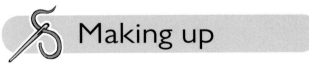 Making up

Do not press. Sew in sleeves. Join side and sleeve seams. Sew on buttons.

Lacy evening scarf

Add the finishing touch to your evening outfit with this delicate silk scarf.

Knitted in a beautiful silk yarn, this long scarf is worked in a simple lace pattern that forms undulating scalloped ridges. The ends are accentuated with long fringes and sewn-on beads.

GETTING STARTED

 The lace design is very simple as only one row out of four is patterned

Size:
Scarf is approximately 12cm wide x 150cm long (4¾in x 59in), excluding fringes

How much yarn:
2 x 50g (2oz) hanks of Debbie Bliss Pure Silk, approx 125m (136 yards) per hank

Needles:
Pair of 5mm (no. 6/US 8) knitting needles

Additional items:
Crochet hook for fringing
Approximately 70 small pearl beads (optional)
Approximately 100 small purple beads (optional)
Sewing needle and matching thread

Tension/gauge:
30 sts and 18 rows measure 10cm (4in) square over lace patt, stretched slightly lengthways, on 5mm (no. 6/ US 8) needles
IT IS ESSENTIAL TO WORK TO THE STATED TENSION/ GAUGE TO ACHIEVE SUCCESS

What you have to do:
Work in lace pattern using decorative increasing and decreasing. Add fringe to each end. Sew on beads (optional).

The Yarn
Debbie Bliss Pure Silk is 100% silk. It is a luxurious yarn in a double knitting (light worsted) weight that has the subtle pearlised sheen of silk and it can be hand washed. There are plenty of gorgeous colours to choose from.

Abbreviations:
beg = beginning;
cm = centimetre(s);
cont = continue;
foll = follows; **k** = knit;
p = purl; **patt** = pattern;
RS = right side;
st(s) = stitch(es);
tog = together;
yfwd = yarn forward/yarn over between stitches to make a stitch

 # Instructions

SCARF:

Cast on 36 sts loosely. Cont in lace patt as foll:

1st row: (RS) K to end.
2nd row: P to end.
3rd row: *(K2tog) 3 times, (yfwd, k1) 6 times, (k2tog) 3 times, rep from * once more.
4th row: K to end. These 4 rows form patt. Cont in patt until work measures about 150cm (59in) from beg, ending with a 4th patt row. Cast/bind off loosely.

 # Making up

Press according to directions on ball band, gently stretching knitting lengthways to accentuate the scallops of lace patt.

Fringe:
Cut 38 lengths of yarn, each 26cm (10in) long. With crochet hook and using one strand of yarn each time, knot fringes along cast-on and cast/bound-off edges, working into each corner st and then into alternate sts.

Beading:
At one end of scarf, highlight the first four garter-stitch ridges in the pattern by sewing on about 35 pearl beads and 50 purple beads at random. Repeat at the other end of the scarf.

HOW TO
WORK THE LACY PATTERN

This is a very simple lace pattern with decorative increases and decreases worked on one row of the four-row pattern.

1 Cast on thirty-six stitches loosely. The cast-on row is worked in this way because the pattern creates a scalloped effect. If the cast-on row is too tight, then this constrains the scalloped effect. Knit the first row and then purl the second row.

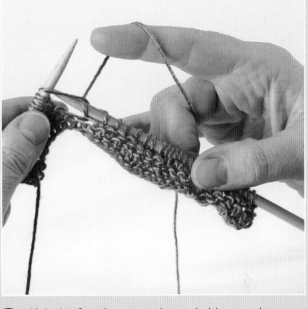

3 Knit the fourth row to the end; this completes the four-row pattern.

2 For the third row, knit two stitches together three times, bring the yarn forward/yarn over between the needles and knit one. Repeat this five times more and then knit two stitches together three times. Repeat this complete sequence once more.

4 The four-row pattern forms a scalloped lace effect. Here you can see the pattern emerging after eight rows. Continue repeating these four rows until the scarf measures 150cm (59in) ending with a fourth row. Cast/bind off loosely in order to maintain the scalloped effect.

Classic waistcoat

This waistcoat/vest has a wonderful retro feel – play up the vintage look by choosing a colour like this mustard yellow.

Worked in stocking/stockinette stitch in an Aran (fisherman) wool yarn, this traditional piece with curved front edges will be a winner in your wardrobe.

GETTING STARTED

Worked in basic fabric but shaping requires concentration

Size:
To fit bust: 81–86[91–97:102–107]cm/32–34[36–38:40–42]in
Actual size: 86[97:108]cm/34[38:42½]in
Length at centre back: 54[57:59]cm/21¼[22½:23¼]in
Note: Figures in square brackets [ ] refer to larger sizes; where there is only one set of figures, it applies to all sizes

How much yarn:
7[7:8] x 50g (2oz) balls of Debbie Bliss Rialto Aran, approx 80m (87 yards) per ball

Needles:
Pair of 4.5mm (no. 7/US 7) knitting needles
Pair of 5mm (no. 6/US 8) knitting needles

Additional items:
5 buttons, Stitch holders and markers

Tension/gauge:
18 sts and 24 rows measure 10cm (4in) square over st st on 5mm (no. 6/US 8) needles
IT IS ESSENTIAL TO WORK TO THE STATED TENSION/ GAUGE TO ACHIEVE SUCCESS

What you have to do:
Work main fabric in stocking/stockinette stitch. Shape curved lower edges of fronts with groups of cast-on stitches. Work pocket linings and inset pockets. Use fashioned shapings for armholes and neck. Pick up stitches and work edgings in single rib, making eyelet buttonholes.

The Yarn
Debbie Bliss Rialto Aran contains 100% merino wool. It has a slight twist that gives good stitch definition for stocking/stockinette-stitch fabrics and it can be machine washed at a low temperature. There are about 20 fabulous shades to choose from.

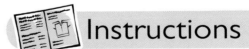 Instructions

Abbreviations:
alt = alternate; **beg** = beginning; **cm** = centimetre(s); **cont** = continue; **dec** = decrease(ing); **foll** = following; **k** = knit; **p** = purl; **psso** = pass slipped stitch over; **rem** = remain; **rep** = repeat; **RS** = right side; **sl** = slip; **st(s)** = stitch(es); **st st** = stocking/stockinette stitch; **tbl** = through back of loops; **tog** = together; **WS** = wrong side; **yrn** = yarn round/yarn over needle to make a stitch

BACK:

With 5mm (no. 6/US 8) needles cast on 79[89:99] sts. Beg with a k row, work 76[80:82] rows in st st, ending with a p row.

Shape armholes:

Cast/bind off 3[4:5] sts at beg of next 2 rows.

Next row: K2, k2tog, k to last 4 sts, sl 1, k1, psso, k2.

Next row: P to end.

Rep last 2 rows 5[7:9] times more. 61[65:69] sts. Work 36[34:32] rows straight, ending with a p row.

Shape shoulders:

Cast/bind off 17[18:19] sts at beg of next 2 rows. 27[29:31] sts.

Change to 4.5mm (no. 7/US 7) needles.

Next row: K1, (p1, k1) to end.

Next row: P1, (k1, p1) to end.

Rep last 2 rows twice more. Cast/bind off in rib.

POCKET LININGS: (Make 2)

With 5mm (no. 6/US 8) needles cast on 15[15:17] sts. Beg with a k row, work 19[21:21] rows in st st, ending with a k row. Cut off yarn and leave sts on a holder.

LEFT FRONT:

With 5mm (no. 6/US 8) needles cast on 16[17:18] sts. P 1 row. Beg with a k row, cont in st st, casting on 2 sts at beg of next 8[10:12] rows. 32[37:42] sts.*

Keeping side edge straight, cast on 1 st at beg (front edge) of foll 5 alt rows. 37[42:47] sts. Place a marker at front edge of last row. Beg with a k row, work 4 rows straight.

Work pocket top:

Next row: (RS) K11[14:15], p1, (k1, p1) 7[7:8] times, k11[13:15].

Next row: P11[13:15], k1, (p1, k1) 7[7:8] times, p11[14:15].

Rep last 2 rows once more.

Next row: K11[14:15], cast/bind off next 15[15:17] sts firmly in rib, k to end.

Next row: P11[13:15], with WS facing p across 15[15:17] sts from pocket lining, p to end.

Work 50[54:56] rows straight, ending with a p row. Place a marker at front edge of last row.

Shape neck and armhole:

Next row: K to last 4 sts, sl 1, k1, psso, k2.

Work 3 rows straight.

Next row: Cast/bind off 3[4:5] sts, k to last 4 sts, sl 1, k1, psso, k2.

Next row: P to end.

Next row: K2, k2tog, k to end.

Next row: P to end.

Next row: K2, k2tog, k to last 4 sts, sl 1, k1, psso, k2.

Rep last 4 rows 2[3:4] times more. 23[24:25] sts. Keeping armhole edge straight, cont to dec at neck edge as before on foll 4th rows until 17[18:19] sts rem. Work 13[11:9] rows straight, ending at armhole edge. Cast/bind off.

RIGHT FRONT:

Work as given for Left front to *. Keeping side edge straight, cast on 1 st at beg (front edge) of next and foll 4 alt rows. 37[42:47] sts. Place a marker at front edge of last row. Beg with a p row, work 5 rows straight.

Work pocket top:

Next row: (RS) K11[13:15], p1, (k1, p1) 7[7:8] times, k11[14:15].

Next row: P11[14:15], k1, (p1, k1) 7[7:8] times, p11[13:15].

Rep last 2 rows once more.

Next row: K11[13:15], cast/bind off next 15[15:17] sts firmly in rib, k to end.

Next row: P11[14:15], with WS facing p across 15[15:17] sts from pocket lining, p to end.

Work 50[54:56] rows straight, ending with a p row. Place a marker at front edge of last row.

Shape neck and armhole:

Next row: K2, k2tog, k to end.

Work 3 rows straight.

Next row: K2, k2tog, k to end.

Next row: Cast/bind off 3[4:5] sts, p to end.

Next row: K to last 4 sts, sl 1, k1, psso, k2.

Next row: P to end.

Next row: K2, k2tog, k to last 4 sts, sl 1, k1, psso, k2.

Next row: P to end.

Rep last 4 rows 2[3:4] times more. 23[24:25] sts. Keeping armhole edge straight, cont to dec at neck edge as before on 3rd and foll 4th rows until 17[18:19] sts rem. Work 14[12:10] rows straight, ending at armhole edge. Cast/bind off.

EDGINGS:

Lower back:

With 4.5mm (no. 7/US 7) needles and RS of work facing, pick up and k79[89:99] sts along lower edge of back. Beg with a WS row, work 5 rows in k1, p1 rib as given for back neckband. Cast/bind off in rib.

Armholes:

Join shoulder seams. With 4.5mm (no. 7/US 7) needles and RS of work facing, pick up and k81[87:93] sts evenly around armhole edge. Work 5 rows in k1, p1 rib as before. Cast/bind off in rib.

Right front:

With 4.5mm (no. 7/US 7) needles and RS of work facing, pick up and k10[12:14] sts from side edge to cast-on edge, 1 st in corner, 16[17:18] sts along cast-on edge, 1 st in corner, 19[21:23] sts round curve to first marker, 1 st in corner, 48[50:52] sts up to second marker, 1 st in corner and 41[42:43] sts up neck to shoulder. 138[146:154] sts.

Next 2 rows: (K1, p1) to end.

Buttonhole row: (WS) (K1, p1) 21[22:23] times, (yrn, p2tog tbl, rib 10) 4 times, yrn, p2tog tbl, rib to end. Rib 2 more rows. Cast/bind off in rib.

Left front:

Work to match right front, omitting buttonholes.

 Making up

Press according to directions on ball band. Join side and all edging seams. Sew pocket linings in place on WS of work. Sew on buttons.

Soft cape

Elegant and understated, this beautiful mohair cape creates a classic evening look.

This neat little cape in stocking/stockinette stitch and a beautiful mohair yarn has a soft collar that loosely drapes around the neckline.

GETTING STARTED

Working on circular needles and the large number of stitches may take some getting used to

Size:
One size fits bust: *81–97cm (32–38in)*
Length from lower edge to collar: *33cm (13in)*

How much yarn:
8 x 25g (1oz) balls of Rowan Kidsilk Aura in Pumice, approx 75m (82 yards) per ball

Needles:
*4mm (no. 8/US 6) circular knitting needle
4.5mm (no. 7/US 7) circular knitting needle*

Additional items:
Stitch markers

Tension/gauge:
*19 sts and 27 rows measure 10cm (4in) square over st st on 4.5mm (no. 7/US 7) needles
IT IS ESSENTIAL TO WORK TO THE STATED TENSION/ GAUGE TO ACHIEVE SUCCESS*

What you have to do:
Use circular needles to hold large number of stitches and work in rounds. Work main fabric in stocking/ stockinette stitch (every round knit). Work collar in garter stitch (knit one round and purl one round). Use paired shaping at intervals to shape cape. Increase at start of collar to give loose shape to fold down.

The Yarn
Rowan Kidsilk Aura is a blend of 75% mohair and 25% silk. It can be hand-washed at a cool temperature and there is a range of contemporary subtle colours to choose from.

Abbreviations:

beg = beginning;

cm = centimetre(s);

cont = continue;

dec = decrease;

k = knit;

m1 = make one stitch by picking up strand lying between needles and working into back of it;

p = purl;

psso = pass slipped stitch over;

st(s) = stitch(es);

sl = slip;

st st = stocking/stockinette stitch;

tog = together

Instructions

CAPE:

With 4mm (no. 8/US 6) circular needle cast on 300 sts loosely. Marking beg of each round, work 4 rounds in k1, p1 rib. Change to 4.5mm (no. 7/US 7) circular needle and work 36 rounds in st st (every round k).

1st dec round: (K2tog, k26, sl 1, k1, psso) 10 times. 280 sts. Work 11 rounds straight.

2nd dec round: (K2tog, k24, sl 1, k1, psso) 10 times. 260 sts. Work 9 rounds straight.

3rd dec round: (K2tog, k22, sl 1, k1, psso) 10 times. 240 sts. Work 7 rounds straight.

4th dec round: (K2tog, k20, sl 1, k1, psso) 10 times. 220 sts. Work 3 rounds straight.

5th dec round: (K2tog, k18, sl 1, k1, psso) 10 times. 200 sts.

Work 3 rounds straight.

6th dec round: (K2tog, k16, sl 1, k1, psso) 10 times. 180 sts.

Work 3 rounds straight.

7th dec round: (K2tog, k14, sl 1, k1, psso) 10 times. 160 sts.

Work 3 rounds straight.

8th dec round: (K2tog, k12, sl 1, k1, psso) 10 times. 140 sts.

Work 3 rounds straight.

Collar:

Next round: (K1, m1, k12, m1, k1) 10 times. 160 sts.

Cont in garter st (1 round k, 1 round p) for 15cm (6in).

Cast/bind off loosely.

HOW TO
USE CIRCULAR NEEDLES

A circular needle is used to make a tubular piece of knitting, as you knit round in a continuous circle. You can cast on and knit whole items on circular needles or use them to pick up stitches and knit a neck or a round shape. Circular needles consist of two short straight needles joined by a flexible plastic wire. They are available in sizes just like ordinary knitting needles and they also come in several lengths; the needles and connecting wire should be short enough so the stitches are not stretched when joined.

1 Cast on or pick up stitches as you would for ordinary knitting using a regular needle. Distribute the stitches evenly around the needles and wire, making sure they all lie in the same direction and are not twisted

3 Hold the needle with the last cast-on stitch in your right hand and the needle with the first cast-on stitch in your left hand. Knit the first cast-on stitch, keeping the yarn well tensioned to avoid a gap.

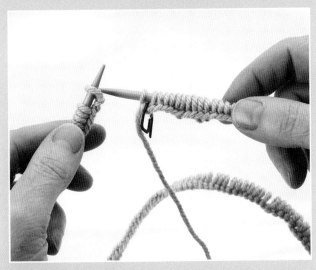

2 The last cast-on stitch is the last stitch of the round. Place a marker here to indicate the end of the round.

4 Work until you reach the marker, checking that the stitches are eased around the needles as you work. This completes the first round. Continue knitting in this way for the required depth of the fabric tube.

Flower hatband

Turn a store-bought hat into a designer look with this amazing knitted flower and hatband.

All you need to decorate a plain hat with a creative floral arrangement is some simple knitting and sewing skills.

GETTING STARTED

Easy shapes and stitches; take care with assembly for a neat finished result

Size:
Band: *60cm (24in) long (adjustable);* **Flower motif**
(with leaves): *approximately 17cm wide x 18cm deep (6¾in x 7in)*

How much yarn:
1 x 100g (3½oz) ball of Patons 100% Cotton DK, approx 210m (230 yards) per ball, in colour A
1 x 100g (3½oz) ball of Patons 100% Cotton 4-ply, approx 330m (360 yards) per ball, in colour B
1 x 50g (2oz) ball of Sirdar Just Bamboo, approx 94m (103 yards) per ball, in colour C

Needles:
Pair of 3mm (no. 11/US 2) knitting needles
Pair of 4mm (no. 8/US 6) knitting needles

Additional items:
0.6mm (24 gauge) silver-plated beading wire
Pack of 6mm (¼in) black glass beads
25cm (10in) of wired organza ribbon 38mm (1½in) wide
Black button 27mm (1⅛in) in diameter
Sewing needle and thread

Tension/gauge:
23 sts and 34 rows measure 10cm (4in) square over st st using DK cotton on 3mm (no. 11/US 2) needles

What you have to do:
Work hatband in moss/seed stitch. Work patterned flower centre using two ends of yarn. Make separate petals in stocking/stockinette stitch using simple shaping. Work leaves in stocking/stockinette stitch. Wire leaves and make decorative beaded wires, then assemble and stitch flower motif on hatband.

The Yarn
Patons 100% Cotton in 4-ply (fingering) and DK (light worsted weight) is pure cotton. It is available in plenty of colours. Sirdar Just Bamboo is 100% bamboo. It is a flat tape yarn in muted pastel shades that will add texture to the floral motif.

Instructions

Abbreviations:

beg = beginning;
cm = centimetre(s);
cont = continue;
dec = decrease(ing);
inc = increase(ing);
k = knit; **p** = purl;
psso = pass slipped stitch
over; **rem** = remain(ing);
rep = repeat;
RS = right side;
sl = slip; **st(s)** = stitch(es);
st st = stocking/stockinette
stitch;
tbl = through back of loops;
tog = together;
yo = yarn over needle to
make a stitch

HATBAND:

With 3mm (no. 11/US 2) needles and A, cast on 10 sts.
1st row: (K1, p1) to end.
2nd row: (P1, k1) to end. Rep these 2 rows to form moss/
seed st until band measures 60cm (24in), or fits around hat,
when slightly stretched. Either graft sts together or cast/bind
off and join ends of band with mattress st.

FLOWER MOTIF:
Central flower:

With 4mm (no. 8/US 6) needles and one end of B and C
tog, cast on 57 sts.
1st row: P to end.
2nd row: K2, *k1, sl this st back on to left needle and pass
next 8 sts on left needle over it and off needle, (yo) twice, k
first st again, k2, rep from * to end.
3rd row: P1, *p2tog, p into front of first yo and into back of
second yo, p1, rep from * to last st, p1. 22 sts.
4th row: K to end.
5th row: *P2tog, rep from * to end. 11 sts.
6th row: *K2, pass second st over first, rep from * to last
st, k1. Cut off yarn. Thread through rem 6 sts, pull up tightly
and sew edges of flower tog.
Petals: (Make 12)
With 3mm (no. 11/US 2) needles and A, cast on 6 sts. P 1
row.

Next row: K1, inc in next st, k2, inc in next st, k1. 8 sts. Beg with a p row, work 3 rows in st st.

Next row: K1, inc in next st, k4, inc in next st, k1. 10 sts. Beg with a p row, work 9 rows in st st.

Next row: (K2tog tbl) twice, k2, (k2tog) twice. 6 sts.

Next row: P2tog, p2, p2tog. 4 sts. Cast/bind off. Sew in yarn end at finish, but leave yarn at base of petal for sewing on to band later.

Leaves: (Make 4)

With 3mm (no. 11/US 2) needles and two ends of B tog, cast on 3 sts. Beg with a k row, cont in st st, inc 1 st at each end of every RS row until there are 9 sts. Work 11 rows straight, ending with a p row.

Dec row: Sl 1, k1, psso, k to last 2 sts, k2tog. Cont to dec in this way on every foll RS row until 3 sts rem. Work 1 row.

Next row: Sl 1, k1, psso, k1 and cast/bind off one st. Fasten off.

so that leaves extend beyond petals, and sew in place. Finish off by folding organza ribbon into a loop and adding to arrangement as shown.

 ## Making up

Press all petals and leaves to correct shape. Wire leaves by threading wire through sts at back, bending back in a loop at point. Note that two leaves will need extra-long wires extending from base so that they extend beyond petals.

For lower beaded wires, take a 30cm (12in) length of wire and thread bead to centre, fold wire in half, bending wire so that bead stays in place. Repeat with two other – 20cm (8in) and 14cm (5½in) – lengths of wire, then wrap another length of wire around all three at base to hold group in place. For upper beaded wires, make two beaded wires – using 20cm (8in) and 14cm (5½in) lengths – and bind tog as described above.

Working over seam and using photograph as a guide, position two leaves and beaded wires on hatband. Pin and sew in place. Pin and sew first layer of six petals in place, then make another layer of remaining petals, alternating position of petals with first layer. Sew flower to centre of arrangement and sew on button to centre of flower. Pin and place two lower leaves with wire at back of hatband,

Beaded mohair bag

Tiny beads, a beaded fringe and a flower-shaped clasp are the motifs of this pretty cross-body bag.

Worked in a glamorous yarn and patterned with beads, this pretty bag with its decorative knitted clasp, beaded fringes and long cord strap is ideal for evening occasions.

GETTING STARTED

 No difficult shaping, but knitting with beads may take some practise

Size:
Bag is approximately 15cm wide x 17.5cm high (6in x 7in), excluding fringing

How much yarn:
1 x 50g (2oz) ball of Patons Orient, approx 150m (164 yards) per ball

Needles:
Pair of 4mm (no. 8/US 6) knitting needles
Pair of 4mm (no. 8/US 6) double-pointed needles

Additional items:
Approximately 508 beads with large enough hole to thread on to yarn
Sewing needle and thread
20cm x 46cm (8in x 18in) piece of lining fabric
Press stud (popper snap)

Tension/gauge:
22 sts and 30 rows measure 10cm (4in) square over st st on 4mm (no. 8/US 6) needles
IT IS ESSENTIAL TO WORK TO THE STATED TENSION/GAUGE TO ACHIEVE SUCCESS

What you have to do:
Thread beads on to yarn. Work bag in stocking/stockinette stitch with beaded panel as instructed. Make flower motif for 'clasp'. Knit cord strap for handle and sew on beaded fringes along lower edge. Sew lining for bag as instructed.

The Yarn
Patons Orient contains 50% polyamide, 30% acrylic and 15% mohair. Its slight brushed appearance is enhanced with a glinting metallic thread that gives the finished fabric a beautiful sheen. There is a small range of classic deep and pale colours to choose from.

Abbreviations:

beg = beginning;
cm = centimetre(s);
cont = continue;
foll = follow(s)(ing);
k = knit; **p** = purl;
psso = pass slipped stitch over;
rem = remain(ing);
rep = repeat;
RS = right side; **sl** = slip;
st(s) = stitch(es);
st st = stocking/stockinette stitch;
tbl = through back of loop;
tog = together;

Note: Before starting work, thread 217 beads on to yarn. Take a length of sewing thread, fold it in half and thread the two cut ends into a sewing needle. Insert end of knitting yarn through loop of sewing thread, then thread beads on to needle and slide down over sewing thread and doubled end of knitting yarn. Push beads a long way along yarn so that you have plenty of yarn for knitting first section before starting to place beads.

Instructions

BAG:

With 4mm (no. 8/US 6) needles cast on 35 sts. K 2 rows.
Beg with a k row, cont in st st until work measures 11cm (4½in) from beg, ending with a WS row. Cont in bead patt as foll:
1st row: (RS) K2, (bring yarn to front of work, slide bead up yarn to needle, sl next st purlwise, take yarn to back holding bead in front of slipped st – called place bead (pb), k1) to last 3 sts, pb, k2.
2nd row: P to end.
3rd row: K3, (pb, k1) to last 4 sts, pb, k3.
4th row: P to end.
Rep these 4 rows 3 times more. Beg with a k row, cont in st st until work measures 35cm (13¾in) from beg, ending with a WS row.

Shape flap:

1st row: K1, sl 1, k1, psso, (pb, k1) to last 4 sts, pb, k2tog, k1.
2nd row: P1, p2tog, p to last 3 sts, p2tog, p1.

3rd row: K1, sl 1, k1, psso, k1, (pb, k1) to last 3 sts, k2tog, k1.
4th row: P to end.
5th row: As 3rd row.
6th row: As 2nd row.
7th row: K1, sl 1, k1, psso, (pb, k1) to last 4 sts, pb, k2tog, k1.
8th row: P to end.
Rep last 2 rows 7 times more. 9 sts.
23rd row: K1, sl 1, k1, psso, pb, k1, pb, k2tog, k1.
24th row: P to end.
25th row: K1, sl 1, k1, psso, pb, k2tog, k1. 5 sts. P 1 row. Cast/bind off.

FLOWER:

Before starting work, thread 5 beads on to yarn as before.
With 4mm (no. 8/US 6) needles cast on 8 sts.
1st row: (RS) Sl 1, k7.
2nd row: Sl 1, k5 (2 sts rem on left-hand needle), turn and take yarn to back.

3rd row: Sl 1, k3 (2 sts rem on left-hand needle), turn and take yarn to back.

4th row: Sl 1, k3, turn.

5th row: Sl 1, k1, pb, k3 (0 sts rem on left-hand needle), turn.

6th row: Sl 1, k6 (1 st on left-hand needle), turn.

7th row: Sl 1, then start by using this st, cast/bind off all sts until 1 st rem, turn.

8th row: Cast on 7 sts.

Rep these 8 rows 3 times more, then work 1st–7th rows again to make 5 petals in all. Fasten off, leaving a long length of yarn.

Sew first petal to last petal to create a flower. Sew running sts through sts at inner edge of central hole and draw up to close the hole. Fasten off.

CORD STRAP:

With 4mm (no. 8/US 6) double-pointed needles cast on 3 sts. K 1 row.

Next row: * Without turning work and RS facing, slide sts to other end of needle and, pulling yarn from left-hand side of sts to right across back, k1 tbl, k2. *
Rep from * to *, remembering to pull yarn tightly across back and always working a k row, until cord measures 140cm (55in) or length required to fit across body. Cast/bind off.

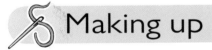

Making up

Using bag as a template, cut out lining fabric, adding 1.5cm (⅝in) seam allowance on all sides.

With WS facing, fold up cast-on edge of bag by 17cm (6½in) and join side seams. Sew ends of cord strap securely to side seams inside top edge of bag. Turn bag RS out. Sew 5 beads to centre and 5 to edges of each flower petal, then sew flower to point of flap.

Fringing:

Make 32 beaded fringes as foll: Take a 20cm (8in) length of yarn and knot close to one end. Thread on 2 beads and knot again, then thread on another 6 beads. Thread yarn into a tapestry needle and sew fringe through lower edge of bag, securing and knotting on inside of bag to leave approximately 5cm (2in) hanging. Place a fringe to the side of every stitch along lower edge of bag.

Lining:

Fold 1.5cm (⅝in) to WS along short, straight edge of lining and sew in place. With RS facing and taking 1.5cm

(⅝in) seam allowances, fold lining as for knitted bag, join side seams and trim seams close to stitching. Place lining inside bag, with WS tog, and sew through lower corners with sewing thread to secure in place. Slip stitch folded edge of lining along inside top edge of bag. Fold under remaining free edges of lining along flap and slip stitch in place.

Sew a press stud (popper snap) to underside of flower and flap point and corresponding section to front of bag.

Long skinny cardigan

A classic design is given a twist with extra-large buttons and a small rever collar.

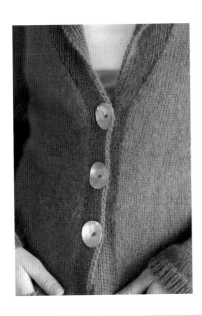

This long-line cardigan in stocking/stockinette stitch has a deep V-neckline and a small rever collar. It fastens with three large buttons just below the neckline.

The Yarn
Sublime Angora Merino DK contains 80% extra fine merino wool and 20% angora. This combination of fibres feels soft and luxurious and there are eleven fabulous colours to choose from.

Instructions

GETTING STARTED

Basic stocking/stockinette stitch fabric but shaping needs concentration

Size:
To fit bust: 81–86[91–97:102–107]cm/32–34[36–38:40–42]in
Actual size at bust: 90[101:112]cm/35½[37¾:44]in
Length: 78[82.5:87]cm/30¾[32½:34¼]in
Sleeve seam: 42.5[44.5:46.5]cm/16¾[17½:18¼]in
Note: Figures in square brackets [ ] refer to larger sizes; where there is only one set of figures, it applies to all sizes

How much yarn:
11[12:13] x 50g (2oz) balls of Sublime Angora Merino DK, approx 119m (130 yards) per ball

Needles:
Pair of 3.75mm (no. 9/US 5) knitting needles
Pair of 4mm (no. 8/US 6) knitting needles

Additional items:
Stitch holders and markers, 3 large buttons

Tension/gauge:
22 sts and 28 rows measure 10cm (4in) square over st st on 4mm (no. 8/US 6) needles
IT IS ESSENTIAL TO WORK TO THE STATED TENSION/GAUGE TO ACHIEVE SUCCESS

What you have to do:
Work welts, cuffs, front bands and collar in single (k1, p1) rib. Work main fabric in stocking/stockinette stitch. Use simple shaping for darts, armhole and front edge. Work inset pockets. Shape rever collar with turning rows.

Abbreviations:
alt = alternate; **beg** = beginning; **cm** = centimetre(s); **cont** = continue; **dec** = decrease(ing); **foll** = follow(s)(ing); **inc** = increase(ing); **k** = knit; **m1** = make one stitch by picking up strand lying between needles and working into back of it; **p** = purl; **psso** = pass slipped stitch over; **rem** = remain(ing); **rep** = repeat; **RS** = right side; **sl** = slip; **st(s)** = stitch(es); **st st** = stocking/stockinette stitch; **tbl** = through back of loop(s); **tog** = together; **WS** = wrong side

BACK:
With 3.75mm (no. 9/US 5) needles cast on 105[117:129] sts.
1st row: (RS) K1, (p1, k1) to end.
2nd row: P1, (k1, p1) to end. Rep these 2 rows twice more. Change to 4mm (no. 8/US 6) needles. Beg with a k row, cont in st st and work 62[68:74] rows.

Shape hips:
Dec row: (RS) K8, sl 1, k1, psso, k to last 10 sts, k2tog, k8. Work 5 rows in st st. Rep last 6 rows 6 times more, then work dec row again. 89[101:113] sts. Work 9[11:13] rows straight, ending with a p row.

Shape bust:
Inc row: (RS) K4, m1, k to last 4 sts, m1, k4.
Work 5 rows in st st. Rep last 6 rows 4 times more, then work inc row again. 101[113:125] sts. Work 9[11:13] rows straight, ending with a p row.

Shape armholes:
Cast/bind off 4[5:6] sts at beg of next 2 rows. 93[103:113] sts.
Next row: K1, sl 1, k1, psso, k to last 3 sts, k2tog, k1.
Next row: P to end. Rep last 2 rows 5[6:7] times more, then work 1st of them again. 79[87:95] sts. Work 45 rows straight, ending with a p row.

Shape shoulders:

Cast/bind off 7[8:9] sts at beg of next 6 rows.
Cast/bind off rem 37[39:41] sts.

POCKET LININGS: (Make 2)

With 4mm (no. 8/US 6) needles cast on
25[27:29] sts. Beg with a k row, work 31[33:35]
rows in st st, ending with a k row. Cut off yarn
and leave sts on a holder.

LEFT FRONT:

With 3.75mm (no. 9/US 5) needles cast on
49[55:61] sts. Work 6 rows in k1, p1 rib as
given for Back.
Change to 4mm (no. 8/US 6) needles. Beg with
a k row, cont in st st and work 52[56:60] rows.

Work pocket top:

Next row: (RS) K12[14:16], p1, (k1, p1)
12[13:14] times, k12[14:16].
Next row: P12[14:16], k1, (p1, k1) 12[13:14] times,
p12[14:16]. Rep last 2 rows once more.
Next row: K12[14:16], cast/bind off next 25[27:29] sts
firmly in rib, k to end.
Next row: P12[14:16], with WS facing, p across 25[27:29]
sts of pocket lining, p to end.
Work 4[6:8] rows in st st, ending with a p row.*

Shape hips:

Dec row: (RS) K8, sl 1, k1, psso, k to end.
Work 5 rows in st st. Rep last 6 rows 6 times more, then
work dec row again. 41[47:53] sts. Work 9[11:13] rows
straight, ending with a p row.

Shape bust:

Inc row: (RS) K4, m1, k to end. Work 5 rows straight. Rep
last 6 rows twice more 44[50:56] sts.

Shape neck:

1st row: (RS) K4, m1, k to last 3 sts, k2tog, k1.
2nd row: P to end.
3rd row: K to end.
4th row: P1, p2tog, p to end.
5th row: K to end.
6th row: P to end.
Rep last 6 rows twice more. 41[47:53] sts. Cont to dec
1 st at neck edge as set on next and every foll 6th row,
AT SAME TIME work 4[6:8] rows keeping side edge
straight, ending at armhole edge.

Shape armhole:

Cast/bind off 4[5:6] sts at beg of next row. P 1 row.
Next row: (RS) K1, sl 1, k1, psso, work to end.

**Keeping neck shapings correct, dec 1 st at armhole
edge on foll 6[7:8] alt rows. 26[30:33] sts. Keeping armhole
edge straight, cont to dec at neck edge until 21[24:27] sts
rem. Work 15[13:11] rows straight, ending with a p row.

Shape shoulder:

Cast/bind off 7[8:9] sts at beg of next and foll alt row.
Work 1 row. Cast/bind off rem 7[8:9] sts.

RIGHT FRONT:

Work as Left front to *.

Shape hips:

Dec row: (RS) K to last 10 sts, k2tog, k8.
Work 5 rows in st st. Rep last 6 rows 6 times more, then
work dec row again. 41[47:53] sts. Work 9[11:13] rows
straight, ending with a p row.

Shape bust:

Inc row: (RS) K to last 4 sts, m1, k4. Work 5 rows straight.
Rep last 6 rows twice more 44[50:56] sts.

Shape neck:

1st row: (RS) K1, sl 1, k1, psso, k to last 4 sts, m1, k4.
2nd row: P to end.
3rd row: K to end.
4th row: P to last 3 sts, p2tog tbl, p1.
5th row: K to end.
6th row: P to end.
Rep last 6 rows twice more. 41[47:53] sts. Cont to dec
1 st at neck edge as set on next and every foll 6th row,
AT SAME TIME work 5[7:9] rows keeping side edge
straight, ending at armhole edge.

Shape armhole:
Cast/bind off 4[5:6] sts at beg of next row.

Next row: (RS) Work to last 3 sts, k2tog, k1.
Work as Left front from ** to end, working 1 row more before shoulder shaping.

SLEEVES: (Make 2)
With 3.75mm (no. 9/US 5) needles cast on 53[57:61] sts.
Work 8 rows in k1, p1 rib as given for Back.
Change to 4mm (no. 8/US 6) needles.
Inc row: (RS) K4, m1, k to last 4 sts, m1, k4.
Beg with a p row, work 9[9:7] rows in st st, ending with a p row. Rep last 10[10:8] rows 8[10:12] times more, then work inc row again. 73[81:89] sts. Work 21[7:19] rows straight, ending with a p row.
Shape top:
Cast/bind off 4[5:6] sts at beg of next 2 rows. Dec 1 st at each end of next and 3 foll 4th rows, then on every foll alt row until 37[41:45] sts rem, ending with a p row. Dec 1 st at each end of every row until 21 sts rem. Cast/bind off.

FRONT BANDS AND COLLAR:
Knitted all in one piece, beg at lower edge of Left front band. Join shoulder seams.
With 3.75mm (no. 9/US 5) needles cast on 13 sts.
1st row: (RS) K2, (p1, k1) to last st, k1.
2nd row: K1, (p1, k1) to end.
Rep last 2 rows until band, when slightly stretched, fits up to beg of front neck shaping, ending with a WS row. Place 1st marker at end of last row.
Shape for collar:
Keeping rib correct, inc 1 st at beg of next row (shaped edge) and every foll alt row to 33 sts, ending with a RS row.
Next row: (WS) Rib 20, turn, sl 1, rib to end.
Work 4 rows across all sts, inc as before at beg of 2nd and 4th rows. 35 sts.
Next row: (WS) Rib 22, turn, sl 1, rib to end.
Work 4 rows across all sts, inc as before at beg of 2nd and 4th rows. 37 sts.
Next row: (WS) Rib 24, turn, sl 1, rib to end.
Work 4 rows across all sts, inc as before at beg of 2nd and 4th rows. 39 sts.
Next row: (WS) Rib 26, turn, sl 1, rib to end.
Work 4 rows across all sts, inc as before at beg of 2nd and 4th rows. 41 sts.
Next row: (WS) Rib 28, turn, sl 1, rib to end.

Work 4 rows across all sts, inc as before at beg of 2nd and 4th rows. 43 sts.
Place 2nd marker at shaped edge of last row.
* Next row: (WS) Rib 30, turn, sl 1, rib to end.
Work 4 rows straight across all sts. Cont as set from * until shaped edge of collar fits up to left shoulder. Place 3rd marker at shaped edge of last row. Cont as set until shaped edge of collar fits across back neck to right shoulder. Place 4th marker at shaped edge of last row. Now cont straight as set for same number of rows as worked between 2nd and 3rd markers, ending after turning rows. Work 4 rows across all sts, dec 1 st at beg of 2nd and 4th rows. 41 sts.
Next row: (WS) Rib 28, turn, sl 1, rib to end.
Work 4 rows across all sts, dec 1 st at beg of 2nd and 4th rows. 39 sts.
Next row: (WS) Rib 26, turn, sl 1, rib to end.
Work 4 rows across all sts, dec 1 st at beg of 2nd and 4th rows. 37 sts.
Next row: (WS) Rib 24, turn, sl 1, rib to end.
Work 4 rows across all sts, dec 1 st at beg of 2nd and 4th rows. 35 sts.
Next row: (WS) Rib 22, turn, sl 1, rib to end.
Work 4 rows across all sts, dec 1 st at beg of 2nd and 4th rows. 33 sts.
Next row: (WS) Rib 20, turn, sl 1, rib to end.
Cont in rib across all sts, dec 1 st as set on every foll alt row until 13 sts rem.
Place 5th marker at shaped edge of last row.
Mark position on Left front band of 3 buttons, first one 10 rows below 1st marker (to allow for roll of collar) and rem two at approximately 16-row intervals, or as desired. Cont straight in rib on these 13 sts, working buttonholes at marked positions as foll:
1st buttonhole row: Rib 5, cast/bind off next 3 sts, rib to end.
2nd buttonhole row: Rib to end, casting on 3 sts over those cast/bound off in previous row.
Cont in rib until band fits down to lower edge of Right front. Cast/bind off in rib.

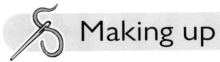

Making up

Sew on front bands and collar, matching 1st and 5th markers to beg of neck shapings and 3rd and 4th markers to left and right shoulders. Catch down pocket linings to WS of fronts. Sew in sleeves. Join side and sleeve seams. Sew on buttons.

Party pashmina

Add a glamorous touch to any outfit with this silky
pashmina knitted in a lacy pattern.

There's no need to spend a fortune on a pashmina for that special occasion when you can make this dramatic wrap in a luxurious silky yarn and stunning lace pattern. Generous fringes at either end add a dramatic touch.

GETTING STARTED

 Simple strip of knitting but concentration needed to keep lace pattern correct

Size:
Pashmina is 48cm wide x 184cm long (19in x 72½in), excluding fringing

How much yarn:
10 x 50g (2oz) balls of Sirdar Flirt DK, approx 95m (104 yards) per ball

Needles:
Pair of 3.25mm (no. 10/US 3) knitting needles
Pair of 4mm (no. 8/US 6) knitting needles

Additional items:
Crochet hook

Tension/gauge:
22 sts and 28 rows measure 10cm (4in) square over st st on 4mm (no. 8/US 6) needles
IT IS ESSENTIAL TO WORK TO THE STATED TENSION/ GAUGE TO ACHIEVE SUCCESS

What you have to do:
Work a few rows in garter stitch (every row knit) at each end for borders. Work throughout in lacy pattern featuring decorative increasing and decreasing. Knot a fringe along short ends.

The Yarn

Sirdar Flirt DK is a mixture of 80% bamboo with 20% wool. It has a tight twist and lustrous sheer that give it it distinctive silky appearance. There is a range of glamorous shades including five trendy metallics.

Abbreviations:

cm = centimetre(s);
cont = continue;
foll = follows;
k = knit; **p** = purl;
patt = pattern;
psso = pass slipped
stitch over;
rep = repeat;
sl = slip; **st(s)** = stitch(es);
st st = stocking/
stockinette stitch;
tog = together;
WS = wrong side;
yfwd = yarn forward/yarn
over between needles to
make a stitch

Instructions

PASHMINA:

With 3.25mm (no. 10/US 3) needles cast on 107 sts.
K5 rows.
Change to 4mm (no. 8/US 6) needles. Cont in patt as foll:
1st row: (WS) K3, p to last 3 sts, k3.
2nd row: K4, *yfwd, k3, sl 1, k2tog, psso, k3, yfwd, k1, rep from * to last 3 sts, k3.
3rd row: K3, p to last 3 sts, k3.
4th row: K3, p1, *k1, yfwd, k2, sl 1, k2tog, psso, k2, yfwd, k1, p1, rep from * to last 3 sts, k3.
5th row: K4, *p9, k1, rep from * to last 3 sts, k3.
6th row: K3, p1, *k2, yfwd, k1, sl 1, k2tog, psso, k1, yfwd, k2, p1, rep from * to last 3 sts, k3.
7th row: As 5th row.
8th row: K3, p1, *k3, yfwd, sl 1, k2tog, psso, yfwd, k3, p1, rep from * to last 3 sts, k3.
These 8 rows form patt. Cont in patt until work measures 183cm (72in), ending with an 8th patt row.
Change to 3.25mm (no. 10/US 3) needles. K4 rows.
Cast/bind off knitwise.

Making up

If necessary, press lightly on WS using a warm iron over a dry cloth.

Fringe:

Wrap yarn loosely around a strip of cardboard 28cm (11in) wide. Cut strands along one edge and remove from card. Taking six strands together each time, fold in half, then use a crochet hook to pull strands from front to back through first st in one short end. Pass ends through folded loop and pull to tighten knot. Rep along both short ends, spacing fringes evenly about 4–5 sts apart.

HOW TO
WORK THE LACY PATTERN

Here is a sample of the lace pattern, working the second pattern repeat across a reduced width.

1 Cast on the required number of stitches, knit five rows and work one pattern repeat. For the first pattern row, knit three, purl to the last three stitches and then knit three.

2 Begin the second row with knit four. Work the following sequence; yarn forward/ yarn over, knit three, slip one, knit two together, pass slip stitch over, knit three, yarn forward/yarn over and knit one. Repeat this sequence to the last three stitches and then knit these.

3 The third row is a repeat of the first row. For the fourth row, begin with knit three and then purl one. Work the following sequence; knit one, yarn forward/ yarn over, knit two, slip one, knit two together, pass slip stitch over, knit two, yarn forward/ yarn over, knit one and purl one. Repeat sequence to the last three stitches and then knit these.

4 For row five, begin with knit four. Then purl nine and knit one and repeat this to the last three stitches. Knit three.

5 Begin the sixth row with knit three and purl one. Work the following sequence; knit two, yarn forward/yarn over, knit one, slip one, knit two together, pass slip stitch over, knit one, yarn forward/ yarn over, knit two and purl one. Repeat this sequence to the last three stitches and then knit three.

6 The seventh row is a repeat of the fifth row. For the eighth row, begin with knit three and purl one. Work the following sequence; knit three, yarn forward/ yarn over, slip one, knit two together, pass slip stitch over, yarn forward/yarn over, knit three and purl one. Repeat this sequence to the last three stitches and then knit three.

7 Repeat these eight rows to form the pattern and you will see the solid diamonds and openwork diamond shapes emerging.

Long gloves with ribbed cuffs

Keep out the chill and look cool at the same time with these classic long gloves.

With their long ribbed cuffs featuring a buttoned opening, these stocking/ stockinette stitch gloves in a soft 4-ply yarn are an essential fashion accessory.

The Yarn
Tess Dawson Merino 4-ply (fingering) contains 100% merino wool. This easy-care, superwash yarn is luxuriously soft and is available in a palette of six delicious colours.

GETTING STARTED

 Easy fabric but pay attention when shaping thumb and fingers

Size:
To fit an average woman's hand

How much yarn:
2 x 50g (2oz) balls of Tess Dawson Merino 4-ply, approx 200m (218 yards) per ball

Needles:
Pair of 3mm (no. 11/US 2) knitting needles
Pair of 3.25mm (no. 10/US 3) knitting needles

Additional items:
2 buttons

Tension/gauge:
28 sts and 36 rows measure 10cm (4in) square over st st on 3.25mm (no. 10/US 3) needles
IT IS ESSENTIAL TO WORK TO THE STATED TENSION/GAUGE TO ACHIEVE SUCCESS

What you have to do:
Work long cuff in double (k2, p2) rib, decreasing for better fit. Work main part of gloves in stocking/ stockinette stitch, increasing within fabric for thumb gusset. Shape thumb, then continue on main part of hand before shaping each finger individually. Leave opening at lower edge of cuff, fastening with a button and sewn button loop.

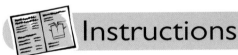 Instructions

Abbreviations:
beg = beginning; **cm** = centimetre(s); **cont** = continue;
dec = decrease(ing); **foll** = following; **k** = knit;
m1 = make one stitch by picking up strand lying between needles and knitting into back of it; **p** = purl;
rem = remaining; **rep** = repeat; **RS** = right side;
st(s) = stitch(es); **st st** = stocking/stockinette stitch; **tog** = together; **WS** = wrong side

RIGHT GLOVE:
**With 3.25mm (no. 10/US 3) needles cast on 60 sts.
1st row: (RS) K3, *p2, k2, rep from * to last st, k1.
2nd row: K1, p2, *k2, p2, rep from * to last st, k1.
These 2 rows form rib. Cont in rib for a further 12 rows, ending with a WS row and placing a marker at each end of

last row. Keeping rib correct, dec 1 st at each end of next and 4 foll 10th rows. 50 sts. Work 9 more rows, ending with a WS row.

Change to 3mm (no. 11/US 2) needles. Work a further 19 rows in rib, ending with a RS row. Change to 3.25mm (no. 10/US 3) needles.

Next row: (WS) P7, p2tog, (p15, p2tog) twice, p7. 47 sts. Beg with a k row, work in st st for 4 rows, ending with a WS row.**

Shape thumb gusset:
Next row: (RS) K24, m1, k3, m1, k20. 49 sts.
Work 3 rows.
Next row: K24, m1, k5, m1, k20. 51 sts. Work 3 rows.
Next row: K24, m1, k7, m1, k20. 53 sts. Work 3 rows.
Next row: K24, m1, k9, m1, k20. 55 sts. Work 3 rows.
Next row: K24, m1, k11, m1, k20. 57 sts. Work 3 rows.
Next row: K24, m1, k13, m1, k20. 59 sts. Work 3 rows, ending with a WS row.

Shape thumb:
Next row: (RS) K39, turn and cast on 2 sts.
Next row: P17, turn and cast on 2 sts.
***Cont on these 19 sts and work 16 rows, ending with a WS row.
Next row: K2, k2tog, (k4, k2tog) twice, k3. 16 sts.
Next row: Purl.
Next row: (K2tog) 8 times.
Cut off yarn, thread through rem 8 sts, pull up tightly and fasten off securely. Join thumb seam.
With RS facing, rejoin yarn and pick up and k 5 sts from base of thumb, k to end. 49 sts. Cont on these 49 sts and work 13 rows, ending with a WS row.

Shape first finger:
Next row: (RS) K32, turn and cast on 1 st.
Next row: P16, turn and cast on 1 st.
Cont on these 17 sts and work 22 rows, ending with a WS row.
Next row: K2, (k2tog, k3) 3 times. 14 sts.

Next row: Purl.
Next row: (K2tog) 7 times.
Cut off yarn, thread through rem 7 sts, pull up tightly and fasten off securely. Join finger seam.

Shape second finger:
With RS facing, rejoin yarn and pick up and k 3 sts from base of first finger, k6, turn and cast on 1 st.
Next row: P16, turn and cast on 1 st. Cont on these 17 sts and work 24 rows, ending with a WS row.
Next row: K2, (k2tog, k3) 3 times.14 sts.
Next row: Purl.
Next row: (K2tog) 7 times.
Cut off yarn, thread through rem 7 sts, pull up tightly and fasten off securely.
Join finger seam.

Shape third finger:
With RS facing, rejoin yarn and pick up and k 3 sts from base of second finger, k6, turn and cast on 1 st.
Next row: P16, turn and cast on 1 st.
Cont on these 17 sts and work 22 rows, ending with a WS row.
Next row: K2, (k2tog, k3) 3 times. 14 sts.
Next row: Purl.
Next row: (K2tog) 7 times.
Cut off yarn, thread through rem 7 sts, pull up tightly and fasten off securely.
Join finger seam.

Shape fourth finger:

With RS facing, rejoin yarn and pick up and k 5 sts from base of third finger, k5.

Next row: P15. Cont on these 15 sts and work 18 rows, ending with a WS row.

Next row: K1, (k2tog, k3) twice, k2tog, k2. 12 sts.

Next row: Purl.

Next row: (K2tog) 6 times.

Cut off yarn, thread through rem 6 sts, pull up tightly and fasten off securely.***

LEFT GLOVE:

Work as given for Right glove from ** to **.

Shape thumb gusset:

Next row: (RS) K20, m1, k3, m1, k24. 49 sts.

Work 3 rows.

Next row: K20, m1, k5, m1, k24. 51 sts.

Work 3 rows.

Next row: K20, m1, k7, m1, k24. 53 sts.

Work 3 rows.

Next row: K20, m1, k9, m1, k24. 55 sts.

Work 3 rows.

Next row: K20, m1, k11, m1, k24. 57 sts.

Work 3 rows.

Next row: K20, m1, k13, m1, k24. 59 sts.

Work 3 rows, ending with a WS row.

Shape thumb:

Next row: (RS) K35, turn and cast on 2 sts.

Next row: P17, turn and cast on 2 sts.

Complete as given for Right glove from *** to ***.

 ## Making up

Do not press.

Join fourth finger seams and side seams to markers, leaving rows above markers open. Make a button loop at top edge of one side of each glove, then sew on buttons to other side to correspond with loops.

Skinny scarf

This scarf takes no time at all and it will soon become one of your favourite knits.

Make this trendy openwork scarf on big needles with cotton yarn and very little effort – the drop-stitch pattern will quickly develop as you knit.

The Yarn

Sirdar Luxury Soft Cotton is 100% cotton yarn in a double knitting (light worsted) weight. It is a delight to work with and feels soft next to the skin.

There is a beautiful colour range with chalky pastels and muted darker shades that make choosing three complementary shades for the scarf an easy task.

GETTING STARTED

Simple to knit in a straight strip and stripes. Drop-stitch pattern can often look untidy until the openwork pattern begins to develop

Size:

Scarf is 13cm wide and 220cm long (5in x 86in)

How much yarn:

1 x 50g (2oz) ball of Sirdar Luxury Soft Cotton DK, approx 95m (104 yards) per ball, in each of three colours A, B and C

Needles:

Pair of 5mm (no. 6/US 8) knitting needles

Tension/gauge:

13 sts and 13 rows measure 10cm (4in) square in patt on 5mm (no. 6/US 8) needles

IT IS ESSENTIAL TO WORK TO THE STATED TENSION/ GAUGE TO ACHIEVE SUCCESS

What you have to do:

Cast on very loosely. Work drop-stitch pattern by winding yarn twice around needle on one row and dropping extra loops on the following row. Work striped pattern. Carry contrast yarns up side of work. Cast/bind off loosely.

Instructions

Abbreviations:
cm = centimetre(s);
cont = continue;
k = knit;
patt = pattern;
rep = repeat;
st(s) = stitch(es)

SCARF:
With A, cast on 17 sts loosely.
1st row: K to end.
2nd row: K to end, winding yarn twice around needle for every st.
3rd row: K to end, dropping extra loops.
These 3 rows form drop-stitch patt.
Join in B. Cont in patt, work 3 rows in B, always catching contrast yarn (by twisting together with working yarn) from 2 rows down at side edges before every row.
Join in C. Cont in patt, work 3 rows in C, catching yarn at sides as before.
These 9 rows form striped patt. Rep them until work measures about 220cm (86in), ending after a 3rd patt row. Cast/bind off loosely.

Making up

Weave in any loose ends along stitches in the same colour as yarn. Do not press.

HOW TO
WORK THE DROP STITCH PATTERN

To begin with, working a pattern where you have to drop stitches off the needle can feel odd, but once you see the openwork pattern developing it makes sense of the technique. This is a quick and easy stitch to work and your scarf will grow at a surprising rate.

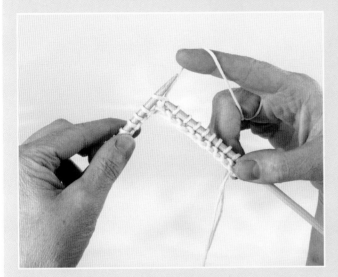

1 Cast on the required number of stitches loosely. The cast-on edge should not pull the edge of the scarf in as the pattern develops. Although the cast-on stitches must be loose, they should also be even. Knit the first row.

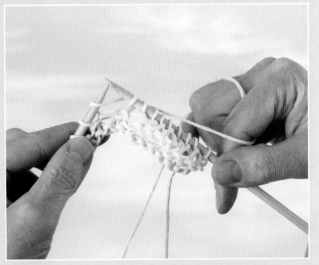

3 Knit to the end of the next row, dropping the extra loop off the left-hand needle on each stitch. This forms the openwork part of the pattern.

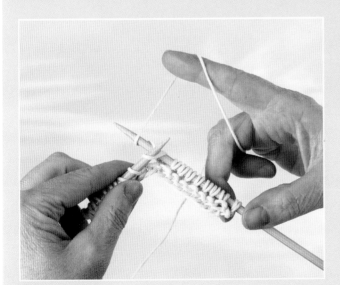

2 Knit the next row but wrap the yarn twice around the right-hand needle (as shown) each time you make a knit stitch. This will give you a row of double loops for each stitch.

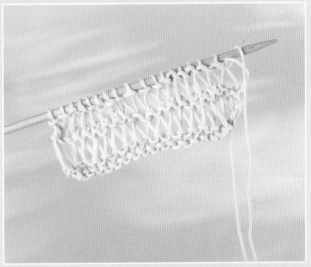

4 These three rows form the pattern and are repeated for the length of the scarf. This creates a row of open stitches intersected by a row of garter stitch. Change colours as instructed in the pattern to create the stripes in this scarf.

Cape-style poncho

This easy-to-wear cape is perfect for slipping over your shoulders on chilly days.

In super-soft Aran (fisherman) yarn, this chic cape with its fold-back collar is self-striped in bands of simple stitches.

GETTING STARTED

Basic stitches and easy shaping make this an ideal project for beginners

Size:
To fit extra small/small[medium/large]
Width around lower edge: *140[162]cm/55[63¾]in*
Length: *53[58]cm/20¾[23]in*
Note: *Figures in square brackets [ ] refer to the larger size; where there is only one set of figures, it applies to both sizes*

How much yarn:
10[12] x 50g (2oz) balls of Sirdar Sublime Cashmere Merino Silk Aran, approx 86m (94 yards) per ball

Needles:
Pair of 5mm (no. 6/US 8) knitting needles

Tension/gauge:
18 sts and 24 rows measure 10cm (4in) square over st st on 5mm (no. 6/US 8) needles

What you have to do:
Work in stocking/stockinette stitch. Work in garter stitch (every row knit). Increase to shape cape at centre front and centre back by making stitches. Pick up and knit stitches around neck to work collar.

The Yarn
Sirdar Sublime Cashmere Merino Silk Aran is an exquisite blend of 75% extra fine merino with 20% silk and 5% cashmere to form a yarn that is extremely soft. Created in Aran (fisherman) weight, this yarn is available in ten luxuriously subtle shades for irresistible, textured knits.

Abbreviations:

alt = alternate;

beg = beginning;

cm = centimetre(s);

cont = continue;

foll = follow(s)(ing);

g st = garter stitch (every row knit);

inc = increase(ing);

k = knit;

m1 = make one stitch by picking up strand lying between needles and working into back of it;

patt = pattern;

RS = right side;

st(s) = stitch(es);

st st = stocking/stockinette stitch

 # Instructions

BACK:

Note: Work in one piece from neck down.

Cast on 52[62] sts.

1st row: (RS) K25[30], m1, k2, m1, k25[30].

Beg with a p row, cont in st st, m1 as before either side of centre 2 sts on every foll alt row to 60[78] sts, then on every foll 4th row to 76[96] sts, ending with a p row.

Cont in 32-row patt as foll:

K16 rows g st, then beg with a k row, work 16 rows st st, AT THE SAME TIME inc 2 sts as before on every foll 4th row to 126[146] sts.

Work 13 rows straight so completing 16 rows of g st.

Cast/bind off loosely.

FRONT:

Work as given for Back.

COLLAR:

Join one side seam using backstitch.

With RS of work facing, pick up and k104[124] sts evenly along neck edge.

Work 17[19]cm/6¾[7½]in g st.

Cast/bind off loosely.

 # Making up

Join remaining side and collar seam, reversing seam for last 12[14]cm/4¾[5½]in on collar.

HOW TO
BACKSTITCH

Use backstitch to join the seams on this poncho, matching the stitches when you place the pieces together.

I Place the pieces to be joined right sides together. Match the rows of knitting stitch for stitch, and pin in place.

2 Thread a blunt-ended wool needle with yarn. Bring the needle through from the back to the front, one knitted stitch down from the starting edge.

3 Insert the needle one knitted stitch back and bring it out one knitted stitch ahead. Pull the yarn through to tighten and form a stitch.

4 Repeat this step as you continue along the seam, making one backstitch cover one knitted stitch. Secure and trim the end of the yarn.

Polka-dot scarf

Red spots on a white background make a striking scarf that's perfect with a red coat.

Edged in garter stitch, this simple wrapover scarf tucks into the neck of a jacket and has a striking pattern of textured polka dots knitted into it.

The Yarn
Wendy Mode Double Knitting is a practical blend of 50% merino wool and 50% acrylic. It produces a soft fabric with the best qualities of both natural and man-made fibres and can be machine washed at a low temperature. There are plently of cool pastel and strong contemporary colours to choose from.

GETTING STARTED

Basic scarf is very simple but working polka-dot pattern may take some practise

Size:
Scarf is 83cm long x 18cm wide (32½in x 7in)

How much yarn:
2 x 50g (2oz) balls of Wendy Mode Double Knitting, approx 142m (155 yards) per ball, in main colour A
1 ball in contrast colour B

Needles:
Pair of 4.5mm (no. 7/US 7) knitting needles

Tension/gauge:
20 sts and 26 rows measure 10cm (4in) square over patt on 4.5mm (no. 7/US 7) needles
IT IS ESSENTIAL TO WORK TO THE STATED TENSION/ GAUGE TO ACHIEVE SUCCESS

What you have to do:
Work narrow borders at both short ends of scarf in garter stitch (every row knit). Work garter-stitch borders (two stitches) at each end of every row. Make polka dots in contrast colour on every 5th and 6th rows of pattern, stranding yarn across back of work.

Instructions

Abbreviations:

beg = beginning; **cm** = centimetre(s); **cont** = continue; **foll** = follows; **k** = knit; **p** = purl; **patt** = pattern; **rep** = repeat; **RS** = right side; **st(s)** = stitch(es); **WS** = wrong side

Notes: When working in patt, carry yarn not in use loosely across back of work. Do not twist yarns together at ends of rows as this will show on RS. Instead carry yarn diagonally across back of work to next row of dots. Join in new ball of A 2 sts in from edge of work.

SCARF:

With A, cast on 39 sts.
K 3 rows. Cont in polka-dot patt as foll:
1st row: (RS) With A, k to end.
2nd row: With A, k2, p to last 2 sts, k2.
3rd and 4th rows: As 1st and 2nd rows.
5th row: K4 A, (1 B, 5 A) to last 5 sts, 1 B, 4 A.
6th row: K2 A, p2 A, (k1 B, p5 A) to last 5 sts, k1 B, p2 A, k2 A.
7th–10th rows: Rep 1st and 2nd rows twice.
11th row: K7 A, (1 B, 5 A) to last 2 sts, 2 A.
12th row: K2 A, p5 A, (k1 B, p5 A) to last 2 sts, k2 A.
These 12 rows form patt. Cont in patt until Scarf measures approximately 82cm (32in) from beg, ending with 9th patt row. With A, k 3 rows. Cast/bind off evenly.

 # Making up

Sew in loose ends neatly, taking care not to let contrast colour show on RS of work. Press lightly on WS following instructions on ball band.

HOW TO
STRAND THE YARN

The polka dots are worked on the fifth and sixth rows of the twelve-row pattern.

2 To begin the first polka dot, join in the red yarn and work one stitch. Pick up the white yarn and work two or three stitches. Take the red yarn across the back of the work and strand it in by taking the white yarn under the red yarn. Continue working with the white yarn to the next polka dot. Drop the working yarn, pick up the red yarn from underneath it and work one stitch. Continue in this way, stranding the red yarn across the back of the fabric and twisting the yarns together to form each polka dot.

1 The polka dots are worked over two rows and are spaced five stitches apart. You need to strand the yarn across the back of the work to keep the fabric flat and smooth and to make the wrong side of the scarf look neat.

Index

Acknowledgements

Managing Editor: Clare Churly
Editors: Jane Ellis and Sarah Hoggett
Senior Art Editor: Juliette Norsworthy
Designer: Janis Utton
Assistant Production Manager: Caroline Alberti